TALKING HEADS

FOREWORD BY **GENERAL PETER COSGROVE**
INTRODUCTION BY **PETER THOMPSON**
EDITED BY **PAULINE TURNBULL**

ABC Books

Published by ABC Books for the
AUSTRALIAN BROADCASTING CORPORATION
GPO Box 9994 Sydney NSW 2001

Copyright ABC TV © 2008

First published August 2008

All rights reserved. No part of this publication
may be reproduced, stored in a retrieval system or
transmitted in any form or by any means, electronic,
mechanical, photocopying, recording or otherwise,
without the prior written permission of the Australian
Broadcasting Corporation.

ISBN 978 0 7333 2348 5 (pbk.)

Cover design by Christabella Designs
Typeset in 11/16 pt Sabon by Kirby Jones
Printed in Australia by Griffin Press, South Australia

5 4 3 2 1

CONTENTS

Foreword — General Peter Cosgrove · v
Introduction — Peter Thompson · vii
Editor's Note — Pauline Turnbull · xi

Peter Cundall — Gardener · 1
Max Walker — Sportsman, writer and raconteur · 24
John Clarke — Satirist · 47
Clive James — Writer · 66
Professor Fiona Wood — Surgeon · 86
Dr Karl Kruszelnicki — Scientist · 107
Dr James Wright — Celebrity GP · 125
General Peter Cosgrove — Soldier · 143
Lillian Frank — Hair stylist and fundraiser · 162
Renee Geyer — Singer · 181
Dick Smith — Businessman and adventurer · 201
Nancy-Bird Walton — Aviator · 223
Kev Carmody — Musician · 241
Denise Drysdale — Entertainer · 260

Acknowledgements · 275

FOREWORD

I'm a 'talking head'. In fact I'm one of about 20 million of them in Australia alone. We are a great nation of yarners—even the most active of us, the busiest of us, the most cryptic of us like to have a yarn from time to time, about ourselves, our lives, our families and our mates and the big events which affect our lives. Even those who are not good listeners are generally good talkers! We don't require that those who tell us their story are famous or infamous, just that they be interesting.

Storytelling is one of the most natural human means of communication, so you might say it is one of the most developed art forms. Those who make their lives discovering and telling stories for the interest and the delight of us all, whether it be in word form or pictures or both, have got special value in the community.

For years now, the men and women of the *Talking Heads* team have brought hundreds and hundreds of stories of Australians, both eminent and unknown, to an eager viewing audience. In a style which has been both relaxed and intimate these stories are now part of the record, of the long history of the show and in the memories of the viewers. Television, the greatest modern communications medium, is ephemeral. Of course we can all keep a visual record and many of us do but TV is also a 'move on' medium—there is always a new story, a new visual experience and cupboards at home are full of old DVDs gathering dust!

The printed word remains the medium of record. We are fortunate that we now have this great account of some of *Talking Heads* stories across the years. That legion of Australians who have avidly watched the program and fretted when, from time to time, they've missed a particular show will find great comfort and satisfaction in reading the selected stories. From my own experience participating in the show, I can promise readers that the editing style has remained true to the unique *Talking Heads* format.

Australians enjoy a good yarn. This book is full of them.

General Peter Cosgrove

INTRODUCTION

Who isn't interested in the lives of others? If you've picked up this book, you're bound to be curious about what others are really like, especially behind the face they present to the world. People are a bit like icebergs. Day to day, we only get to see the visible tip, but most of us want to know what lies beneath the surface.

There's a particular fascination in knowing more about the lives of notable people, too. The *Talking Heads* guest list is made up of many household names. They have made headlines for their achievements and successes and sometimes their failings. Some have even been nominated for Australian of the Year. Yet, although these people are in a way familiar, in another sense we don't know much about them at all beyond their attachment to a particular cause, role or occupation. What were their childhoods like? Who influenced them? Where did they fall along the path? Why did they set off down their chosen paths, anyway? What were the other turning points along the way? Where does family fit in? What were their darkest times and their best moments?

The funny thing is that it's pretty rare that conversations of this sort occur, even among close friends. The modern pace of life doesn't afford much time to sit down with our friends and really enter into their inner worlds, especially in a sustained way. They're most likely to occur during some time of crisis when help and understanding are being offered. So, oftentimes, the response we get on *Talking Heads* when we talk to people about the finer detail of their lives is 'I haven't thought about this for a long time or in this way before.'

One thing that fascinates me is the way that people think about their past and then tend to 'reconstruct' it in their imaginations. We become the editors of our own stories and we choose the meaning we attach to incidents and the relationships that shape our world. So, did it really happen as we think it did? Where does objective reality lie? Are the attitudes we form about the past fixed or fluid?

Talking to people about their lives is also a means of constructing social history. The people who make up our guests on *Talking Heads* are products of the times in which they've lived. In this book, their stories have traversed the pioneering days of aviation, to the devastating impact of the Great Depression, war and concentration camps; from migration's impact on nation building through to the struggle for indigenous land rights; from popular music and entertainment through to the quest for improving peoples' lives through medicine; from sporting prowess to philanthropy.

One thing that's changed in the past generation or two is people's willingness to talk about themselves. The modern media world is a fishbowl of reality shows, gossip, internet sites like Myspace and Facebook and chat shows where people hang out their intimate washing for public airing. Much of it is produced for purely voyeuristic entertainment. In some respects this trend is healthy in that in the past it was commonplace for people to hide a lot from others. Openness probably goes with greater honesty. But, on the other hand, we are dealing with matters of personal boundaries. When people agree to be guests on *Talking Heads*, they are making themselves vulnerable. They need to know that we will respect their privacy and limits. It would be easy to intrude too far.

As you look over the lives of the outstanding people in this book—it's inevitable that you will see patterns. What are some of them?

Childhood often meant trouble. Clive James' father was killed in an accident on the way home from war. He was there when his mother received the news. In later life, he sought out his grave in Hong Kong and 'it was a big moment for me'. Max Walker didn't see his mother for five years after his parents' divorce. 'I couldn't understand it for a long time and you do feel a lot of rejection.' Peter Cundall says, 'We rarely ever spoke to our father. He was a person to be feared.'

Quite a few were loners, especially as children. Dick Smith was told by his mother that he marched to the beat of a different drum. 'I loved being by myself. I really hated school in the early days ... I've never been any good in a group.' Dr Karl Kruszelnicki: 'I was too geeky. I would wear sandals with socks. Still do ... But that sort of separated me from my fellow schoolmates. And the other thing was that I was a wog. And they were all Anglos. And there was just this big gap.'

Mentors matter. John Clarke made a film *Man and Boy* about someone he worked with at a service station who called him Walter and everybody else Ted. 'He was very encouraging to me in a way that made me wonder whether or not he'd recognised something in me,' he reflects. 'Encouragement is like a book voucher. "Here's a voucher. You don't have to spend it yet." So it's up to you what you do with this encouragement.'

They pursue their passions. Nancy-Bird Walton says: 'They say something happens to my face and my eyes when I get in an aeroplane.' Burns surgeon, Fiona Wood: 'I am mad, passionate, obsessive. I think there has to be a level of fight as well ... that you will not be deflected from your path.' As television medico Dr James Wright opines, 'If you've got a goal or some passion in life, you'll outlive all the other guys.'

Manic energy and a determination never to give up is commonplace. Lillian Frank tells of how her husband says she's 'possessed' with her desire to raise funds. Clive James admits to hyperactivity. 'I overdo it. I don't have to work this hard or do so much.' Peter Cundall says old gardeners never die. 'They just very slowly turn into the most magnificent compost.'

They want to give back. In their own way and in their own spirit, they live by the motto of Fiona Wood's school *Non Sibi Sed Omnibus*. Not for oneself, but for others.

So, I hope you enjoy these stories, as the team that made *Talking Heads* certainly has. After more than three years of making these programs I realise more than ever that as we get to know others, we understand ourselves a little more.

Peter Thompson

EDITOR'S NOTE

As you probably know, each *Talking Heads* program featured filmed location sequences of the guests' early lives, their career highlights and current situations, followed by Peter Thompson's questions. It was always hard telling the stories of inspirational Australians in just half an hour of television time.

Behind the scenes, producers and editors frequently agonised over which fascinating anecdotes or stories to cut to make the material fit the allocated time slot, and still keep the flow of each episode accurate and entertaining.

The chapters in this book include extra material we simply couldn't fit into the program. The collection draws on interviews that each of our guests recorded on location with one of our field producers, as well as the conversations in the studio with Peter Thompson.

We've made adjustments to account for the translation from the spoken to the written word, and to clarify answers where needed, but I hope we've retained the different styles of conversation that made each of our guests so individually engaging.

Our guests were all very patient and generous with their time. Most endured calls over several months to organise a shooting schedule, then a background telephone chat, on-location filming and an interview, as well as the studio interview.

It's been a privilege to be a researcher on a program that illuminates the lives of so many talented, funny and brave Australians, and to have been part of the Brisbane-based production team that made *Talking Heads* from 2005 to 2007.

Pauline Turnbull

PETER CUNDALL
Gardener

Screened 26 March 2007

Peter Cundall is an Australian legend—the avuncular face of ABC TV's *Gardening Australia* has been on our airwaves one way or another for almost forty years. At Tasmania's Royal Botanical Gardens he keeps Australia's most famous vegie patch.

He also writes to five deadlines a week, and supplies the photographs for all his articles.

> I've loved taking photographs ever since I was a kid. But I couldn't afford a camera. I got my first camera about 1943 or '44 and then, of course, I had a brownie box. I've always loved not just photography but trying to photograph unusual things—anything that was interesting. As far as I'm concerned if I can catch a difficult thing like ... two ladybirds copulating, it's an amazing sight because other ladybirds try and get in on the act. And when you look at a group of ladybirds trying to copulate together you can understand instantly how they came to design the Sydney Opera House.

Childhood

I was born in Manchester, 1927. My parents didn't have a home, but used to move around and just kind of hire a room. There were six children ... total poverty. I think when I was about two we moved into more or less our own home, which was a council flat. And I remember—I must have been about four—my mother gave me some peas. Now in those days we used to eat dried peas, still do. We'd soak them, and they'd swell up, and occasionally, if they were left, they'd shoot. And my mother gave me some, and I actually planted them, and to my amazement, they actually came up. That was my first gardening experience. Later on I tried different things; I watched people gardening—I used to talk to old geezers in greenhouses, and they'd give me lots of advice about what they were doing and why they were doing it.

Just before World War II started every home in Britain installed what they called an Anderson Shelter, an air raid shelter for protection against shrapnel. It was really nothing more than a kind of galvanised iron tunnel, a little one, with flat bits at either end. And they said, 'That's not enough; what you should also do is have soil piled on the top'. So I went down to a piece of land that was vacant and dug out what they called sods, square pieces of turf, and stacked them all round and backfilled inside with soil to protect the shelter. It was bombproof. It was brilliant. But I couldn't help but notice that on the top, which was flat, was magnificent soil. So I had a little garden up there, it was only 8–10 square metres, but I grew carrots and parsnips and beetroot and lettuces and a whole range of different vegetables, up in the air, because of this magnificent soil.

School

When I went to school it soon became humiliating. We were all poor—there were thousands of poor—but we were the poorest of the poor, but I never knew it. As a child, remember, you don't know you're poor; you just know there are certain things you can't get. I remember at school, for example, we were given free milk for the poor kids, whereas the rest had to pay a ha'penny.

And on one occasion, after the first year, the teacher said, 'Right now, we want the list of all the poor children. Will the poor children please stand up'. I remember sitting there for the first time in my life as a five-and-a-half year old, just feeling suddenly ashamed. And I didn't stand up. And as a result, I never got any milk for the next six years. I used to sit there in the class watching everybody drinking milk because they thought I didn't want it—yet I loved milk.

In the morning when we went to school we used to have a slice of what we used to call barm cakes, which are nothing more than round pieces of bread like a flat loaf—and that was all. I'd have one for breakfast, and I'd take a barm cake for school usually with something on. I used to love beetroot barm cake sandwiches. And we'd have an evening meal, just a light one. We never had a proper big meal except on a weekend. But at school there were free meals for the poor children. We used to have a little ticket and we'd go to a local church and get appalling food that stank, but we used to eat it—because if you didn't eat it, you never got any pudding, and all I wanted was the pudding.

Parents

My mother was an extraordinarily powerful woman in the sense that she'd known extraordinary poverty as a child. I remember she told me that when she was five, her first job was minding babies. I mean a five year old with one bottle full of water with some sticky condensed milk in it to feed them. And as a result of this poverty she, like me, had an extraordinarily strong social conscience all her life.

My mother was a great humanitarian, but my father, like most males of that period—and most males now for that matter—was extraordinarily self-centred. He also basically—because he couldn't get a job—had a fairly miserable, shameful kind of a life. And of course he hit the grog too.

The Depression

I remember walking round with him looking for work. They had to go around because they couldn't get the dole unless they had proved they had been to so many places. And so it was desperate because quite often he had to walk miles to some factory to try and get a job even when he knew there were none. And he got sick and tired of signing the little chits that would prove that he had been looking for work. It was a depressing business.

He hit the grog for a start. He'd come home, and sometimes he was quite violent with my mother and it was terrible. Sometimes I'd be lying in bed, as a six and seven year old, listening to my mother screaming and this terrible noise of him hitting her and wondering why I was lying in bed so stiff. And, of course, it was fear and apprehension. All children want more than anything is security—that's all. And this destroyed it.

We rarely ever spoke to our father. He was a person to be feared. He was a violent man; but you must understand, in those days blokes often bashed their wives, it was quite common. It affected my mother a lot because eventually when he disappeared—as he did during the war—quite often some local women who'd been bashed by their husbands would come and see her. You'd see these women with these blackened faces where they had been bashed. And my mother actually used to organise other women to go to the place where the bloke worked and show him up. They would bring his wife along to where he was having his meal and say, 'Look what he's done'. And later when he came home they'd be waiting for him and he knew it and they'd bash him up. Nobody ever thought of calling the police.

All this taught me a lot about how to live and how to survive. For a start, I developed a hatred of poverty. I understand it, I know what it's like, yet it helped me to survive too. In other words, if you're poor, you learn to make do, to do things yourself. But at the same time, as long as you live, you never forget poverty and what it does, and how it makes you feel. There's a shame to it in a way.

Remember, where I lived, everybody was poor. Everybody. Everybody was a socialist in the part of Manchester where I came from. I hardly met anyone that voted otherwise, you know, until I was about fifteen.

A library card

In Manchester, we didn't get a library card until we were eight years old. And that, to me, was the magic moment of my life, because that introduced me to the most wonderful paradise. The first book I borrowed was called *Just So Stories* by Rudyard Kipling.

A quite conservative council years earlier decided that there must be a public library within reach of everybody and, in fact, wherever anyone lived in Manchester—and it's still the same, I think—there were three libraries within easy walking distances. And I remember going to the library for the very first time and being sent home because I had dirty hands, but I didn't care. You copped a lot and that's part of this poverty, I suppose. That's it, you do accept it. So I washed my hands and went back and got my first book and read it and went back again and they said, 'Oh no, you're only allowed one book a day'.

And then I found myself reading everything I could and trying if possible to get into the adult section. And eventually ... the luxury of having two books and sometimes being able to borrow three or even four books. Not only that, we all read anything. Remember, in those days there was no television, radio was limited, most of the activities of children were out in the streets. And we'd exchange books and read out to each other. It was a philosophy, it was a kind of a culture, if you like, of reading and, of course, the libraries were always full. When you go into a public library the thing that you smell is the smell of the glue in the book. It's a kind of sickly, horrible smell, but to me it was the sweetest smell in the world.

I got my first job when I was twelve years old. I was still at school but it was as a milk boy so I used to get out of bed in the morning at half past five, deliver the milk on a bike, work until a quarter to nine, go to school, come back at lunchtime, spend an hour washing bottles, and then after school I would be back again, washing bottles and what they call capping, putting the caps on the milk bottles. So I did that every day except for weekends. Then I worked the entire weekend. I left school shortly after that, and I basically ran wonderfully wild around Manchester.

A wild boy

I left school at twelve because that was in 1939 when the war came, and we were evacuated. And because I was a bit of a delinquent at the time, I didn't last long when I was evacuated and was sent back home after two weeks. So I was running wild. It was magnificent. That was the most brilliantly educational period of my life, running wild in Manchester as a twelve year old and not going to school. It was lovely.

I learnt about people. One thing that my mother used to say right from the very beginning: 'You must always watch people. Never mind what they say, but you must watch what they do. Learn to watch people and watch their behaviour all the time'. I used to go and watch people.

Sometimes I'd go to little quiet places, like even an old quarry, or a clay pit, I used to sit there and just think. I remember when I was going to school I used to wag it just to go there to think. And I could never quite explain when the head teacher asked, 'Peter, why is it this week you've been away for a day, then another day, and then half a day?' And I said, 'I just wanted to think, sir, I just wanted to catch up', and he didn't understand.

I didn't think I was odd. I was like any other kid. But I just felt that sometimes you want to get away from lessons and sit there and just think and look at things. I remember looking at weeds growing. I was amazed at the extraordinary vigour of the way a weed can grow in almost pure clay. In a claypit you can see the roots. I used to think, Where does that energy come from? Wouldn't it be marvellous if we could get our plants to grow like that?

I was about fourteen when I got a job working as a store boy at the railway. And working in the railway workshop stores was one of the most unbelievably boring experiences I've ever had. Fortunately after two months they sacked me, when they discovered, to my amazement, that I was red/green colour blind. When I went in to be tested, they looked at one another after I'd tried different colours, and said, 'I'm sorry, pal, but we can't have you on the railways if you're colour blind; otherwise, you might be walking into a train against the signal'

When I was at school, we had art classes, which was mainly drawing with crayons, but of course, because of my colour-blindness I drew all sorts of strange pictures. And I can remember how teachers used to stand behind me saying, 'Oh Peter, oh Peter, where did you get that from?'—because I would look at the sky and see only the colour that I saw. And they'd say, 'Oh Peter, the skies are not purple', but that was the colour I could see. I remember I used to love what used to be the local gypsies—they used to come along and park nearby—and I remember once drawing a gypsy camp with caravans and horses, and people sitting around the fire, and they said, 'Oh Peter, that's a beautiful drawing but the colours are so weird'.

The Blitz

I became what they call an ARP [Air Raid Precautions] messenger boy during the Blitz. That meant I was placed in a big warehouse and my job was to report any fires that took place. I remember incendiaries coming down through the roof once. And I thought, Right, and off I raced—because there were no telephones, the lines had all been blown up—running to the fire station. And I'm running through streets blazing on either side, the electric tramwires were down, arcing and jumping all over the place. I thought, Hang on, why am I running to the fire station? And I ran back and threw a sandbag on them. That's when I was fourteen. It was my first experience of war, and also the first experience of my hatred of war ... the total idiocy of it. I mean, Wilfred Owen called it 'the pity of war', but I call it 'the stupidity of war'. It is utterly stupid, and I think I learnt that even in the Blitz when I saw huge buildings destroyed.

I was delivering milk on one occasion to this house. I was about to go into this little street, and a policeman stopped me and said, 'Where are you going, lad?' I said, 'I'm going to number 14'. He said, 'There's no number 14, lad, off you go'. I said, 'Well, I've got to deliver the milk', and I went past him. And of course, there was just an empty space and a pile of rubble. And I thought, What am I going to do with the milk? I drank it, actually. But I did see a group of people walking away earlier with blankets round them talking to each other and saying strange things like they did in the war, 'Are we downhearted? No, we're not downhearted' ... That sort of cheering up stuff.

I was about sixteen when I became a tram conductor. It's almost like a performing art—you'd perform before a load of passengers. And my experiences there were extremely interesting, the way I started to understand people and the way they behaved. So it was absolutely fantastic. But one of the big problems about being a conductor on a tram is that you've never finished: as soon as you've collected all the fares and handed out all the tickets, everyone has gone and another lot has taken their place, and so it goes on all the time.

A love of music

I've always had the most incredible interest in music, which has been to me the driving force of my so-called artistic life. In Manchester we were very fortunate: we used to have the most brilliant orchestra called the Halle. So from about seventeen I used to go to concerts on a regular basis. It was a magnificent orchestra. They used to play lots of new works as well as traditional works, so I got to know quite a lot of European classical music. I was into Mozart and Chopin and Beethoven and Schubert, and all these with great enjoyment. And it had its great effect later on because I didn't realise I was almost memorising some of these works. It was only later—just after the war when I was in prison, in solitary confinement in Yugoslavia—that I was able to while away the time by listening to Mozart in my head. And I was amazed at what we can remember, because it wasn't just the themes—and the tunes, if you like—but after a while you can hear other counter melodies as well.

I used to listen to all kinds of music including popular songs. I used to sing them. Remember, too, that there was an enormous amount of music in our area. Every second kid could play a mouth organ. I'd loved to have done so but I could never quite get the suck and blow of a mouth organ. I'd always find I was sucking in my own spit; it was horrible.

Conscripted

Just towards the end of the war in 1945 I was conscripted, then posted to Austria. That meant I was passing through France and Germany—I mean, it was town upon town that was totally shattered and destroyed—and that's when I first came into contact with people who'd just been liberated from concentration camps. It was appalling.

Just after World War II in Europe and the liberation, my job was guarding SS guards from some of the camps, and I was also in contact with many of the people who had been in the camps. I listened to their shocking stories. That had an incredible effect on me. Particularly talking to those Jews, communists, socialists, democrats, and the Seventh Day Adventists and Jehovah's Witnesses that had been in the camps. Particularly the Jews, because their only crime was being Jewish. And to be a Jew in Europe under Hitler was a sentence of death, make no mistake about that.

We were stationed in an old monastery in a place called St Paul in southern Austria, only 6 kilometres from the Yugoslav border. One day I met a girl of such exquisite beauty and she asked me to take her for a walk. What I didn't realise was that people were going backwards and forwards over the frontier illegally, and it helped her to move around if she had a soldier with her. And so I went over the border with her. That's when I was picked up by Tito's partisans and was put in the nick.

Surviving solitary

The only problem about solitary confinement was it was extraordinarily boring. I overcame it to some extent, although I only had a tiny cell. I'd move my blanket from one corner to another every day, so it became almost like another world, you know. Remember, I was only nineteen years old. When I first went into that cell I remember looking round and thinking, This is the first room of my own I've ever had in my life, so there was a certain sense of elation about it.

I had my music and I used to listen to Mozart. It sounds mad, but, I mean, you can actually listen to music in your head. And the amazing thing was this: that as I listened, I could sometimes hear the other melodies coming in as well. It was quite a remarkable experience. They wouldn't let me whistle, so I used to whistle silently to some of the tunes that were in my mind. But it was music that carried me through.

When I was released, in a place called Sežana near Trieste, I was interrogated by British intelligence to find out what had been going on, and then posted to Vienna. And was picked up again, in the Russian-controlled Grey Zone. This time I was without a pass; I think the Russian military police took pity on this strange young man because they let me go.

Court martial

I think it was almost a joke. All I know, because of six months' absence in Yugoslavia, I was marched before a group of army officers and the senior officer said to me, 'You are really an absolutely wretched man, aren't you?' And I said, 'Yes, sir'. And then the sergeant major, to my amazement, stepped forward and said, 'I'd like to give evidence in this man's defence, sir'. And the officer said, 'That's very unusual, sergeant major. What do you have to say?' He said, 'Sir, I'd like to point out ...' and then he told them how I'd spent the night with the young woman who had taken me over the border yet I was still a virgin. Quite clearly they were shocked. In fact, the senior officer said, 'Is it true? Did you not experience carnal knowledge?' And I said innocently, 'Well, her name wasn't Carmel, sir, it was Angela'.

It was a bit of a shock when I left Austria and was sent almost immediately to another war zone—the Palestine War—I was posted to Gaza. And for the first time I met some Jewish settlers. I suppose the thing that shocked me more than anything else—and it was quite illuminating—was that some of them were quite racist in their attitude towards the Arab people. And of course I've learnt since that quite often the very worst tyrants can be ex-slaves.

Not an officer

They're another class, the officer class. You didn't want to be part of it. I used to resent saluting. They used to explain that it's just a polite way of passing the time of day. But if you didn't do it you got into strife. I resented it and still do. I never call anyone 'Sir' and I certainly don't want anyone to call me 'Sir'. I've always believed—it may sound strange—I've always believed that I've never met anyone better than me or anyone worse than me.

I mean, I've gone through the process of almost, being almost intimidated by power and by wealth and by highly educated people. I remember going to a Halle concert in Manchester once and I was almost awestruck at the university students who used to sit right along the front row with their scarves and thinking what great and powerful intellectuals they must be. I remember walking behind them and listening to them talking. And I'd never heard such pretentious rubbish in all my life. And I thought, Hang on, what am I so awestruck about? I mean, they were talking so stupidly amongst each other and so pretentiously about the concert and about Beethoven and Tchaikovsky, and their conversation was just so full of emptiness.

Joining the Australian army

Eventually I got back to Manchester. A couple of years after leaving the British Army I saw a little tiny ad in the paper, and it said, 'Volunteers wanted for the Australian army'. The last thing I was going to tell them was that I had been an infantryman. I said that in fact I had been a military librarian. They said, 'You are exactly what we need. Have you ever heard of Bondi?' They told me right on the beach is the most magnificent military library. I said, 'Where do you sign?' However, when we got to Melbourne, they put the whole lot of us in the infantry. They said, 'There's a draft going to the Korean War'. We all felt a bit conned, but then again we were more or less resigned to it.

During World War II, I had met a group of Australian soldiers in Kent. Some of them had recently been released from a camp they had been prisoners of war—and I remember watching them. They all had their slouch hats turned down all the way round and they were just so quiet, so self-confident. When I talked to them they were just so marvellous. I mean, these were the men of the second AIF, the greatest Australians, and wonderful men. And when I talked to them, they were so kind to me. They hated any form of pretension, any form of dishonesty, and any form of snobbery. And they impressed me. From that experience I thought I'd like to go to this place where these blokes come from. I knew nothing of

Australia, apart from what I'd read in that very first book by Rudyard Kipling, which included a story called 'How the Kangaroo Got Its Hop'.

I couldn't believe it when I arrived in Australia in 1950. I couldn't take my eyes off the sky. I'd never seen anything so blue. It was so intense. And it was so strange. Australia had a different smell. I remember walking through the streets of Melbourne and then walking from central Melbourne—or basically from Royal Park, where I was stationed—to St Kilda Beach. It was almost magical. But it was the smell—the smell of fruit and milk bars. I mean, a milk bar is an Australian development, I already knew that. And so there were these amazing milk bars where you could go and get a milkshake or a cup of coffee and things like that. But no, I just thought it was so absolutely marvellous. It was like a dream.

I found that there was a great feeling of equality around the place. Again, it was a complete lack of pretension. Things are different now in some ways. People seem to be becoming a little bit more Americanised in Australia. They're also a little bit more awestruck by powerful people, these days. In the past they never were.

After coming back from Korea, I was training soldiers. By this time I had developed such an extraordinary hatred of war that, even though I was supposed to be training soldiers for war, I was really training soldiers to survive. I used to say to them, 'You must never volunteer for anything'. That's what soldiers do in a war: they protect each other and they do everything they can to survive.

Shortly afterwards, still as a soldier, I was posted from Sydney to Tasmania, and I became a weapons instructor for national servicemen. It was a completely new life. By this time, I'd married, and there were no children at this stage. Later on the children started to arrive. I then moved to Launceston and settled there in a war service home. Of course, Tasmania is the perfect gardening place. And as soon as I left the Australian army I could hardly wait to get stuck in to it. I put a little ad in the local paper saying

'Gardens cleared, pruning', all that sort of thing. And I was amazed: I got about thirty replies in two days.

While I was in the Australian army, what I did, in Japan or in Europe, I went to see gardens whenever possible and looked at great gardens and small gardens and talked to gardeners, especially in Japan, where I was greatly influenced by Japanese gardening techniques.

Communism

It was the cruelty of the Korean War—all these dead people in villages that had been totally destroyed—that really appalled me so much. And I was afraid, like many other people, of a nuclear war breaking out. So I became involved in the peace movement and out of that joined the Communist Party. It was, I think, my way of doing good.

While I was in Launceston, long after I'd left the army ... I retained a tremendous sense of justice. I've always had a great feeling that it's possible to abolish poverty, and supported equal rights for everyone. So I was actually looking for a political party that more or less reflected these ideals, and that's why I joined the Communist Party. In fact I went looking for them, and at first I couldn't find them. Eventually I joined and became quite active. But it was during that period while I was putting out leaflets, even writing them and printing them myself, that I realised there was a major problem there: that basically, Stalinism, as it was, had actually spread throughout different communist parties everywhere. What was happening was weird. Within the Soviet Union and the other eastern European socialist countries, it was a privileged position to be a communist and so they had privileges. So people were joining these parties simply to get these privileges, whereas in the west there were people like myself joining the Communist Party for idealistic reasons.

I even left gardening work and went and got a job in a certain factory because I'd heard that the conditions were very poor and very bad. So I deliberately went in there to try and improve the working conditions. It was terrible: a foundry with appalling conditions. There was no protection at all for some of the workers. Eventually I was sacked from that job, blamed for something I hadn't done, and I couldn't believe it. They just sacked me. They said, 'Just don't come back'. However, I did. I came back the next day. It took a lot for me to do this. I was trembling but I stood at the door. As the workers were coming back in I said, 'I was sacked for no reason yesterday. What are you going to do about it?' Everyone was a bit frightened, and they all went inside and they didn't speak to me. But believe it or not, within twenty minutes the whole lot walked out. That was the first turning point. They actually improved conditions. I went back for a while, but eventually they got rid of me.

By then I was known as an agitator of the worst type, and never to be employed. So I couldn't get a job, and I went into gardening fulltime. The very people who wouldn't employ me in their factories would have me working in their garden because I wasn't agitating the other workers; I could only agitate plants.

Into the media

One day, I happened to be pruning the roses of the manager of the local radio station. Afterwards he said to me, 'Look, we've just started a new thing'—this is late 1960s—'it's called radio talkback. How about coming on our station and giving people gardening advice over the air?' So I did and, believe it or not, the switchboard was absolutely blocked with callers. For me it was the beginning of a new career.

In late 1969, the ABC invited me to do an audition for a little television gardening program called *It's Growing* that went to air before the 7 pm news on Friday night. So I prepared for it in the most intense way. I managed to get an idea of what the studio looked like, and even made a replica of the special demonstration table they used. When I arrived down there for the audition they said, 'You've got to do exactly four and three-quarter minutes'. So I did a miniature rock garden and how to plant it. And that was my introduction to television. I did the *It's Growing* program for two or three years.

And then in about 1972 they decided to expand the idea of television gardening with a program called *Landscape*. This was an outside broadcast unit with a huge van and people running everywhere. That was interesting because it was the very first time anywhere that anyone had actually landscaped a garden from scratch on television. That was done in black and white. In 1974, I won a Churchill fellowship to go overseas and study television gardening in colour in the USA, Britain and South Africa. When I went to the United States to see their gardening television, they had none. Then I went to South Africa to study television gardening and they didn't even have television in South Africa at that time!

Landscape went until 1990 and then state gardening programs became national with *Gardening Australia*. I remember how one ABC official from Sydney said to me, 'But you realise, of course, that with your unfortunate accent you could never ever be the main presenter'. So I said, 'Why not?' He said, 'Trouble is, it's unfortunately rather working class'. I don't know what happened, but the bloke who said that has long since gone, and I'm still here.

An activist in Tasmania

I suppose because I had been an infantry soldier in three wars—in World War II, the Palestine War, and also in Korea—I became absolutely anti-war. I realised what a total waste of life it was. And this was one of the reasons I became so active in the anti-war movements, and why I wrote and printed pamphlets and handed them out. It was mainly against nuclear war. That was the great fear everywhere in those days. It was a period of extraordinary activity. I used to sit up all night writing and then printing leaflets. Then I'd go out at night and distribute them, in letter boxes at different houses.

I became deeply involved in the campaign against the Vietnam War. I was one of those carrying a sign—even on my own at times that said 'Bring our troops home'. I mean, I was also happy to welcome them when they came back—I thought that they had suffered. And since then we've found out that the Vietnam veterans have suffered far more than any others. I think it's terrible. Many are going though a terrible experience now.

I also got involved in the environmental movement. Because I'm an organic gardener I'm deeply aware of the problems of chemicals in the soil and poisons in the atmosphere or on the plants that we eat.

I have long been involved in the campaign to stop the destruction of our forests, destruction of our wilderness areas, to save a river— the Franklin River. I was deeply involved when they attempted to dam the Franklin River. When they tried to put up a giant, stinking, toxic pulp mill at Wesley Vale I never hesitated. I was right in the thick of it. Right now I'm deeply involved in the campaign to stop them putting up another even bigger pulp mill in the beautiful Tamar Valley.

The Tamar Valley is where I live with my family and thousands of other families. And they're hoping to build a pulp mill there— one of the biggest in the world—and it's going to produce not only toxic fumes from its 200-metre chimney stack, but it's also going to use the water supply for the whole of the West Tamar region. Then when they've polluted it, they want to pump it out into the sea. And that's the sort of campaign that I've become involved in, and I'll never stop fighting against this mill.

Living in Tasmania

Tasmania is probably the most looted place on earth. It's also one of the most beautiful places, and that's the thing that strikes me time and time again.

When I first arrived here in 1955 I went to Queenstown, and it was a kind of ghastly moonscape. I couldn't believe that the industry could be so terrible—this was damage from a copper smelter. Up north near Burnie it was a huge semicircle of discoloured water, in the sea, where they were pouring all this paint waste into the ocean. I couldn't believe that pollution and contempt for the environment could be so brazen. You have to speak up. If you don't speak up you get buried, it's as simple as that.

I actually love Tasmania so much that I never want to leave it—I don't even want to go to the mainland—it is the most marvellous place. But I supposed I've learnt a lot here. I've learnt more about gardening. Remember that Tasmania is not like England. It's more like Portugal—a Mediterranean climate. It's not all that cold, although some people may think so.

This is one of the greatest gardening places on earth. It's got this extraordinary climate where we can even grow subtropical trees like citrus quite well and also the hardiest alpine plants: the whole range. We can grow the most magnificent vegetables. Remember that these particular bands around the earth, around 40 degrees north or south, are the most prolific and fertile bands on earth because of the day length, which varies. This is very important. Also because of the kind of climate that we have. For example, the temperature where I live, it's about 24 degrees in summer, and it drops to about 14 at night. It's great. And in winter we get about twenty frosts and that's it. During the daytime it'll rise to 12 or 13 or 14. Ours is a brilliant climate for growing every kind of vegetable and fruit apart from tropical ones.

Gardening changes

The most dramatic change of all I've seen is people turning to organic growing. That's growing fruit and vegetables and ornamental plants without any poisons whatsoever, and without any disruptive chemicals. That's happening now, and that is the most revolutionary change. Remember, thirty years ago, you'd go into a nursery and all you could smell was the chemicals, the toxins that were used—there were rows of them. You don't get that now.

I'm part of it. I'm part of that change; I've pushed and pushed. On *Gardening Australia* we don't use poisons and we don't use chemicals. We broadcast that and tell everybody, 'This is what you can do. You don't need poisons to grow great stuff'.

A celebrity gardener

People think it must be lovely to be famous. But it's not! It's a bit embarrassing because people think they know you so well that you can't have a conversation in public without somebody barging in. And when they do, they do it quite innocently. Quite often I bury myself behind a newspaper in an airport and keep out of sight as much as possible. I try to be polite to people because I realise that when people come up to talk, it's a great compliment. But it can be also quite disturbing if I go out with my family and we are having a meal—some people come to the table and stand there. They want all sorts of information about their gardens. And that can be embarrassing at times.

I believe in many things, like saving the environment and preventing the destruction of forests, so I'm quite ruthless about getting up there and speaking out. And if my position as a well-known person helps people to listen better, that's fine by me.

I've always had very strong feelings about what I considered to be major problems in the world, and I believe the basic cause is greed. Greed for everything. Consequently, when they invited me, to my amazement, to address the National Press Club in Canberra a few years ago, I said, 'What for? What do you want me to speak about?' They said, 'Anything you like'. When I heard that my speech was to go to air live, it was a great opportunity, so I said to the audience—many of whom were gardeners, who had come along to listen to something on gardening—'If you think I'm going to be talking about gardening you've got Buckley's'.

Instead I spoke about my thoughts about greed. How greed for power, greed for money, greed to control people, is the greatest threat to the world today. Greed is the major responsibility for wars, for the destruction of the environment, for the pollution of rivers, and above all for keeping people all over the world miserable and poor. And so I spoke with great passion about that and to my astonishment, within a matter of about a week or so, the letters flowed in from all over Australia, every one of them positive. Some people said, in fact, that they were listening and crying as they heard it because they believed it to be so true. So I don't feel so lonely about my hatred of greed and what it is and what it does.

I have an optimism about what people are willing to do. The greatest force in the world today, believe it or not, are these countless groups of people in every country almost—even in China—that are doing things to protect their local environment and to try and protect the earth. It's happening and of course it is developing everywhere. But we're approaching a kind of razor's edge right now. The fools are in charge, but it's the wise people who are shouting warnings!

Life today

The main driving force in my life is not necessarily gardening. That's just one of the things that I do with great passion and enthusiasm. But I'm involved in just about everything else. I take a burning interest in current affairs, in what's going on in the world. I read every newspaper I can. In fact, I read them incessantly, apart from the business pages and the sport pages, which I chuck away.

I'm interested in everything. In fact, the first thing I do every morning, I go to one of my computers. This is the great thing about technology—you can go just about anywhere in the world instantly. So, the first place I go is to look at Steve Bell's cartoons in *The Guardian*. They're always funny, and they're always a little bit vulgar. And then, of course, I go immediately to the news pages, and

I read the news from just about everywhere in the world—America and Britain, and of course Australia—and I find out what's going on, because I'm totally dedicated and addicted to current affairs.

I'm still making radio programs—I started in 1968 and I've never stopped—so every week I do a radio gardening talkback for ABC Radio and it covers the whole of Tasmania. And the terrific thing is the immediate contact with people. I know what they're thinking, what they want to know, what their problems are, and actually I use many of those ideas for the television program.

I suppose in a way some of my busiest times are sitting on my bum actually writing, typing away there, sitting behind a computer. I have about five deadlines a week—scripts, magazines and newspapers. It's mainly about gardening, and every column's different. And throughout the year, I try and present even the same kinds of jobs in a different way or from a different angle. I do love modern technology. I've got about six or seven computers simply because my friend makes them for me. I use them all. I use them for different purposes and I now find, for example, that I hardly use any paper, although I'm writing continuously. So I'm writing columns all the time, but I simply belt them out and email them to the newspaper or to the magazine for which I'm writing, with photographs I take myself.

A concert performer

One day I got quite a surprise when someone rang me up and said, 'Look, we'd like you to take part in a concert. It's a composition of the great French composer Messiaen'. It was a very difficult piano piece called *The Catalogue of Birds*, with Michael Kieran Harvey, who I think is one of Australia's greatest pianists. They wanted my voice mainly to read the prose about birds and the environment in which they lived. The composer became greatly concerned in the late 1950s about the destruction of the environment. So, my job was to stand there to introduce some of the pieces, by reading the prose of Messiaen.

I'll be collaborating with Michael Kieran Harvey again, in Brisbane at their wonderful music festival in July [2007]. The pieces are by Bach and several modern composers, and my role is to do a kind of narration—to recite different poems or different forms of prose, such as my own. 'Stand in despair anywhere old-growth forest has been clear-felled. All life has been replaced by blackened, poisoned desolation. Animals and birds have either fled or been killed, and baits are laid waiting for those that should return. And in these tortured places, the devastation is brutal and total. And this is what greed looks like.'

It's going to be something that's quite new for me. Why would I, an eighty-year-old geezer, go in to be spruiking at a concert? But I'm trying it out and seeing what's happening.

Growing older

The most important thing of all for most people as they grow older is good health.

I've not changed my priorities, just some of them have become more urgent. The older you get, there's a certain urgency to things. But what I've stuck with and the thing that I'm concerned about more than anything else is the health of ordinary people. The last time I went to a doctor, because I was sick, was 1951. Why? Because I'm determined to stay healthy. That's the reason I don't drink. Not because I've got anything against the grog, but I like a clear head all the time. And I certainly don't smoke, because I don't want to die a horrible death of lung cancer. But the most important thing for anyone is to stay healthy. And as for myself, I'd never, ever wish to be a burden on anyone.

I never think about retiring. As far as I'm concerned—look, I'll go on forever, until someone taps me on the shoulder and tells me to bugger off or until I suddenly think, I've got better things to do. Old gardeners never die; they just very slowly turn into the most magnificent compost. But what a marvellous, active brew it is!

It's the sheer joy of seeing things grow and helping them to grow, even harvesting the stuff that you've grown yourself, no matter how old you are. Look at me, an old geezer, and yet experiencing that same joy that I had when I first saw those peas poking through ... I mean, last week I put some carrot seed in. It was up yesterday and it gave me that same lovely jolt of happiness: Boy, they're up.

It is a good life, if you're doing what you like doing. Believe it or not, I actually like not only gardening; I take a kind of a fiendish delight in pulling out weeds—ripping them out. There's a certain sadistic satisfaction in pulling them out roots and all and saying, 'Got you!' that keeps me alive.

MAX WALKER
Sportsman, writer and raconteur

Screened 19 February 2007

Max Walker is a great sport in every sense of the word. He played first-grade Aussie Rules for Melbourne and Test cricket for Australia, one of only a handful of players to reach such dizzying sporting heights. His passions extend to art and architecture, and he's also one of the country's best yarn spinners, a skill he developed early in life, as the son of a publican.

> One day there, there was even a prostitute that lobbed in the hotel and the police were involved. My sister's moneybox and her records had been taken and so the police arrived, and they had a fair idea it might have been the moneyboxes and the records in behind this door ... and I'm about ten, eleven years of age. I look through the crack in the door, the two police go in and there's Francy Anne Sullivan, there she was, larger than life, stark naked on the bed, two constables trying to sort of bring her down, now what do you do? She's got a high heel shoe in each hand. I can't believe what I'm seeing here. I'm going to get Boston buns for the next twelve months retelling this story at school. I guess that was one of the first big stories I got to reshape and retell to get better and better.

Childhood

My story began across the horizon, across Bass Strait, in Tasmania. As a young fella—elbows like razor blades, legs like fluorescent light globes—I went to the Lansdowne Crescent State School ... very happy time there. Played a bit of footy and a bit of cricket. In fact, I think the footy jumper was the same one my old man wore twenty or thirty years earlier.

I spent a fair bit of my life in the backyard of the Empire Hotel, the Institute of Experience. We had the good, bad and ugly there at any particular stage on any day. Sure there were fights. I hypnotised a few chooks out in the fowl yard, I used to play backyard cricket. A never-ending stream of clientele would come out for a nervous one and this snotty-nosed little kid would tap them on the shoulder and say, 'Mister, do you feel like a bowl or a bat?' Occasionally they would want to bat and that's when I used to bowl the throat ball, into the expansion joint between the two slabs of concrete, the cork composition ball would climb vertically, hit them in the throat. They'd go back to their beer on the counter and their Gladstone bags and tell another yarn. The old man would sell more beers. It was a never-ending stream. The times I got to bat, I hit one of the best cover drives of my life back then ... 45 degrees, like a tracer bullet, straight at the women's toilets. There was a dead beer bottle lying outside the external wall of the women's toilets, redbrick; it climbed vertically, took eleven louvre blades out of the women's toilets. Now I don't know whether that woman achieved what she set out to do, but I know it frightened the absolute living suitcase out of her. And that was when I was introduced to sledging. This woman, teeth still intact, blue rinse hairdo, what she said to me, it seared my eyebrows. My boxer dog Paddy—sable colour—he went down on all fours, put his paws over his ears; I mean, he couldn't cope either. Yes, we had all sorts of fun in the backyard.

You know, one day, and I couldn't believe it, I'd come home from school, 3.30 in the afternoon, and there's two pretty close to sixty-year-old people—and I call them old people because I was only a young person. It was a guy obviously not with his wife. Now I didn't know that, but when his wife arrived I realised that there was something wrong in the dynamics. And then his wife absolutely king hit this guy. It's the best right cross I've ever seen. I've just gone, 'Whoa!' And he's out like this—horizontal! And then these two women, they're pretty close to sixty, are rolling over. It was rock'n'roll wrestling. You should have seen it. There were high heels, stockings, garters, you know, lipstick, and language like sledging; you wouldn't believe it. Of course, this is the rich tapestry of life. You go back and you tell the kids at school. 'What did you do?' 'I went home and I did my homework.' 'I went home and there's the biggest blue you've ever seen taking place in the back bar.'

In the main bar in the early days closing was at six o'clock, and then later on it went to ten o'clock. But there were the odd occasions when the licensing squad would raid the hotel, and the big no-no was the proprietor could not be caught at any cost. They tried and they tried to get Big Max, my old man, but he was good. He used to hide out the back, in the garages, underneath boats, in amongst crates, in the cool store, and they never got him.

I cherish all of those stories, experiences that are inside my head, that 3½ pound blob, the 'neck top computer' as I love to call it. It's the most awesome piece of technology on the planet. All of those stories, all of those images, all of those relationships, it helps storytelling as a writer. But it also makes it more interesting to be around, it gives you a different perspective, you can understand why people do things, you can see someone that's alcohol fuelled. For example, they won't take no, they go forever, the non-stop cigarettes, all of that stuff. You see everything. How incongruous was it that I, the son of a publican and a master builder, went to The Friends' School, which was a Quaker school. Quakers don't believe in alcohol. They don't believe in individualism either.

The sounds of cricket

Some of my fondest memories were being there as a young teenager amongst the clan. They were drinking beer and we were listening to the fabulous, almost romantic sounds of John Arlott, the gravel-voiced Englishman, and the silky smooth Alan McGilvray talking and commentating on Test cricket—England versus Australia, The Ashes—in many ways they lit the fire in my belly that made me want to be a Test player. It was a fantastic time for me.

I spent a lot of time growing up alongside my Uncle Charlie. He could do anything. On a Friday night he would take me down to the newsagent and we would buy the broadsheet, *Eagle* comics, get me a *Phantom* too. We wound our own copper wire coils and we built our own crystal sets. You'd lay in bed at night, with the headphones, your ears would be pinned back, and you'd hear the commentary—McGilvray, Arlott, South African Charles Fortune—they were fantastic. You'd wake up with your ears pinned back but happy in the knowledge that Australia had done well overnight.

Family

We weren't a big family. Mum, Dad, my sister, Lexie, who was about twenty-one months younger than me. In fact, in many ways she was a better kick, she was a better cricketer, she was better than many of her boyfriends that she brought home. They were a bit young, fourteen or fifteen, and she used to say, 'Why don't you go down there with Max, you'll get a kick down there'. She used to outmark them too. She was great sportsperson in her own right: she was a sprinter, a high jumper, played hockey, netball, softball. She was a lot of fun.

Divorce

You feel, in one sense, how can this be happening to me, why aren't my parents together? As you get older you understand the perspective and the dynamics of relationships that make these things possible, but I guess you don't live a lie and so you break up. That's what happened. I couldn't understand it for a long time. You do feel a lot of rejection. Yet today my mum and I are closer than ever.

I stayed with my dad. Lexie stayed with us for a while and then she moved on up to Sydney for a few years. We were a bit all over the place. And I remember one evening a door swung open; I was about to play in a State Premiership match for Friends' School versus Launceston Church Grammar and, you know, you're taught as a kid, don't get into strange cars. The door opened and there was my mum—I hadn't seen her for about five years. We'd exchanged some letters, but so we actually came back together again there that night. I finished my schooling, got matriculation, went to Melbourne to play. I stayed with my dad for a little while there and it seemed a much better thing to actually move in and stay with my mum, so we lived in this little maisonette in Brunswick and you'd put the hot coals in for the hot water and put too many in and the hot water would boil over. I stayed in half a bungalow up the back of the house.

Illness

As a ten- or eleven-year-old kid I spent a very dark period of my life ... I spent a lot of time on my back, about six months actually. I was diagnosed with rheumatic fever. It was very painful, I fell down a few stairs, I couldn't walk, I couldn't get involved in footy practice.

I first understood that something was wrong; I used to be able to kick 40 yards in the old days when I was about ten or eleven, and yet I could only kick about 10 metres, and then I went back home after footy practice with my Uncle Charlie, and I fell down the stairs; my legs wouldn't work ... A massive symptom there. They just wouldn't work, day after day, and so I spent six months on my back in bed, old cardboard box folded up so that you could actually put your legs through it and the idea was to not have any weight on your legs.

But the worst part was being told I was not able to play sport. It was devastating. The doctors said to me, 'You'll never play sport, you can't play sport, you have got a weak heart'. I remember once, about three months after I was back on my feet, and back at school, playing footy out on the street with a few other kids. I came inside with a sweat; the old man looked at me, and my mum looked at me and said, 'You can't do that, you mustn't go out there'.

Fortunately I was like any other kid, full of mischief and keen to play and I didn't listen to them. History, I guess, will judge me. I didn't have a weak heart: I bowled up the hill into the breeze with an old ball on a flat wicket many a time, and the heart stood up well. Even managed to send a few Englishmen on their way.

Dad—Big Max

Big Max was—gosh, what a footprint he's left on my life. Always telling me that I could do things. You know when someone puts their arm around you and says, 'Look, I think you're good enough' and seriously, genuinely means it, that's a massive amount of support. As older people we should do that with our youngsters, just give them a chance, give them confidence. Big Max was a great friend as well. He spent hours throwing a ball to me in the backyard. We'd go to sports grounds; he could see that there was some future for me as a batsman. It didn't actually turn out that way, although I made quite a few runs for North Hobart.

He was a master builder. He wanted me to be an architect; he sent me to a Quaker school. And as he said, if he'd had the same amount of opportunity as me on the mainland, he reckons he would've got as many kicks in VFL footy and he certainly would've taken more wickets in Test cricket. I know that for a fact, because he told me so over and over again. And the number of people who would come in to the pub and say to me, 'Son, if you're half as good as your old man you'll be a champion'. You reckon that didn't 'p' me off? That was a huge incentive. I think somewhere along the line we might've levelled out.

I never fell out with my old man. If I look back on life, he might have only ever once really couched a heavy sentence at me and I think he might have whacked me on the back of the knuckles with his huge builder's hands. It was a gentle touch. I was probably about ten or twelve at that stage ... I can't really remember. We never had much conflict at all in our life. He said one day to me, 'Son'—he'd come back from watching me play footy—he said, 'Now, you've got to get the ball. If you haven't got the ball you can't kick it, you can't make an impact'. And I'm going, 'Dad, Dad', and he said, 'No, listen to me, you must have the football'. 'Dad, Dad', I said, 'It was my turn to be goal post today, that's why I didn't move!' I was only about nine or ten. Big Max didn't like to be seen. He'd hide behind cars, behind trees; he thought he'd bring me bad luck.

Crossing Bass Strait

When I was a kid Bass Strait represented a huge barrier, it was like a big brick wall in the psyche. To expect, as a Tasmanian, you could go to the mainland and be successful wasn't that easy to accept. In fact, a few times before I left, I was told, 'You can't hope to go to the mainland and be a VFL footballer and a Test cricketer and an architect'. And I said, 'Look, there are no guarantees'. And if I had bought into that psychology, I wouldn't have come and what a disappointment that would've been. It's nice to be able to create your own opportunities because there are no guarantees in life.

I had a knock on the door, as a seventeen year old: Norm Smith, AFL/VFL coach of the century, was at my doorstep. A Form Four it was called back then. Really it was just an airline ticket. 'You get a kick, son, when you get to the mainland and you won't have to use the second leg. You don't get a kick, you do use the second leg and you go home very quickly.' Fortunately for me, to have a man like Norm Smith come into my life, I think he was the greatest man that

I ever met. He had a huge impact on my life, way ahead of his time in terms of thinking about individuals and treating them differently. And for me, to play in the MCG, to walk out on the ground ... there were more people at the MCG than the whole of Tasmania!

The MCG

The first time I walked onto the MCG was like walking on air. The huge roar of that great grey concrete colosseum—marvellous! As a kid you dream about that sort of stuff. This day I ran out, Don Williams played his 250th game ... I didn't know whether the streamers were out there for his 250 or my first, but I was floating on air. I just strolled out and ran a round of the MCG. I lined up against a guy named Noel Teasdale, won a Brownlow Medal for North Melbourne. He had a leather patch on his forehead, a massive leather patch, covering up a metal plate. And I thought, Gosh, that's got to be to hold his brains intact ... I didn't tell him; I mean, he was 17 stone and I was about 12½ stone, wringing wet. That was my introduction, and I got my hand on the ball first. But then his chest and his fist took me about 10 metres the other way. I remember lying in the middle of the MCG thinking how neatly I fitted inside the circle, cumulus nimbus clouds overhead, and I still hadn't realised that dream of my first kick in VFL footy. It's been a great journey.

Next match I played [Graham] 'Polly' Farmer, who was great. I watched him all day that day. John Nicholls ... I knew my nose was broken five minutes into the first quarter because the pointy part was under my right eye; there was blood streaming down the JohnCo shorts. And the fourth match I was introduced to the squirrel grip by Teddy Whitten, the great number 3 for Footscray, who became a mate. We hosted *The Footy Show* together ... a dear friend. Mr Football, a larger-than-life character.

My first year at Melbourne, interesting time—from seconds to Under 19s, back to seconds and the seniors. I was the last player picked on the supplementary list: number 46 on the back; it felt comfortable. And then next year, a huge burden—for the rest of my career, I wore number 1.

Study @ RMIT

The Melbourne Football Club organised for me to go to the Royal Melbourne Institute of Technology to study architecture. I needed to get a kick playing for Melbourne to study there. I needed to pass because my marble had rolled out: I was conscripted. I was off to Vietnam if I failed. Now, do you reckon I was motivated? Too right I was!

I pursued a career in architecture because of my dad, Big Max. He was a master builder and he said, 'Son, there's not much money in building. You should be an architect; that's where the dollars are'.

I begged to differ a little bit there. But I designed Maxy's Motel at the age of thirteen. He lovingly constructed a beautiful western red cedar drawing board and a T square to go with it … a bit boxy, square, not that aesthetically pleasing to the eyeball, but it had a cool store and a few rooms and a front bar and that was the beginning of a love affair. And I suppose I'd been building huts and cubbyhouses as a youngster. Then to actually go on and study architecture, it did seem a natural progression. Big Max had a passion and a preoccupation for excellence in building, and a lot of that rubbed off.

I also studied nude drawing. Now the theory being, if you could sketch the human body naked, you could certainly design a triple-fronted brick veneer.

My formative years as an architect were spent in the Public Works Department, Research and Development group, Melbourne.

Melbourne cricket

Football was my ticket out of Tasmania, but cricket was really my passion. I was a batsman, scored a couple of hundreds for North

Hobart before I crossed Bass Strait. I played cricket for Melbourne, which is a 150-year-old plus cricket club. They had six shield batsman. I batted 10 in my first match. They did not have a bowler. A man named Clive Fairbairn, chairman of selectors, reckoned I could make it as a bowler. 'Fairy', how can I ever thank you?

Another guy named Jack Ryder, the King, he looked beyond the right arm over left ear hole, with the legs crossed at the point of delivery. He was a selector and I guess had a fair say in me first of all playing for Victoria and then Australia. Thank you, Jack.

The whereabouts of the nickname? That came about from a *Sun Herald* newspaper article, picture of me from the kneecaps down, legs crossed, top right-hand corner inset of about 25 millimetres square, that was it: 'Melbourne's tangle-footed bowler to play first Shield match', and then it became 'Tanglefoot' and then 'Tangles'.

The baggy green was a massive dream. Most kids in my class wanted to be a Test cricketer, they wanted to be a league footballer—it was natural. I used to be able to feel the texture of the baggy green and I could run my fingers over the coat of arms in gold braid. I could feel the freshly cut grass at the MCG and the weight of 5½ ounces of leather in my hand. It was everything to me as a kid—and to have it come true. Wow!

The baggy green arrives

None of the media grandstanding that we see now with an old legend giving the new player a cap and telling him, 'Son, this is what the history's about. This is your hand on your heart. This is where you've got to take this thing'.

Brown paper bag, short-sleeved jumper, long-sleeved jumper, blazer, tie and cap, and I tore it open. I couldn't wait to take that cap back and show the old man because it was a dream come true. I walked through the flywire door and I pulled the cap on tight and the old man's standing there in builder's overalls, the red pencil and the nail bag and the hammer. I said, 'What do you think of that?'

He said, 'Not bad'. And then he said, 'Come here'. And he wanted my cap. He had a grade one hair cut, lawn mower straight over the top ... baby boomers, they put the black gear on now and they think they look trendy, don't they, with that sort of hair cut. He was way ahead of his time. And he did, he pulled it on. He had a bigger head than mine and he beamed, 'What do you think of that?' And I said, 'Not bad'. But when I looked deep into those pale blue eyes, they welled up, and a tear ran down over his cheek and it seemed like eternity before it hit the ground and dissipated ... it was at that moment that I knew when I walked on to the hallowed turf of the MCG the next day, I wouldn't just be pursuing my dreams but I'd be taking his. Because as a seventeen year old he was a schoolboy prodigy in both football and cricket. He was signed up by the St Kilda footy club and the Essendon footy club, but his mum was a very tough old lady; she said, 'Son'—one of nine kids—'if you get in that ferry to cross Bass Strait, it sinks, you're dead, I've lost a son. You are not going'. Not many people are as strong minded as that. So a decade and a bit later we go together to manifest our destiny.

To play VFL footy, AFL footy and Test cricket, that is about the ultimate dream. In hindsight to have been able to achieve that, it is wonderful. I don't think you could do it now. The football clubs at AFL level, they own you. The same with the itinerary for Test cricket, one-day international cricket: it's continual, it is a globe trotting exercise. And as cricketers they've got financial advisers, image, accountants—they're all there, massive. Whereas footy in the winter, cricket in the summer, it seems fairly simple. Simon O'Donnell was the last to play both; he played football for St Kilda, one-dayers and Test matches for Australia. There was myself; I think Keith Miller was just a wonderful player; Sam Loxton was another one. But there wouldn't be ten, I don't think, who would've played both—it's an interesting group to be amongst.

At the MCG

There's the roar of the crowd when you play footy; it's a huge mass of humanity roaring their lungs out. Now at cricket you go down to deep fine leg in front of Bay 13 and you can hear the humour come across the crowd.

There's a different sort of fitness. Football is confrontational, it's full on. Cricket, you need to stand out under the hot sun, you get sunburnt, you get dehydrated just when you relax, a catch comes your way.

But in many ways, the lessons I learnt in football were able to be transferred into cricket. It gave you a sense that you could do anything, football, and in front of a huge crowd, so I didn't get stage fright when I played Test cricket. And as Ian Chappell said, 'Don't talk about it, son, just go out and prove you're good enough'. And in my second Test match, not that I'm into the numerics of the game, sixteen overs, eight maidens, six for fifteen. I guess that was my ticket to being accepted.

The MCG has been the axis of my life now for the best part of four decades. It's still amazing to walk out onto the hallowed turf, the rush of memories. VFL footy was one thing, a fabulous learning curve for me. But to play my first cricket match for Victoria and then to pull on the green baggy cap for the first time for Australia, to pick up eight wickets against England—that was incredible. As a young student of architecture I painted the seats at the MCG, about 40,000 of them; I worked in the scoreboard with a dear old fella named Joe Caneer. Wonderful memories indeed. In fact, later on I became a commentator with Alan McGilvray on the ABC, a little chook house of a structure at the back of the old members' stand. And then alongside Richie Benaud, 'Welcome back, marvellous contest between bat and ball'. Rich experience. The MCG has been a huge part of my life for such a long time.

A cricketing era

I never really wondered about the era I was born into. I doubted whether I was good enough to play amongst that team. In the mid '70s we were rated as the best cricket team in the world. Ian Chappell was a great captain. For Maxwell Henry Norman Walker to sit in a dressing room with a Dennis Lillee, a Rodney Marsh, the two Chappells, Doug Walters, Keith Stackpole, Ian Redpath ... Gee, you've got to pinch yourself.

And, yes, I was the support act. I rarely got the new ball. My role was always up the hill into the breeze with an old ball on a flat wicket. Jokingly I'd say that Lillee and Thommo would play them in; I'd have to separate them. But I loved my lot in life.

Sixth Test match 1975 [England v Australia], Dennis Lillee broke down. I can remember taking the third new ball. There was just Geoff Dymock and myself, and I managed to take eight wickets. I remember saying to Ian Chappell on the way out after tea, 'Don't do anything stupid like telling me to have a rest, because you're never going to crank start this body again. I'll just seize up down at deep fine leg, at Bay 13' ... Bay 13 is one of the great places on the planet—they embraced me, later on it was Merv Hughes, before that, Dennis Lillee ... The energy that comes across the fence down there is marvellous to be part of.

Back in those days we didn't have the same media coverage. The intensity is beyond belief now, but there were only a couple of newspapers and some radio, and a limited amount of television. I think each game took on a different value. You played for your place in the side for the next Test match. And if you were good enough you got selected for the next tour to England or the West Indies or New Zealand. Every game was more loaded; there were more opportunities for the players. Now they play fifty or sixty one-day internationals a year, seventeen or eighteen, twenty Test matches ... Bradman only played fifty-two Test matches; Steve Waugh, 167, scored a couple more centuries than Bradman, took three times as long.

I think the emotional connection between player and public was different back then. The players today, they receive $1 million or $2 million, some of them perhaps even $3 million.

We went to England in '75 for $2700 less medical insurance and tax. We weren't in it for the money. We were there for the camaraderie, the victory and the spoils that go with it. A wonderful experience. I wouldn't change it for anything, but it is a different relationship to the crowd today. And with it goes an enormous responsibility ... way beyond the fence. If you're the voice and face of a product, and you're going to take half a million dollars for it, then that's pressure; you live your life in a goldfish bowl.

World Series Cricket

Nothing happens unless there is a need. And I think there was a breakdown in communication between the players and the Australian Cricket Board (ACB) back then. I think we were asking for $400 extra. Our pay packet had stayed the same from 1972 till 1977. Gough Whitlam had taken the prices of almost everything through the roof. Basically, we were told, if you do not like the scenario, there are another fifty to sixty players out there who would give their right arm to play for Australia. And they would. Just that none of them were as good as Ian Chappell and Dennis Lillee. And of course, Kerry Packer, he had a different scenario. He wanted prime time television to involve sport. It would be a magnet for marketing. The ACB said 'No'—consistently said 'No', so he created a competition for the very best players in the world above and beyond what was already there. That is, Test cricket. But emotion got in the road, fences were starting to be built around 'we own the players, they can't do that'. Ended up in court—£250,000 bill.

Kerry Packer fought the whole cricket community, and won. That was a costly exercise but the state of the game today I believe wouldn't be as good as it is now if it wasn't for the intervention of Kerry Packer, who created an innovation and a creative environment where things could happen ... white ball, black sight screen, coloured gear, microphone at the base of the stumps, lipstick camera three-quarters of the way up the off stump, spin cam, marketing ... 'Big boys play at night'. It was like being a cowboy in the Wild West. There were some friendships broken, and a lot of emotion involved. But I think when you look back at the impact of Kerry Packer on the game, maybe Bob Parish, the administrator, Sir Don Bradman and Kerry Packer, who had had a bigger impact? It would be hard to go past Kerry Packer.

Playing life/private life

It was not a healthy template being a Test cricketer. In our day it was written into our contract that your wife was not allowed on tour until the last ball of the last Test match was bowled. If you were away for five and a half months, as we were in England, then you'd be another three and a half months in the West Indies. You might as well have been in the UK for a normal Shield season: three or four months you'd be in Perth, Adelaide, Sydney, Brisbane. So it is a strain. Probably, ideally, back then, better not to have been married.

It cost me a marriage, standing at fine leg and third man in another part of the world for thirteen years. There were three children involved. And, basically, to say 'Look, it's not working', what do you say? I wouldn't wish that on anyone.

It became easier to be apart than to live together. And you grow differently too. I mean, if one is anchored in one place in Australia and then all of a sudden the other partner is exposed to the world and travel and all sorts of things, we just didn't grow together.

But now with the amount of money, players are encouraged to take not only their wives but their families around, and I think quite rightly so.

Losing Lexie

Lexie was my younger sister and she was probably more talented than me in all areas. In the classroom she was certainly in the top one, two or three in her class; as an athlete, just naturally gifted harrier—actually ran second to Pam Kilburn, who was a 400-metre runner for Australia in the Olympic Games—played hockey, anything. She was very, very gifted and yet at thirty-eight years of age, went to the footy, was sick during the early part of the week and then had a heart attack overnight. Not a conventional heart attack, but a burst aorta. By the time I arrived on Sunday, about eight o'clock in the morning, my mum had phoned me and said, 'Look, your sister's not going to make it'. And I thought, Gosh, have we got a barbecue on? She said, 'No, she's had a heart attack'. So I raced out to her house and the guys were just shutting the ambulance doors and said, 'Sorry, mate. She didn't make it'. Incredibly I actually went on air and did *Wide World of Sports*, the Sunday edition, for two hours—and I thought, Well, she'd want me to do that. Didn't realise the gravity, you never do, and then the penny drops. I walked back to make-up and Annie, one of the girls that works with us, she said, 'There's something wrong, isn't there?' And I said, 'Yes. My sister died'. And then I lost it. But up until then I was bulletproof, I could do anything. Now I'm much better at saying 'No'.

Out of the game and into the media

Retirement with a capital 'R'—it's a nasty word in any sportsman's life. To me the timing picked itself. It was 28 December 1981, the same day my third son, Shelden, was born, and I had an Achilles tendon injury. The Doc couldn't guarantee I would stand up in the next match, so I retired. And within forty-eight hours the ABC said, 'How would you like to be a commentator on radio?' I'd never done that before. But in life you've got to throw yourself out there. You've got to challenge yourself. There were no guarantees. I said 'Yes'. For four days in a row, no commercial breaks, Drew Morphett and myself commentated on this game in front of a couple of hundred seagulls plus a few stray cats and dogs and a few relations, down at Kardinia Park at Geelong. Soul-destroying. You couldn't do a Bill Lawry and say, 'Big crowd in, the atmosphere's electric here', because it wasn't. So we had to verbally create some sort of excitement, some sort of drama, and by the end of that summer I got a great opportunity. I was invited to sit alongside Alan McGilvray, who was the doyen of ABC cricket commentators, along with, say, Charles Fortune and John Arlott. They were perhaps the big three voices in the game during the '60s and the '70s.

Once I had stopped playing cricket I was invited to work on *World of Sport*, the old Channel Seven icon with Lou Richards, Jack Dyer, Bobby Davis, Jack O'Toole—I mean, there was an amazing cavalcade of characters that used to front up regularly at the Dorcas Street studios.

That was my introduction to media. But the big step up was when I did an Aeroguard commercial way back in 1977, the first year of World Series cricket ... 'Have a good weekend, Mr Walker'. I use it too!

Now that is a long time ago, but I think the camera liked me, or it appeared to. And I was headhunted by Channel Nine from Seven, and the ABC in terms of radio. I ended up hosting *Wide World of Sports* on the Nine network for sixteen years. That was fantastic. It looked as though I might be a newsreader for sport. But, being a slow-talking Tasmanian with five broken noses, I wasn't going to make the grade. Plus the bouffant hairdo, I mean it just didn't work for me. Became a cricket commentator. That was a fabulous journey. Television was make it up as you go, have fun, it'll translate down the lens, and I think it did. It's a much more scripted, tighter way that they go about making television these days, and from a distance, in my opinion, perhaps lacks the energy of what we had back then. I think it was a great time to be on camera ... You know, red lights, tight underpants and a bit of make-up.

Television was perhaps more real back then. Graham Kennedy once said the most difficult thing to do on television is tell a lie; I mean, your eyes move, your nose twitches, the corners of your mouth ... and it's so true, and I think if you're having fun on the set or down the barrel of a camera, then most certainly your audience is going to ... That's why *The Footy Show* in the early days was a huge success.

I hosted *The Footy Show* with a bunch of rogues—Sam Newman, Teddy Whitten, Lou Richards, Dermott Brereton, Mal Brown—on a Sunday afternoon, legends in their own lunchbox. They had no brief to their club; they would say anything. And they would cause a story, even make it up. And I remember hosting the very first night-time *Footy Show*, which was the precursor for the huge, massive cash cow that Channel Nine has produced, and Eddie McGuire and Sam Newman. But the very first one, Lou Richards had the King of Moomba's crown on, sitting in a burgundy velvet chair with gold trim, and Sam Newman turned up five or ten minutes late. Teddy Whitten was off the long run and Mal Brown was very abrasive in his comments, and Rex Hunt from Channel Seven turned up to give the Most Valuable Player Award away, to Gary Ablett, and I think that show rated twenty-five points. Over two hours with no advertising, we took on *Footy Marathon* from Channel Seven; you could see it was going to be big. And, gosh, to be part of the evolution of that ... came as a sense of fun, no more, no less.

Sport as business

Look, sport's no longer a game. You used to play sport because you loved playing sport, you used to love to win, but now, it's a big business, and it can be a nasty cycle that goes around. You need to have notoriety to be part of a marketing campaign; there are millions of dollars, there's sponsors, there's vested interests that come in, and pressure; whereas my dad said to me many years ago, he said, 'Son, don't get these in the wrong order. Be very, very passionate about what you do; the fame and the fortune will follow'. He said, 'If you get the fame and the fortune in front of a passion, you'll muck it up'. How right was he?

Life today

I have been doing motivational speaking now since the mid '70s. I love motivational speaking. I love to lift the bar, stretch capabilities ... To make a difference in peoples lives, and to make an emotional connection. I guess as an old fast bowler and as a batsman, the roar of the crowd, the initial feedback, the energy—it is beautiful to be a part of. And if I did not genuinely like people, I do not think I could do it.

It's easy to get pigeonholed as the genial giant from Bay 13, right arm over left ear hole, dear old legs crossed at the point of delivery, the bowler who makes you laugh all the time. But a lot of time is spent speaking to corporates about lifting the bar, stretching capability, communication. I use mind maps all the time. I'm a frustrated architect, so I love the felt pens, imagination and association, bringing ideas onto the table. I get to sit in the engine room of some of the most dynamic companies in Australia and offshore. You hear their thinking about what they're going to do into the future. That's a privilege. I would never betray their trust. It's like going to university and actually getting a fee to go to university. So I love that, love writing, love photography, love art, pen and ink and pencil, watercolour wash. So, never enough hours in a day, 168 hours in a week; gosh, I'd love it to be 250 hours.

Writing

The world's full of self-help manuals—there are books, there are a whole lot of motivational speakers out there—and you can only really buy, or connect, the information that works for you. So, sure the cover might look good, there's a lot of fact, a regurgitation of a whole lot of things, many times you can actually tell where it's come from. But we're talking to real people in business, on a daily basis, from all parts of the world. They're good enough to share their thoughts and their problems, sometimes heartaches, expensive ones, but they're good enough to share how they've solved their problems.

I got into writing almost by default—no one in television could write like I speak, and along the way I have written fourteen books. We have sold a million copies. Today the book business is different. It is just as important to be able to sell as it is to write. The nicest thing that has been said about my books is that 'we can hear that slow Tasmanian drawl from five broken noses just peel off the page'.

Architecture is no longer my vocation, but it is still a passion. I love what they have done to my beloved MCG. And I guess you have to be a little careful where you say this, but I reckon Federation Square is absolutely fantastic. You look at the Square itself: it's a community hub, it's a magnet, it brings people together, it's very user friendly. Big events like World Cup soccer, they're celebrated right there in the square. I think it's wonderful for Melbourne.

The Melbourne Sports and Aquatic Centre was barely an idea when Jeff Kennett asked myself and a handful of others to sit on the trust here. But what a life experience to be involved in the schematics and then to see it built. It is a fabulous facility. It inspires people to break world records. People from all over the world look at this multipurpose sports centre, and they consult. Beijing's had a look at it.

Art

I've loved art for a long time, almost all my life. I designed Maxy's Motel at the age of thirteen. It wasn't until I studied architecture at the Royal Institute of Technology that my passion developed. A wonderful lecturer named Joe Bradley introduced me to fine arts. No matter where I travelled in the world I sourced out architects and artists and art galleries. Try to get a bunch of cricketers on tour to go to the Museum of Fine Arts in London? You've got to be joking.

I'm an ambassador for the National Gallery of Victoria and it's beautiful to be able to go and visit all of the exhibitions and to be able to talk about them. There are more people coming to the National Gallery of Victoria, and the art is better than the Guggenheim in Spain. So to have that here in Australia when we don't appreciate just how good it is … but I think as time goes on, it will gain more and more notoriety on a global scale. If you ask me what art I like, sure, I love the Impressionists, but my love, personally, hands on, is watercolour, it's pen and ink and pencil. I love the thick and thin lines; positive and negative space. This is a legacy from architecture school. The ability to take an idea, imagination, association, put it on a page, see it grow into two dimensions and then finally into three dimensions—that's architecture. But when you see a great piece of art, you don't need a handbook to tell you what it's about. Everyone's interpretation or perspective on that piece of art strikes a different emotional chord, and when that happens you know that you're going beyond just recreating an image or some imagination out of your mind. It will touch the heartstrings; it will put its hand on your heart.

I have five children. All of them enjoy their art, but the two girls in particular, young Isabella and her older sister, Alexandra, are very passionate. Mum, Kerry, she has always had a great love of art, loves to travel, loves to go to art galleries. So how lucky are we in Melbourne?

I've been an admirer of Picasso's work for a long time … That theatre of the mind, the economy of line, the juxtaposition of geometry, the use of colour … Incredibly unique, authentic, very different. I suppose we are lucky too in Victoria, the National Gallery owns the *Weeping Woman*, one of the most famous. I think, if we are honest, Picasso is one of the most important artists of our time. To be able to walk around a gallery like this with so much space, it really showcases how good the man was.

Patron of blind cricket

The blindies, my mates, they're terrific. They play cricket with a passion, just like the rest of us. The ball is the core, obviously, it used to be a wickerware sphere with bottle tops. Roll it along the ground, it will make a noise. These days, there is a plastic ball with ball bearings and washers inside—there was a moment about trying to change into the twenty-first century with a sonic ball. This ball came together like a hand grenade: you pressed the button ... Now, blind cricket is made up of six guys who cannot see at all, totally blind, and the rest of the team, up to 12.5 per cent, doesn't give you much. So they press the ball ... talk about research and development ... and it goes beep, beep, beep, beep, beep, beep, beep. Well, the six totally blind guys think it's a huge truck backing onto the ground. They run off the ground. That didn't work. But today they play Test matches. In fact, probably incredibly, the best blind cricketer in Victoria wins a Max Walker Medal. A lot of blokes would say, 'That's pretty appropriate for you, Maxy!' But they're fantastic; I mean, I gain so much inspiration from them, and they play international matches now and it was wonderful to be able to present the caps to the blind players and say, 'Look, this is the same cap that Victor Trumper, Donald Bradman, Alan Border, Steve Waugh wore'.

A lucky guy

A lot of reasons to be happy ... Mind you I have my moments of introspection and, I guess, the world shuts down. There are so many people in my life on a weekly basis I get to meet. A lot of the relationships and conversations are very short. But for me, at the end of that energy—and it does sap your energy—to sit in a room, in a hotel and look at the ceiling and think, Wow, that's white, that's great.—There's nothing there, your mind is clear again. I love to dump my thoughts down on paper every day, three or four pages, not a journal and not a to-do list, but just how I feel, angry or sad. It's amazing when you open up the power of the universe what can hit the page. Then over time, it will take shape, it will morph itself into something stronger and it might even be a gut feeling about someone, some concept, some business, and you're allowed to be wrong, but often we go to a doctor, we go to our parents, we go to our boss to work out what's right when there's this innate voice inside us that sometimes we tend to reject. Have you ever walked in a room and said, 'Oh, I don't know about that bloke' and three months later you've been proved right? It's funny, it's … again, it's trust. Trust your instinct.

At this stage of my life it's nice to be able to choose the difference between what is good and what is not good. You can't do everything, and I guess in a strange way, all of my passions have begun to come together, the love of art and photography and writing and speaking, background in media—it makes me happy, and it makes me smile.

> All in all I wouldn't change anything. It's been an incredible journey. I've been a very lucky guy. Sport has helped shape who I've become, who I am. Along the way we've laughed a lot, we've had a bit of mischief, we've won some great battles, probably even shed a tear or two, but isn't that what we love about sport?

JOHN CLARKE
Satirist

Screened 29 October 2007

Satirist John Clarke is known to the world through *Fred Dagg*, Clarke and Dawe and *The Games*, amongst many other hits. He writes, acts and directs, and has been a success at all three. John's sharp wit has challenged the status quo for years on a host of television programs that began with the bucolic Fred Dagg, who had seven sons all conveniently called Trevor.

> Trevor was just a name I always liked. It was a good name to yell out and Fred did quite a lot of yelling. If I lost my place in what I was thinking or saying I used to yell out at the dog or Trevor; it's a good name to call out. There were a lot of Trevors in New Zealand at that time. There were certain things that just seemed to me funny, certain words that are funny. 'Trouser', for example. TR. Maybe it's TR.

Growing up in NZ

I grew up in a city called Palmerston North, which sits in the middle of a large and at that time very prosperous rural district called the Manawatu. And Palmerston North was a very nice place to grow up in. It was just after the war, it was safe and everybody was the same. My dad ran a shop. There was a chain store called McKenzies and my father ran the local branch of it, and my mother was a writer and performer in local repertory productions and so on. And my sister, Anna, and I went to the local school, ate three times a day and so on, pretty conventional.

I would go along and see my mother in these plays, and sometimes if they were a bit short-handed I'd be standing in the wings handing people a chair or a piece of paper, and in dire moments, when some kid had got the flu or something, I'd be frogmarched into some small role. But I do remember that the theatre and the theatre people were quite different from the other people in the town, and they were extremely amusing, and very generous.

If you have a parent who does something, especially if it's slightly unusual, you do secretly know that that is a legitimate human activity. I don't think I yearned to do it, but you do see what your parents do and you do come to understand that that is something you can do. I didn't do it until much later, and I didn't do it in the same way, but it is an influence because it's a door you can look through.

I'm like both my parents, I think, because my dad, who wasn't a performer, is quite performative in his personality and in his modes of communication. He wasn't mad keen on *Fred Dagg*, but that didn't bother me because my priorities were to learn as much as I could, and earn a living and do stuff. I loved *Fred Dagg*.

I don't know why he took that view.

When I was a kid, I listened to adults a lot. I was quite intrigued by people, and I was quite interested in adults and the way they talked. And I was aware that humour is one of the elements in the way that they were communicating, and if you didn't get it, it didn't matter, because it wasn't jokes, it wasn't people telling jokes, it was just a way of behaving. I had a couple of uncles who were very good at it, and who were hilarious and who'd tell terrific stories and they'd have people on.

I think your family is a fairly big influence on every aspect of your life. You certainly learn some drama from my family. It was a pretty dramatic sort of place to be. My sister and I grew up in this apparently completely bland time, place and family environment, but it turned into something much more dynamic than we thought, which is, you know, interesting. Our job is to find the pluses in the position we were in and there's plenty of learning to be done there.

When I was about twelve, my father got promoted to head office and we shifted to Wellington, which is the capital of New Zealand. I went to a boys' only private school, and that school was less good educationally. I think I was quite well educated at the age of ten, and not particularly well educated at the age of seventeen. By the time I left school, I knew basically what I had learnt at primary school, plus how to shave.

There were a couple of teachers who were quite well disposed and there was one who had been a friend of WH Auden, the poet, and who opened my mind to all of that, particularly Auden and [Louis] MacNeice. Of course, in stories as he told them, I learnt more about him, because I knew him a bit and I didn't quite know who Auden and MacNeice were, but later on when I was at university I retrospectively was a little more confident reading their stuff because I felt I knew who they were ... because I knew their friend.

When I left school and went to university I had to have a serious look at where I was up to by comparison with the rest of my generation, and I was somewhat dismayed to find that I would've been better to go to university after primary school. A little young perhaps, but I would've got a lot more out of it.

In the shearing shed

I worked in shearing gangs when I left school because I left school slightly early, and I had nothing better to do until university started. 'Irreconcilable differences' is what the magistrate said. We parted our ways. I was in my last year at school so I hadn't forfeited anything, and I had the enormous benefit of not being at school anymore. It is possibly a very good school now. Schools go through phases. It just wasn't very good at the time.

It was a great life working in shearing gangs. You went all around the place, you worked very hard, you were with people who neither knew nor cared who you were, so you had to make your way with them, and that was interesting. Later, through university, I often worked in shearing gangs during the Christmas period because the money was good, and if you're shearing sheep, it is piecework: you get paid by the sheep. So if you were any good, you could go all right. And the way that you learnt to shear sheep in those days: you learnt at lunchtime and at smoko, you jumped on the board and had a go. And somebody would take an interest and say, 'You're standing the wrong way round' and 'You hold it by the other end' and so you learnt. And so by the end of my time I was shearing sheep. But when I was a rousie it was great. I loved the whole life. That was probably my experience that is embedded in *Fred Dagg*.

University years

I was at Victoria University, in Wellington, which was beautifully situated halfway up one of the major hills, so you could be at university and you could have what these days would be million-dollar views. We used to sit chatting about ontological matters, while the whole of the city was there like an amphitheatre below us. It was a fantastic place, and I met marvellous people at university.

I went to university in 1967, and in 1968 I was in the stage crew of the annual revue, which was a pretty big thing at the time, and the following year I was in it. And that was the first time I really went on stage as me. And I really did feel, Oh, this is quite good. I quite like this. And the following year I was in semi-professional shows in town. And so throughout 1970, with some very talented people who I still know, we wrote basically a stage show a month or every six weeks because we had a fairly small audience in Wellington. And we learnt quite a lot about very fast turnaround and relatively topical material.

Partly to put myself through university, I worked in an all-night petrol station. And there was a bloke there who ran it, about whom I later wrote a film [*Man and Boy*]. He used to call me 'Walter', which was based on Walter Mitty, because he thought I was a dreamer.

He was very encouraging to me in a way that made me wonder whether or not he'd recognised something in me, which he may have; or whether or not I was an opportunity he hadn't taken in his own life; or whether I was just a person he got on with and understood a bit. I don't know. Anyway, I always thought I wanted to write something about him because it's—the first relationship you have with someone who is not a member of your own family, and who likes you because you're you before you've worked out where you are—it's that sort of thing, and I was very grateful to him.

He didn't go to our theatre show. In a way, we had a relationship that could only work in the petrol station. So maybe our context was so specific that it evaporated off the patch.

He called everybody 'Ted', so when somebody would come into the petrol station he'd go out and say, 'Yes, Ted'. And the person would say, 'Fill her up', or whatever it was, or 'My name is not Ted', or 'How did you know my name was Ted?' Or something like that. And when we were shooting this thing—we were shooting down in a building opposite the Flagstaff Gardens, which is not there anymore—and the guy who ran the petrol station said to me, 'What's this about?' And I told him and I told him about this guy and he said, 'He called everybody Ted?' And I said, 'Yes'. And he said, 'Was their name Ted?' And I said, 'No, he called them Ted regardless of what their name was. He didn't know what their real name was'. He said, 'He called them Ted anyway'. He said, 'That's weird'. He said, 'I call everybody George'. So he thought it was quite strange that someone would call everybody Ted but completely natural that somebody would call everybody George. That's funny but it's not a joke.

Early influences

My influences, like anybody my age, would include, number one, *The Goon Show*, because my generation grew up listening to *The Goon Show* on the radio. I would describe it as essentially a Second World War show. It comes out of the anxiety and madness and stupidity and so on, and it's the crumbling empire, and it's a whole lot of other things. So there's Milligan and Sellers separately. And then there was Peter Cook and Dudley Moore.

When I was at secondary school in about 1965, I think, Peter Cook and Dudley Moore came on New Zealand television. And then when I left university I went and worked in television as a film assessor. And I discovered that these films were still there—there was no such thing as video tape; everything was filmed—and we had the capacity to watch them several times. So we could go downstairs and lace these things up, and I watched Peter Cook and Dudley Moore shows, and Alan Bennett's show *On the Margin*, and all these things innumerable times, and I got paid as well, which was rather nice.

In Peter Cook's case—and he would be an influence on anyone of my age in my field—the thing that he teaches you, I think, is to be yourself, because you're always aware of the 'Peter Cookness' of what he's doing. He's not really a great actor; he's playing—he's always trying to get Dudley Moore to laugh, for example. You're always aware of these things. And he's not trying to be someone else; he's not Peter Sellers.

So I think there were various signs to me that said, 'Work this thing out and do it your way'.

Overseas

In 1971 I went overseas because I didn't quite know what else to do. I was possibly bored. It was impossible to get into television or radio positions at that time; they were still tightly held by people from Rent-a-Pom or somewhere. I don't know where they got them, but there were Program Prevention Officers in spades, and they weren't letting too much local stuff go on. So there was maybe a sense I had to wait for the wheel to turn a little bit. And I went away to do other things in the meantime.

I went to various places, including London, where I lived for a couple of years. I met Helen in London. While I was in London, a friend who is an actor came back one day and said she'd auditioned for a film in which they were looking for men, and she'd put my name down to go and do an audition. And I went along and I met Bruce Beresford and Barry Humphries. And we had a talk and did quite a lot of laughing. And they offered me a part in this film, which was the first *Barry McKenzie* movie, and they basically said, 'Come along whenever you like and do stuff'. They were very generous. They took me aside and they said, 'You should think about doing this for a living'. And it had never occurred to me that that would really be possible. And they explained to me that they thought it was and I had to do it in my way, but they would be interested to see how it all went. And they both stayed in touch with me over the next few years.

After I met Bruce and Barry, I came back to Australia, and then I went back to New Zealand. And I was giving it a go, and some things work and some things don't. You don't need any help when things are working, but when things are not working, it's sometimes hard to gather yourself and get a grip on what the lesson is there for you and how to go on. But if somebody like that has said to you, 'You should do this for a living. You're actually good at this', it helps. It's a secret but it's a pretty important one.

Encouragement

Encouragement is like a book voucher or something. 'Here's a voucher; you don't have to spend it yet.' So it's up to you what you do with this encouragement. So, for example, someone might encourage me when I was ten, but I was too confused to understand quite how that could be applied.

And a couple of times I've been slightly stopped in my tracks by people encouraging me. I think that was the importance of Bruce and Barry, because I didn't quite know what I was doing at that stage in my life. I was rather a silly person, and I got involved in that film, and they basically pulled me aside, and I thought about that. And then when I went back to New Zealand, I thought, I will do that, that is good advice, and this is where the seed should be planted.

So I did do that. And I remember meeting Barry at an airport about five years later in Sydney, and I went up to him and I was going to say, 'Barry, you probably don't remember me, but …' And I got to about the second 'R' in Barry, and he said, 'John, I think this Fred Dagg stuff you're doing in New Zealand is fantastic'. He knew all about it. Not only did they encourage me but they kept a bit of an eye on me; they knew what I was up to. And I took the course that they thought was a perfectly natural course to take, but it was a difficult thing for me to work out how to take it because it was a way through the trees that hadn't been done before in that particular way, at that particular time.

Back to NZ

When I went back to New Zealand in 1973, I, amongst other people, was asked to provide satirical material to current affairs shows. I did it basically as Fred Dagg, which was a character I'd developed on stage before leaving New Zealand in '71. And by the middle of 1974, although sporadic and basically still an amateur project, it was working quite well.

Helen and I got married in 1973. She was teaching. Had she not been teaching, we wouldn't have made a living, because I couldn't make a living out of this, even though it was working quite well. I think I probably made a living doing it for the first time in 1975. And I thought, Righto, now I had better work out what I am doing and what its best uses are, and also how to make a living at doing it.

In 1976 I did a national tour and began to work out what next to do, because by this stage I had done regular television, I had had a couple of shows of my own, but the television system was struggling with how that was going to work, and I'd released records, and I'd done books, and where to next? There's a finite number of things you can do in a relatively small market, and I wanted to go somewhere else and see if I could do something a bit different.

Australia

As it happened I'd been to Australia a number of times. I'd lived here in '73 and I'd go to Sydney from time to time. And I'd encountered two people on ABC Radio—Bob Hudson, who was on what was at that time 2JJ, and Robyn Williams from *The Science Show*. And both of them had found my early recordings and had begun to play them, so they invited me to do stuff on their programs. And I said, 'Well, who's ever heard of me?' And they said, 'My audience has heard of you. I've been playing your records for two years'. So with great generosity they introduced me to their audience, and in no time flat I was doing quite regular things on ABC Radio, which was a glorious fluke because I hadn't understood previously that radio is a writing medium. And at this stage we had our first child and I wanted to stay at home as much as I could, and I was sick of touring, I cannot tell you.

I learnt a lot and I wrote a lot more than I had ever written previously.

I had been doing these characters which came out of the New Zealand experience. And I knew these characters terribly well; I could slip in and out of them quite easily and I didn't need to write them, I could make stuff up. I adlibbed most of those things and I had half an idea of where I was going to go, but it was mostly casual or, to use a technical term, 'sloppy'.

Radio is where I worked out how to write a cogent piece.

When I came to Australia I tried to stay away from the things that I had done a lot of in New Zealand in the previous years, but I felt myself drifting back into television in the early '80s because I was removed from ABC Radio for reasons that were never made very clear to me, but which went like this: question one, 'Can you please stay off politics and current affairs?' 'Well, not if I'm doing something every day I can't.' (I was doing a daily broadcast.) Then it was announced that they didn't have any money, so you know, the usual lie and crap. But when I started drifting back into television I drifted back in with a much better idea of writing.

The Gillies Report

The Gillies Report was a terrific creative experience. It came from a stage show that Max had done—and we'd all contributed various elements to—and it was decided to go to television. And it was a mixture of writing and performing, and I was certainly doing both and enjoying both. It was weekly turnaround. It was satirical. There were some seriously bright people involved in that show and it was terrific fun. It was exhilarating and exhausting.

'Farnarkeling' emerged because, in the first series, I used to do some little sporting inserts. And in the second series it was a bit hard to choose a sport because it was winter and the various states have got different sports. You were pretty safe with tennis and cricket and swimming and stuff in the summer. But in the second series I invented this ridiculous sport with a superhero, Dave Sorenson, who was a bit on the injury-prone side and he would very often come to grief, in some spectacular way. And it was full of bits of language that had always amused me and had nothing to do with sport at all.

It was based on the fact that I would very often be in the car, and I'd flick the radio on and hear the back end of a sports report that had strange terminology in it, but the cadence of it made me understand roughly what had gone on. I was pleased that Australia, or New Zealand or whatever it was had done so well, but I didn't understand what the code was. I wasn't up on the terminology and had never heard of anyone involved. So I thought, it sounds real, that's what's happening here, so I just did a sport that sounded real. And I just tried to do it straight and it sort of caught on.

Playing with Peter

Peter Cook was in the *Barry McKenzie* picture and I met him again out here in about 1987 because he came out for a comedy festival and he liked playing golf. And he and I got to go out and play quite a bit of golf because it was a nice break. And he was hilarious company.

He was probably my comedy hero, so I thought I'd died and gone to heaven. This was pretty good fun; and he was a pretty good golfer. In fact, the last contact I had with him was that he was in Queensland doing some golf-related thing, and he rang up and he left a message and I rang him the following day and he wasn't terribly well. And I said, 'Oh, sorry to hear that'. He thought he had the flu, and I said, 'That's no good, Peter'. He said, 'Well, last night', he said, 'we did go to the bar. And when I left the bar at the hotel here, I came back to the unit we are staying in, across the tennis courts', and he said, 'I must have activated a tennis ball serving machine, because I was quite suddenly struck by many thousands of tennis balls at a wide and unsettling range of angles'.

So even when he had a hangover he just riffed away. The minute the conversation started he was making it fascinating, just fuelling its fun, you know? We shared a dressing room in 1987, and he had a copy of the newspaper that I had a column in. And he said, 'That's your column?' He said, 'You should perform that'. And I had written the interviews as a thing to read. And he said, 'No, it's better than that, it's a great idea, you should perform those'. So I thought, Mmm. That's when I formed the idea that became radio when Bryan [Dawe] asked me to go back on radio. It was Peter who picked the thing out of the newspaper and said, 'That's got a bigger life than you've written it for; that's a very good idea'.

Clarke and Dawe

I asked Bryan to read the questions—he was running the department that employed me—and Bryan's got a supernatural understanding of speech rhythm; he's got a terrific voice and we found the same things amusing. And so we did it on radio for a while. And then I was asked to do something on Channel Nine, on *A Current Affair*. And I took that idea over there and said, 'That's the idea I'd like to do, please'. And it was a pretty weird idea for television, quite surreal.

Jana Wendt, who was hosting it, liked the idea. And Jana's rule was 'Don't show me anything until I see it live on air'. So we always got her genuine response, which was very intelligent of her, because the audience read her. A lot of presenters, if they doubt something, they distance themselves from it, and it might've sunk without trace if we'd got one of those presenters, but she was terrific. She got it. She liked it and she got it, and she helped.

And we have now been doing it for about twenty years. And we'll get it right if we stay here long enough.

The interviews began on Channel Nine; they've been on radio pretty much the whole time, and then they went back to ABC TV on the *7.30 Report,* which is a terrific home for them because the program gets the agenda up and most of the other interviews look very, very similar—it's the grammar of television that people are reading.

Health and shirts

I was approached to do a project about men's health and I went to the Cancer Council of Victoria and spoke to them about the messages that needed to go out. Bryan and I hosted these shows, which were really a call to arms. They were trying to get men of exactly my age to get a checkup. And I was completely typical of the problem: I'd never had a checkup. And they got some men who were going to get a checkup on camera, and I thought, Well, I can't very well talk to them afterwards if I don't do the same thing. So I went and got a checkup as well. And I learnt quite a lot about the work of the Cancer Council and so on, and I've done a lot of other work for them in relation to their anti-tobacco campaigns and things.

The shirt came about because I was playing golf and working outside, and I used to get a short-sleeved shirt with a little pretend collar—a kid could design a better collar. So I wanted to design a shirt that went higher up the back because I'm genetically designed for being in Scotland or Ireland, where the sun shines every second Shrove Tuesday; I'm not actually genetically designed to be here at all. So I'd begun to get little basal cell carcinomas pinged off me, burnt off me, nothing dangerous, but a lot of them were just around the neck and on my shoulders because I spent my childhood outside. We weren't allowed in until it was dark.

So I went to the Cancer Council and got their advice about how best to approach what the requirements ought to be and would they stock it? And they said, 'If it's successful, it will be copied, and we won't have a problem with the fact that it's copied because the issue for us is to get as many people to wear long-sleeved shirts and get them to look after their skin as possible'. I said, 'Fine', so it got copied. We don't make it anymore. We just needed it to shift the paradigm. It had a slightly higher collar and it had long sleeves and it had a slightly scalloped shape at the bottom so it covered your hand a bit and it was made of a fabric that was very light and which screened out 99 per cent of UV.

The Games

The idea behind *The Games* is a pretty good one, I think, because it chooses a real event, and therefore the program has to finish. In our case we wrote it as a satire, tried to play it as a drama, and shot it as a documentary. And we used our own names because people use their own names on television, and therefore we believe what they say. Coupled with the completely ludicrous prospect of organising the Olympics, it's a huge unnecessary mess. And then you get this golden fortnight when the most beautiful people in the world come and run around in their underpants. And it's very, very telegenic, and it works like a beauty.

That was a project I wrote with Ross Stevenson, who is very, very clever, is a wonderful radio talent and used to be a lawyer, so he has a very clear structural understanding of what's going on, and I don't have much. So we'd be thinking of something and wouldn't it be funny if … and he would say, 'I bet you that's happening', and he would invariably be right. Then we had people leaking to us. We couldn't very often use that because it would be clear where it had come from and somebody would have got into trouble, but at least it fortified our observation that there was nothing too silly we could say if we said it with a straight face and if there was an arena in the background.

Huntaway Films

Huntaway Films is a production company I formed with two friends, Sam Neill, the struggling New Zealand actor, and Jay Cassells, who'd been a film lawyer and producer. We did an adaptation of two of Shane Maloney's excellent novels. Sam directed one and I directed the other. David Wenham played the lead in both and if ever you're going to do anything, that's a pretty sound principle: get David Wenham to pay the lead in both. And it was great fun. They went through the roof. The ABC knocked them back. I think possibly they had one of those awkward positions, which only the ABC has, where you want to do something, you've got the money, but it's allocated in August and you have to shoot it in two financial years in order to make the budget work, and if you can't do that, you have to make part of it in Brisbane and do the sound in Guam, and they couldn't quite wrap their heads around it. The reason the films won the ratings is that the ABC audience went to Channel Seven and watched them largely because they adore David, and David's so fantastic.

We set up the film production company because we would often sit around at someone's kitchen and be talking about things that we would like to do if we had a film company. So we decided that we'd better put the umbrella up in the garden and then see if we wanted to go and sit under it. It originally came from a desire to do some things with New Zealand short stories, because we all liked New Zealand short stories rather a lot, but we haven't got around to that; we've been a bit busy, and Sam lives in a plane. He's everywhere all the time, so we have an AGM whenever he lands.

The Book of Australian Verse

It's a favourite project of mine. I've often been bored doing something else that I was being paid to do, and late at night I've gone to the computer and had another fiddle with the poets.

The thesis is that these poets were in fact the genuine model for quite a lot of subsequent world-famous poetry, so it took me back to the poets themselves, which is great.

Dylan Thompson, a martyr to the turps—in his case, for example, my mother had a record of Dylan Thomas reading 'A Child's Christmas in Wales', which is a brilliant piece of writing. And I thought, Well, 'A Child's Christmas in Wales' is fantastic and I love it, but it's not my Christmas because my Christmas has no fir trees, no snow, no snowmen, et cetera. It's got salads and we are all at the beach, basically. So I'm trying to do his style of writing to describe my Christmas, so that book is full of things like that. And it's quite an interesting exercise, a lovely thing to do to basically walk in someone else's shoes, because you liberate stuff in yourself and you have great respect for footwear.

7.30 Report

We come in once a week and do an interview for the *7.30 Report*. We conventionally arrive at about 4.30 having spoken briefly about what subject matter we're going to cover. We'll probably have two scripts with two separate interviewees. We dress up; normally the top half is better dressed than the bottom half. Then we enter the beautification area, where we experience the miracle of make-up. Then we tumble into the studio. We shoot both, then we work out in editing which one is more appropriate to news stories of the day and in the mix of the program, and which one we think is funnier. We're not great political experts; we're not pretending to be wiser than anyone else in the community. But we need to be concise, we need to be reasonably accurate, and it's not an ad hominem argument. It's not an argument that says, 'This is a completely worthless person'; it says, 'This argument doesn't work', or, 'This is not the full story', or, 'This doesn't make sense to us', or, 'This person's saying this, but it's really that person that's driving the argument'.

Seagrass

I'm on a conservation body whose concern is environmental degradation in Western Port, the very large bay next to Port Phillip Bay. There are some serious environmental problems down there, and I've been making a documentary for the Seagrass Partnership that I'm on. And that's been interesting because our board is full of remarkable scientific expertise, of which I have none. I think I am the only person on the board whose name is longer than what follows it. So I do quite a lot of listening about the science.

The problem is that the whole area had a huge sponge-like filter at the top called the Koo-Wee-Rup swamp, and it slowly filtered out anything in the water and then let the water seep down into the bay. Humans removed that entire swamp to make it easier to get from Gippsland to Melbourne. As a result the water has come into the bay much faster and has done much more damage. There's been a lot more erosion, and the area where the swamp was is now very dry and crumbly. And when waves bang into it, it's now crumbling into the sea. So there's a lot of muck in the sea, a lot of turbidity, and plants can't photosynthesise and the seagrass is dead in that area, and the fish that used to use that as a nursery are not there anymore, and the birds that used to eat the fish are not there anymore. And it's a pretty big problem.

The Dagg Sea Scrolls

The other thing I have been doing this year is developing a website, because as a result of my advanced age, I've now got a life that's made up of various chapters and I needed somewhere where all the strands of that could be drawn together. So that business of assessing your own archive is something that ... it's probably a metaphor for my age but that is where the *Fred Dagg* project comes from.

When I was shooting *Fred Dagg* in New Zealand there was no video tape, so nobody could possibly have pressed 'record'. And quite a lot of it has gone missing, because there was one copy on film, and if somebody borrowed it and didn't put it back, it's gone. So we did a big survey of what was left. And I went back, and remembered shooting it back in those days, which was pretty good fun, and in a couple of cases I did it myself, because there was no camera operator and all that, and that project is about remembering those days. There were certain bits of *Fred Dagg* that I don't remember having done, which I saw and thought, That's me, but I don't remember doing that, and other bits of *Fred Dagg* that are very like what I do today.

I loved doing *Fred Dagg*, so to me it's a kind of indulgence to watch it. I do feel now that a lot of what I did in it, quite a lot of ideas were being tried out and instincts being backed and bad habits being formed. One of the nice things about *Fred Dagg* is that the people who saw it at the time couldn't record it, so by remembering it, they've helped invent it. It's a pretty precious place to be in people's memory. But as to the work itself, it taught me everything I know, really, I think, because I did all sorts of things, I did every sort of television I could think of and I had a bit of a play. I was doing stuff that was so little, they didn't stop me.

Ambitions

I don't know that I've ever been sufficiently ambitious to spot a mountain and think, Oh, I wouldn't mind going up there. I'm on a level place, really, if that's the metaphor. I think I'm on a plain and just amusing the other people who are on the plain. I don't think I've ever had an idea of what my ambitions were in my field. I think my ambition is to make a living, work with interesting people, and say the things I want to say.

If you're going to have people's attention you'd better know what you're going to say to them. That is a bit of growing up I had to do after *Fred Dagg*, I think. I needed to work out what I genuinely thought about the world, and if I was going to be providing a satirical perspective, what it should be questioning, what it should be suggesting, how it should be presenting its arguments.

I couldn't have done any of it without Helen. She's a very, very honest and highly intelligent person. She doesn't look at my work in the sense of going along or anything, but she's an awfully good judge of me and she's a pretty smart unit. I think I'll keep her on.

She'll test my ideas out. I don't mean looking over your shoulder when you're doing the work, but dealing with the you who's doing the work is sometimes pretty important. She's the brains of the outfit there, no question.

You need your work to be creatively interesting. I spent a lot of time at my work, because if you're walking down the street, there's still stuff going around in my head that I'm basically processing as part of my work. My work needs to be very interesting to me. I'm lucky enough to be doing something that I do love, so to be bored at your work is a bad result. I spent my secondary school years bored at my work and it wasn't a happy picture.

> I think humour does give people a lot of pleasure. I've certainly had a lot of pleasure from the comedy that I've loved in my life, and I like the humour in everything. Humour doesn't have a better friend than drama, for example. There's a lot of humour in life and there's very often a lot of humour in quite serious situations and quite serious subject matter. But aside from anything else, it's nice to actually be able to make a living out of the thing that got me kicked out of school.

[P.S. In May 2008 John was inducted into the Logies Hall of Fame in recognition of his contribution to the Australian television industry.]

CLIVE JAMES
Writer

Screened 6 August 2007

Clive James is one of the most recognisable Australian writers. For years his trademark voice, manner, style and wit have made us laugh and helped us see things afresh. His work covers television, essays, fiction, poetry and music.

These days Clive divides his time between 'the two best places': England and Australia. As a successful writer, he still lives with the daily tension of waiting for inspiration.

> A writer is a hell of a thing to have in the house because he's nominally there, but suddenly he glazes over. It's because he's thinking. The writing's coming. If he's sitting there doing nothing, he's working and it's very, very hard to convince your family, if you're a writer, that you're sitting there doing nothing but you're working, that it's on its way. Because you look exactly like a man who's ready to carry something heavy upstairs, you see?

What's in a name

I was born in Kogarah, Sydney, in 1939. And the other big event of that year was the outbreak of World War II, which for a while did not affect me, but eventually it did.

My mother and father called me Vivian after a Davis Cup tennis player in the 1938 team called Vivian McGrath. And then about a year later *Gone with the Wind* came out, with Vivien Leigh in it, and my sufferings began because I had this girl's name. I got chased by other boys and beaten up, and eventually I got sick of it. At about the age of eight or nine I asked my mother for another name. My mother, being my mother, said, 'Okay, which name?' And we went to the movies together and there was a movie with Tyrone Power in it playing a character called Clive, and I quite liked the sound of 'Clive'. It was an unusual name but I liked the sound of it. I asked for that. She gave me that. I was the only Clive in Australia so I got chased and beaten up again.

The Kogarah kid

A chapter in my first book, *Unreliable Memoirs*, I think is called 'A Kid from Kogarah', and some of the journalists picked it up and called me 'The Kogarah Kid', and I was rather glad about that. It sounded like a comic book character, which I sometimes see myself as. 'The Kogarah Kid comes from an unknown suburb.' Kogarah is still unknown because no one could pronounce it. There are people in Sydney who can't pronounce the name Kogarah correctly. It's still the way it was. It's a small, humble suburb. I see myself as someone who came out of nowhere on his mission to save the world, you know? The caped crusader. I go for it. It all depends on these humble origins. Actually, they're not that humble; it's a perfectly respectable little suburb. It's like so many Australian suburbs. It's very, very attractive, and it's an attractive place beside Botany Bay, pretty much where the convicts came ashore, actually.

The memories

As I get older, I remember more and more about being young. My memory gets clearer about the far past. On the other hand, I couldn't tell you what I was doing last week. But I can remember the rhythm of life in Kogarah, which largely consisted of waiting for the weekend so you could go and play in the quarry at the top of the street or go down the bottom of the street and play in the park, and then the swamp, which was the wetlands leading to Botany Bay.

And I can remember being out there in the wetlands, building cubby holes. I remember the smell of lantana and the way that it scratched you. I remember more and more about the years of growing up. And I suppose it was a kind of heaven, but I had to grow up and look back on it to realise how privileged it was. That's the essential point. We were living in a dream world.

My father was a mechanic who spent most of the '30s out of work because the Depression hit Australia so hard. My mother worked on the production lines. And they had a tough life. They had to wait for a while before they had me.

I was an only child, and that was probably the reason why I didn't have many friends. I was a difficult youngster. I think I was the despair of my mother in many ways. If there was a broken milk bottle half a mile away, half-buried in the mud, I would somehow find it and jump on it. I was that kind of child. I'd come home and my mother would fix me. On the other hand, she would do anything for me, and I got used to getting what I wanted, which is bad training for being with other people, especially other young men. And I wasn't notably successful at being gregarious. I would've liked to have been, but I wasn't. I think I was pretty hard to put up with. I think I was obnoxious, actually. I hate to say it.

My first job: I had a paper round. And I found out immediately that I was unfit for any kind of disciplined, responsible activity. I lost the papers, I lost the money, and the man who was employing me said, 'This is hopeless', and then terminated our arrangement.

The personality

I have a histrionic personality. If there's limelight, I will somehow manage to get myself into it. My character was already on display during the war, while my father was away. The first birthday party I went to, I think I was about four years old. There was a birthday party going on up the street. I wasn't invited. I invited myself. I sat on top of the plank fence, at the back of the party, and made sure everybody could see me. It was the beginning of my career in show business and I was hard to miss ever since. I've got it in me. I'm a performer. I also like being alone. I like solitude, so I can write. The two things conflict. All through my life this conflict has been going on: one to be in the limelight, to be performing, to get the laughs; the other to be alone, to study, to read. The two things combine, I hope, or contest always. And it's the way I am. I don't think it can be traced to anything. I think you've just got it.

My father

My father volunteered to go and defend Australia from what were thought to be the onrushing Japanese hordes. And guess what? The onrushing Japanese hordes actually materialised, and he fought in Malaya. He was captured in Singapore, and spent the war as a prisoner of war. And he was lucky to survive it. And he got right through to the end of the war, and then he was killed in an accident on the way home.

I never knew him. There's a photograph of my father with me in his arms, in about 1939, I think, 1940, before he went off to Singapore from which he never came back. And there I am, I'm tiny, and that was the only photograph of us together. So I know him only by repute. I can tell he must have been quite something by the way my mother grieved for him and missed him. I was there when she got the telegram that said he wasn't coming back from the war. And I saw the full force of human grief released in front of me. And I could tell from that, that what she was missing was someone important. And as my life has gone on, this thought has dominated it more and more.

I was six years old and there was nothing I could do about it. And I think that probably marked me for life. I'm really trying to pay them back. It was an accident and I try not to dwell on it, because I saw what dwelling on it did to her. My father was a prisoner of war of the Japanese; he went 'into the bag' in Singapore, went to Changi, was lucky not to get drafted off to the railway in Thailand; in fact, he went with the other group that went to the home islands, to Japan. He spent the whole of the war on the docks in Kobe. It was a hot spot; it was hard. There were many deaths but he got through it. And he survived the war.

But then the Americans with typical generosity and, unfortunately, with typical impetuosity, laid on a flight of B24 Liberators to fly our prisoners home so they wouldn't have to wait for a ship. Unfortunately, it was typhoon weather and a typhoon caught the B24 that my father was on somewhere above Formosa and it crashed with the death of all aboard. His body was eventually taken to Hong Kong, where it's buried now.

It was an accident, it was cruel to my mother, but I was too young to understand.

They were corresponding, after the prisoners were released in Japan. The first thing that happened was correspondence, uncensored correspondence, passionate letters ... the emotions involved are such dynamite that I can hardly talk about them.

The impact

First of all the impact on my mother had an impact on me. I could see what despair looked like. She kept going and she brought me up. My mother was a very focused woman, a very responsible woman. But she missed him terribly. Half of her potential for life had been destroyed, and I was there and watching it. And in many ways I've been making it up to both of them ever since.

I don't think it's so much guilt; it's a recognition of the role that chance plays in human affairs. The dice roll and sometimes they roll right over you and across someone very near you. And that's what happened. And it gave me a sense from a very early age, the age of six, that I was living on borrowed time. Ever since, I've lived from day to day. I have no expectation that the future will last another twenty-four hours.

I was vividly impressed by the fact that chance had removed him. But I wouldn't say that I dwelt on it; I was just aware of it. I was a war orphan and I suppose in many ways I used it for advantage; it helped establish a character for me—I was the 'war orphan'. I didn't curry sympathy on it, but there were certain privileges accrued, and they went on accruing. In fact, I got in to university because I was a war orphan. Because I didn't even get a Commonwealth scholarship, I got in on a Repatriation scholarship, so tertiary education happened because my father got killed. Another reason for guilt, you might think. I wouldn't say guilt was the right word. I didn't do it, the Americans didn't do it, the Japanese didn't do it. Chance did it: a storm. He was caught in the weather.

Mother

My mother, luckily, was a very frugal, well-organised woman. And she eked out her war widow's pension, which was never very lavish, with smocking babies' frocks. Smocking was very intricate stitching. My mother was very good at it. She made a pittance with that, added that to the pension. It was enough to bring 'me' up, but we didn't have a lot of money.

I tried not just to make her proud of me, but him proud of me, if he'd been there. Mind you, this took time. I spent my youth being as callous as any other boy towards his mother; neglectful of her feelings. I went away without a qualm to Europe, even though she hated the idea of my leaving. But she was big-hearted enough and intelligent and imaginative enough to realise that I needed to make the break; otherwise, I would've stayed a mother's boy. So I got on the ship and sailed for Europe in about 1961. And there she was on the dock, and once more, for the second time in her life, watching the only man in her life leaving on a ship.

Schooling

I was naturally a bad student, I think. There was a school called the Opportunity School in Hurstville, and I rather shone there because half of the day was devoted to playful activities and I was good at playful activities; I was never very good at the other stuff. And this became obvious when I got to Sydney Technical High School and I couldn't do maths very well and eventually not at all. And that became a pattern throughout my life. I've never been very good at the set course, as it were. I was fairly small physically and to stay alive in the playground I had two courses of action: one was to outrun the opposition, which was difficult because some of them were athletes, and the other was to sit down and organise a discussion group. And eventually I chose the second course, told stories and got away with it. And I've been doing the same thing for the rest of my life.

I turned out again to be a natural show-off. I ran the school newspaper, but I didn't think of myself, One day I'll do this: I'll be a journalist.

I went to Sydney University and enrolled in the Arts Faculty because I thought the Arts faculty would be all about drawing and painting, and to my surprise found out there were things like literature. I was continually being surprised by what they asked me to learn.

At Sydney University I did quite a lot of performing and writing, but I didn't think of myself as a writer.

But when I met my first poets, I knew instantly what I was going to do with my life, because I wanted to be them. They were all cutting classes, sitting around in the Women's Union, reading poetry books, speaking incomprehensible stuff littered with famous names which weren't famous to me. I was very keen to find out what they were talking about, but I knew I wanted to be part of it. Somehow I knew then—this wonderful world of glittering talk and allusion to poetry, and quoting poetry—the whole business. And it was a way of getting girls. All the really attractive girls seemed to like the literary guys. And I knew I wanted to do it. But also, it began to occur to me that it was what I could do. I wasn't a natural athlete, although I looked like that. I can say it safely now that I am a physical wreck. When I was young, you would've sworn I was going to be an Olympic swimmer, you know. I had the V-shaped surfing hero, but I couldn't do it; I had no real gift for sports, no gift at all for music, many things I wasn't gifted at.

I could write a bit. I had this turn of phrase. I was smart enough by then to know that my turn of phrase was what I had going for me. But I still didn't know I was going to make a living at it. And it was a long while before I did.

Secret men's business

This is very secret, intimate stuff and we shouldn't really be talking about it, but the following is true. While I was at Sydney University Germaine [Greer] had just arrived from Melbourne covered with starry glory because, you know, she'd been working with Barry Humphries in Melbourne, and she was already famous. Everybody knew she was a famous wit because she was striking, beautiful, this striding Valkyrie of a woman. And she grandly announced that she was going to take my virginity. Somebody told me this, and I ran. It is not true that I hid up a tree. I hid behind the tree! But I did hide. It was a big mistake. Time went by, about another year, and I realised if she really wanted to take my virginity, it was a very good idea. And I tried to remind her of it. She threw me out of her apartment. I never got a second break.

I began becoming a professional writer at the end of university. I was asked onto the *Herald* as an assistant literary editor, for the *SMH* on Saturdays. It was a rather grand title because all I ever did was rewrite stuff that was being sent in from the country. Always in Australia there's someone in a bush town who has written a novel which is 600,000 words long and fits into three suitcases, and finally he brings it to Sydney. And they used to end up on my desk. And I would find bits of it to rewrite and we would put it in the newspaper. It was very, very good training but I still didn't think of myself as a professional writer. And I didn't really become one until years later, after I'd got to England and got nowhere in London for the first three years, doing a variety of odd jobs.

London

I sailed for London in the early '60s with the intention, the bold intention, of staying away for five years. It was regarded as sheer bravado that I said this. It turned out to be longer than that. I had three years of bohemian—that is, unsuccessful, feckless—existence in London before I was saved by going to Cambridge.

I think in those days a lot of us thought, correctly or incorrectly— I now see incorrectly—that Australia was a sort of permanent backwater for what we wanted to do. The truth was that Australian culture was already booming because of the influence of the migrants, and the influence was just beginning to show. And in the following decades, especially under the Whitlam administration, Australia became the efflorescence that we now see, which stuns the world. For a small nation of twenty million people we have an extraordinary cultural impact on the world. That was already in the wind but it took intelligence to see it. And I didn't have the intelligence; I was too damn dumb. I just got on the ship and went because everyone else did. And, being me, I landed in Britain with no money, and I couldn't get back again. I grandly said I was going for five years. In fact it was fifteen or sixteen before I could afford to get back to Australia.

So as with so many things it all happened by accident. But the impulse that sent us, well, I think free countries do that automatically. They export the kind of people who like to wander. Other kinds of people don't like to wander. The smart thing to do in 1961 was stay here. Les Murray did it and Les is a gigantic poet, a truly great talent. He didn't need to go abroad because his imagination can do it for him. I think people like me, we actually gained from going abroad because we weren't smart enough to guess what it was all like. We had to go and see it. And one of the consequences of seeing what the world was like is that you see what Australia was like. So that was very valuable to me, so I don't apologise for it. But I don't say it was an especially smart move. I got on the boat because everyone else got on the boat.

Australians abroad

It was a sort of *Animal House* scenario, and I was the animal. I was in the same house as Bruce Beresford, and Bruce was a cut above the rest of us, because Bruce had clean clothes and he earned a salary. No matter what happened, Bruce would go out to work. Sometimes he would work in a steelyard. He would bring home the money the rest of us were living off, because we would borrow from him. He was a kind of male den mother in that way. Also, Bruce was fantastically attractive to women—I think I can say that safely now—and we envied that. And eventually that whole ménage moved on. We moved across the road to Mulberry Road in Kensington, and Mulberry Road was a house full of Australians. The girls were upstairs, the guys were downstairs; in the backyard was Brett Whiteley, living in a state of magnificence in Holman Hunt's old studio.

The whole house used to belong to the Pre-Raphaelites, and Holman Hunt had a studio out the back. And now Brett was in it with his beautiful wife, Wendy, and he was doing these pictures of her in the bath which subsequently became some of the most famous pictures of the Australian artistic movement. And Brett was this sort of golden-haired god, and Wendy was this dream figure. And they would emerge from this shed, studio, fully dressed to go to dinner with Sir Kenneth Clark or something, Brett in his black jacket and Wendy looking like a million dollars, because what she had on cost a million dollars. And the rest of us were standing there open-mouthed, realising there was another world that we were missing out on, and we would be very lucky to get in to.

But of all the whole bunch that were around there envying Brett, Bruce [Beresford] was always the most likely one to make an impact, because he was very well organised, very realistic. And when the crucial moment came, he was the one who realised the way to finance the first *Barry McKenzie* movie was to go back to Australia and get it financed there. And he did it. And the *Barry McKenzie* movie succeeded and it began the modern Australian film industry as we know it today. You should never underestimate the impact of that film.

Getting in to Cambridge

I had to do all this hand to mouth stuff in London because I was really, really broke. You couldn't go on living off Bruce forever, just because he was organised and handsome. So I would do casual jobs. I could work in market research, for example. I got a job where you go stand in the street and ask people whether they prefer the cap of the tomato sauce bottle to be attached to the bottle with a little bit of plastic, or free so it can be unscrewed and thrown away. The answers to those questions were usually manufactured by us in the pub, because instead of asking 100 Norwegians you'd go and make it up and get fired. Which I did!

I got fired from a lot of things. I worked in the library and I got fired. Stacking books—I couldn't stack books properly. And I could never arrive on time. And I worked in a sheet-metal factory driving a crane, and I dropped a big stack of metal sheets very near the foreman, who didn't take it kindly, so I left that job early. I accumulated enough experience in two or three years to prove I couldn't do anything else except write. So it was very lucky that I went to Cambridge.

The great George Russell, who died quite recently, was the great professor of medieval romance, philology, old English, middle

English all that stuff at Sydney—and he was one of my professors. And even though I was a rotten student for him, and never did the work, he smiled fondly on me, I think because I entertained him and he was actually very advanced in every way. And George said, when he knew I was going to sail for Britain, 'If you get into trouble there, drop me a line and I'll fix you up at Cambridge, because you know if you really get into a mess', he knew I would, 'you should go back and do university properly because you've been just pretending while you were here'. He was right about that.

And I did get into a mess, and I did write to him, and he did fix it up with Pembroke College in Cambridge. And I walked in and got a university place, and I'm very, very aware that there are many people in Britain who might resent that. I got in on a fix. I got in through his influence, and immediately I became a bad student again, but at a higher level. George Russell did that for me.

I was smart enough by then to know that my turn of phrase was what I had going for me, because what I wanted to do was get established as a poet. I knew I wouldn't make a living at it, but at least I wanted my poems published. And editors spurned my poems as if they were infected, and I was a total flub. And until I got in to Cambridge I never really had an outlet for my poetry. And then things changed, because at Cambridge, once again, I could skive off the way I skived off at Sydney. And once again I could write poems for the university newspapers the way I did in Sydney. And once again I had become a literary figure and a Review figure and a Footlights figure, the way I had in Sydney, but I could do it all more intensely.

I knew more and I was slightly older than the other students. A couple of years at that age is a big advantage. And so Cambridge became my stamping ground. It was a happy hunting ground. And I did so much there for the university newspapers and stuff that it began to be noticed in Fleet Street. And I spent more and more time writing for Fleet Street, which is the reason why my PhD never got very far.

One of the first big pieces I wrote for *The Times Literary Supplement* was about the American critic Edmund Wilson. It was about 11,000 words long and they printed it all. And it created quite an impact, and people wanted to know who had written it. And one of them was Graham Greene. And Graham Greene sent me a note saying he was glad to see his own opinions of Edmund Wilson put into print so eloquently. And I was so flattered I sent Graham Greene one of those six-page letters you should never send. Never respond at length, because they haven't got time, and I never heard from him again.

It was the first time I experienced having said the right thing at the right time. And I got a taste for literary journalism. It's a very addictive taste, and that's where it started—on the way out of Cambridge—my transition into Fleet Street, which is essentially the story of how I didn't do my PhD. I started a PhD; it never got anywhere because I went to work. Finally, finally I went to work.

Becoming a writer

Earning a living from writing wasn't all that easy, even though I was working like a dog. And I had a lot of energy in those days. I could hit four or five deadlines a week, working all night. And then in 1972 I was asked to be *The Observer*'s television critic. And that was a big move, because I wrote a weekly column about television, and *The Observer* was reaching a million of the brightest people in the country. It was the perfect audience; it was my pulpit and I could talk about anything because television talked about everything. And it was a dream platform. And I did that for ten years and everything branched off from that, really.

Sometimes journalists say, 'First he was a critic and then he became a performer', which is not quite true, because I was already a performer. I was a guest quite early on. I was quite a good guest. I could actually relax doing it. I made a lot of guest appearances, and I also did a series.

I was asked by Granada to take over a program called *Cinema*. I was so green in those days, I thought Granada Television was in Spain. In fact, it was in Manchester. And I took the show over from Michael Parkinson. And I did about thirty-nine of those shows. But what I never stopped doing was writing.

Even when I was doing a lot of TV, for the next twenty years, I was still writing literary reviews and stuff like that. Writing poetry, I always write poetry. I'm always between poems and a poem will be the last thing I write when I fall off the twig. I still did that.

I still wrote songs with my friend Pete Atkin. They're under his name: Pete Atkin's albums. But I wrote the lyrics, and I'm very proud of them. I can be proud of them, I can boast about them because they were failures commercially. And these six albums of songs, I think, are some of my best work.

They're mainly about doomed love. But they were also about the world, and about war, and about terror, and all these things. And they're some of my most wide-ranging writing, as a poet lyricist. I really can't write better than I can in the songs, but I feel the same way about some of my TV programs, my *Postcard* programs.

Television

It became clear that I was doing more and more TV; I couldn't go on being a critic. So I switched in 1982. From 1982 onwards till about the millennium I did hundreds of TV shows in the studio or out on the road.

For me, the *Postcard* format was the best thing on TV because it gave me a chance to write as well as I could, and I did about thirty of them over twenty-five years. They were very carefully written. I really can't write better than that. I like to bring the same concentration and attention to detail in the writing to everything I do. I'm fundamentally a writer. It's what I do.

All the time I was working in television I never quit being a literary journalist. Literary journalism never paid, still doesn't, but I thought it was valuable. Still do. The trick's to keep it going while I was working in TV. Somehow I managed it.

The writing process

My writing day is that I just sit there and I wait, and if at five o'clock in the evening you're still waiting, don't panic; it'll come next day.

It remains difficult, but I have to do it. I get up in the morning and I wait for inspiration, and sometimes I wait all day. Sometimes it never comes. And you have enough guilt from the wasted day to make sure that you write the next day. There's no secret why most writers are drinkers. The tension is awful because maybe it won't come back tomorrow. You don't know how you do it anyway. Nobody knows how they turn a phrase. It's a gift, and suppose it doesn't come back tomorrow?

I've never had a long block. The way I've actually developed as a writer, over the years, is I've learnt not to panic when it won't come. Because when it doesn't come, that's part of the process. That tension of not being able to do it means somewhere in your brain you're sorting out something that's too complex for immediate expression, but it will be when it's sorted itself out. The expression 'sleep on it' comes out. Sometimes I work in my sleep. I know I do because I wake up more capable of expressing what I have to say. But to become a professional writer, it's necessary to reach the stage where you can live with the tension when it's not happening, because that's part of the process.

Philip Roth once said that the minute a writer is born into a family, that family is doomed. And it's quite profoundly true, and I value my family, and I have a pact with them that I never talk about them. And I go along with that pact willingly, because I want to preserve my relationship with them. And I would destroy it if I started writing about them, but it's not that I'm not proud of them. On the contrary, what I can't really see is why they put up with me.

I haven't really been a very satisfactory husband and father. My attention is always elsewhere. I'm conscious of it and they are.

I don't find any tension between being funny and being serious myself. But the reputations that result from these two activities can conflict in the most disturbing and frustrating way.

I'm not really a comedian and I don't even tell jokes. If I do anything funny it's because I've expressed something real in a very short space. The result is, if you make an article interesting enough on that level, so you're saying something complex but some of it comes out funny. And you get this reputation as a comedian, then journalistically these two reputations get in each other's road: 'He can't be serious because he's funny'; 'He can't be funny because he's serious'. I've lived with that for the whole of what I laughingly call my career. I'm still living with it.

Being Australian

I've still got my Australian passport, which is a real sign of patriotism because there are so many countries you can't just walk into, including Britain. You land at Heathrow with an Australian passport and you go in the 'Other Passports' queue. Sometimes it's a mile long. You look across; there's this tiny queue for the EEC, people are flying through it. Ex-SS tank commanders being greeted with laurel wreaths. You stand there resenting them. But I'm still very proud to have that Australian passport. As for what you take with you of the Australian character, that's in dispute, and it's always going to be in dispute. The attempt to define Australian national characteristics, national values, is a political talking point. And what the people who are politically talking about it don't realise is there's no end to the discussion.

Being Australian has affected everything I have done. And as I've got older, and stayed away longer, I got more and more interested.

I don't want to give the impression I've got a pocket full of airline tickets, but I'm back in Australia five or six times a year, so

I'm practically here. And you get accumulative multidirectional jet lag, but the advantage is you're living in the two best places, Australia and Britain.

A mother's son

My mother was here and I was there, largely, but she kept herself informed. And when I started coming home, after sixteen years, I'd tell her everything that I'd done. And I kept that up all the way to the nursing home, as it were. I would actually come and visit her in the nursing home and say, 'Mum, I just got photographed with Margaret Whitlam', and keep her up to date to prove to her that I was doing well, because I knew it was important to her. She was always worried about other things. Always worried about whether my socks matched or whether I was warm enough over there in England.

And she was always desperately worried that I'd never really got my qualifications. I'd got these strange university degrees, but she didn't think they qualified me for anything. She was right: they didn't. That bothered her. And finally, not that long ago, Sydney University gave me an honorary doctorate. And I arranged for Mum to be taken from the nursing home and be in the Great Hall at Sydney University in a wheelchair while I gave the address to all the graduates, and got my own honorary doctorate with the big hat and the robes. And then I walked towards her down the aisle, in my big hat and robes, and I could see this light in her eyes as I approached, and I knew what she was thinking ... she was thinking, At last he's got his qualifications.

Father's grave

I never searched it out for years, actually; something was keeping me away from it. Then in 1982 I was in the press corps that followed Mrs Thatcher through China. We came out of China through Hong Kong and I got a cab out to the Sai Wan War Cemetery and found his grave. And it was a big moment for me. It was the dates on the tombstone that did it, because it was then I finally fully realised that my life was already much longer than his. So it was like I was the father and he was the son. And I cried the big tears that day. And I've gone on visiting that grave ever since. And I've got older and older, steadily realising that I'm leading the life he should have had, which I think is probably one of the motors for my what could be called hyperactivity. I overdo it. I don't have to work this hard or do so much.

The writer

Writing, for me, is still it. It has always been the basis of everything I do. I'm a writer who performs, not a performer who writes. I love the act of writing. It's still a thrill for me. I do the first draft longhand because I want to see what I've crossed out easily. Because sometimes the bit you crossed out is the bit you should put back. I honestly don't count the number of books I've had published. It's somewhere between thirty and forty, and the range goes from poetry across through novels, to essays, collections of essays, travel books.

I suppose my most important thing, for myself, is poetry, because that's the one that earns me absolutely no money.

I haven't been exactly showered with prizes over my career, but I did get the best one, which is the Philip Hodgins Medal, in 2003. And as the premier literary award in Australia, in my view, I was very glad to get it for my poetry, which is a double thrill.

Of course, I think it's all wonderful, but the book that really counts for me is my big book, *Cultural Amnesia*. It took me forty years to write this thing: thirty-seven years to get ready, three years to actually write it. And everything I know is in here, and I hope I've made it entertaining, but to me it's very serious, and I can only say if you don't buy this book, you'll get warts.

When I retired from the small screen in 2001, I actually started working harder. I wrote my big book and I also started developing my website: clivejames.com. I still don't know what it is. It's half space station, half university campus. I do know that it's a clearing in the jungle. The web is an enormous mess. There has to be some place where young people can come and be absolutely sure that everything they see is high quality, it represents humanism and the adventure of the mind. And I think it's going to be my contribution in old age. It certainly makes me feel young again, working on it.

I started planning this website in which there would be moving pictures as well as words and radio and everything. And I was planning it before I realised it couldn't be done. It physically could never be done when I was thinking of it, because narrowband couldn't do it. But while I was planning it, someone invented broadband, and it was on. In about 2001 we started to build it. And for me it's the ultimate means of expression. It's a wonderful thing to have discovered at my age. I just wish I had another thirty or forty years to develop it. But I've made a cunning plan. If I invite enough good stuff in, people won't notice when the central bit—me—goes silent and I quietly fade away. There'll still be a lot of interesting stuff there.

The intellectual adventure

What I tried to do in my big book, *Cultural Amnesia*, was transmit the adventure to a new generation. For me the intellectual adventure is the supreme one. Maybe it's because I'm the only one I'm equipped for, but I still believe it is. My stroke of luck is that I'm consumed by what I do and will be to the end.

I think I'm trying to say that liberal values are worth transmitting for themselves. That culture is worth pursuing for itself. If you don't have the attitude that these things are consuming and important for themselves—they're not utilitarian, they're not for gain, they're not for any other purpose, they are for themselves—unless you have that, you shouldn't be doing them.

A free society will necessarily produce things you don't like. It will necessarily be scary, be terrifying. Somewhere in the middle of it there's got to be something that represents civilisation—liberal values, humanism—and I think that's what we should be after. Somebody has to do that. If you're cut out for it, you should do it.

> What I do had better be fun, because it's all I do. Journalists often ask—they want you to say that you spend your life fishing for sharks and chasing loose women. What they really want to say is they can't believe that you're getting enough out of what you're doing, and I say reading and writing, for me, is exciting, and they glaze over. But reading and writing, for me, is exciting, or are exciting. The most exciting things I can think of. And now, as I reflect, as we move into the twilight zone—what my friend Bruce Beresford would call 'the Departure Lounge'—the time comes to sum up your life. I have to say that I've been lucky in that I'm amused by what I do—sufficiently amused.

[P.S. Clive is currently working on his website, clivejames.com, while writing the fifth volume of his memoirs and preparing for the publication of two books of poetry, *Opal Sunset* and *Angels over Elsinore*.

He says his recent book *Cultural Amnesia* has become essential reading for serious students all over the world!]

PROFESSOR FIONA WOOD
Surgeon

Screened 14 August 2006

Plastic surgeon Fiona Wood became a household name in the aftermath of the 2002 Bali bombings, with her spray-on skin coming to the rescue of burns victims airlifted to the Royal Perth Hospital. The dynamic mother of six, who was made Australian of the Year in 2005, grew up in the coal-mining communities of west Yorkshire. Her father worked down the mine, but was determined his children wouldn't have to follow the same path.

> My father was very keen that we should explore our potential in terms of sport, and academically. He himself was a very academic sort of character in that he had a scholarship to go to grammar school but wasn't allowed to pursue that by his family. So he has a mind like a steel trap. He felt very strongly that we had to explore our potential, and education for him would give us a choice in life, so that when we got up in the morning we enjoyed what we did. He didn't have that privilege and he was very keen that we did.

A Yorkshire lass

I was actually born in the west of Yorkshire. It was lots of very small villages all clustered around a pit, and they were all related to that given mine. I was the third child. My older two brothers were born at home in the village of Upton. By the time I came along my parents had moved to another mining village: Frickley. I was born in the closest hospital, which was in Hemsworth.

My father is 'Big Geoff'. When we were kids he was known by everyone in the area as Big Geoff, and my brother was Little Geoff. He was brought up in the nearby mining village South Kirby, where he went to school to about thirteen, fourteen. From there he went down the mine—he was a pony driver initially with his brother Cyril, who was a couple of years older—and he worked down the mine until he went for National Service. But my understanding is that they were exempt from that after the Second World War—being miners, being primary industry—so they had to sign for certain things like tail-gunning or despatch riding or whatever, in order to get into the air force. So he went into the air force for five years. He was a great sportsman—a soccer player, in fact. He played for Nottingham Forest at one stage, very briefly. Then he had a bad injury, he broke his leg, and found himself back down the mine.

He hated it; he didn't like it at all. And it was very obvious to me as a young child that he was significantly grumpier when he got home from work than the days he didn't work. So the mine to him did not represent anything other than a means to an end—and the means to the end was to feed and clothe his family.

One of the memories of my father is at a stag night. He was in his thirties and ... in fact, it was a documentary called *The Wedding on Saturday*. And part of this was this stag's night, was that they were discussing what their children would do, what opportunities they had. My father, Big Geoff, stood there swaying in the breeze, because there'd been a fair bit of amber fluid flowing, and said, 'Well, you know, I won't be satisfied until I see one of my boys in dark blue and one in light blue rowing under Putney Bridge in the Oxford and Cambridge boat race'. And there was a lot of discussion about that, very vocal, 'Who are you to think that your kids could do that?' I think my father's response always was, 'Who am I not to? Who are any of us not to dream? If we don't dream how could we ever know what could be possible?'

I think a lot of people should look back and really appreciate what's special about their childhood because it's made them as they go forward in life. I think I was just extraordinarily lucky to have the parents that I had … that really, even in that quite austere environment, they could see that there was something special in everyone. Certainly for them in their four children there was something very special worth nurturing. I think if everybody stands back and really looks hard then the vast majority of us would find that. And it's something to hold on to because it gives you that strength going forward.

At the time I was being brought up in the mining area, it was very transitional. As a young girl, I remember, there were some impending concerns that the industry and the environment and the lifestyle were not sustainable. That certainly was subsequently confirmed by Margaret Thatcher.

I remember, when we were young, the social aspects associated with the collieries. Sport very much ran the communities around the collieries. We were all encouraged to explore sport certainly as a way to learn how to work, if nothing else. If you want to get better you train harder; it's not rocket science. If you want to achieve a goal then you work for it. And so that was very much in the ethos. I ran for the collieries. You ran under their colours, whether it be Frickley or Hickleton Main. I ran for Frickley colliery, although apparently I wasn't the original 'Frickley Flier'—my brother David is the real one, he keeps telling me. Then I ran for Hickleton Main and I ran against the Grimethorpe guys. In fact, on my way here today I was listening to the Grimethorpe Colliery Band, because again, with the music, the whole thing was based around mines. But it was all starting to come apart at the seams, I guess.

I remember being very impatient, sitting on my dad's shoulders waiting for union leader Arthur Scargill to shut up with his speeches to the miners on the Saturday afternoon, because we were there to run, you know. We were here to do the business, and what was he going on about? In retrospect it was obviously quite a difficult time, and by the time I went to university at seventeen, and came back, we were right in the middle of the prolonged strikes. Things were very, very different and they've never recovered.

A changed community

There certainly was a strong sense of community. It's never recovered from that period in the late '70s—and the disintegration, if you like, of those communities—because the unemployment soared as a result of the mine closures.

I think from a political point of view it's really interesting because we're all influenced by our genetics and our environment. For me, when I was working in the NHS [National Health Service], I had no concern about working as hard as I could, and doing the best I could ... and the concept of private medicine never entered my mind. So I think there's a lot of those things that stay. I was brought up in a very working class environment and as far as I was concerned that's what you did; life was about working. I always felt myself very fortunate that I didn't go down the mine, that I didn't work like my mother, in the fields picking brussels sprouts on a winter's morning. So for me, working was a privilege. And the concept of pursuing that to look into private medicine or things was something that didn't even cross my mind.

Mother

My mother's been a fantastic role model and mentor all my life. She worked all her life, and still has trouble not working—she's well past seventy now. She was very much a go-getter. And again, you make your luck in this life. My dad's saying is 'The harder you work, the luckier you get', and she kind of is the living proof of that. She left school very young as well. Her exit strategy in the environment was the WAF, then she came back, married Dad, ended up with the four of us and worked. In her early life, she worked in the fields, picking brussels sprouts, beetroot, that kind of stuff, working in youth work. She was very proactive in the youth club and educated herself. She'd left school early but got qualifications, both in the WAF as a PTI, and then in youth work.

I must have been twelve, and there were significant changes taking place in the educational system in Yorkshire at the time. My eldest brother had gone to secondary modern school, my next brother had passed his eleven-plus and gone to grammar school, but I was in a situation where I wasn't allowed to take the eleven-plus and I was going to go to comprehensive school. My mother, working in youth work, thought that this was the thin end of the wedge and that it wasn't a positive development from an educational point of view—wrote to Sir Alec Clegg at the time, who responded that I wasn't university material so I should stop worrying. My mother thought that was an inappropriate response. At the time we had a friend who was a policeman, who was involved in security of a school in another village—these villages are all within a couple of miles of each other—and it was Ackworth, and this was a Friends School—Society of Friends, Quaker—and I used to walk past and think, Oh Mum, I would love to go there.

Ackworth Friends School

They had these Harry Potter cloaks that went down to the ground with pale blue woollen lining and a little hood. And they all looked so happy and wandered around in this ethereal fashion. I had no concept of what a private—a public school in England—a private education cost or anything like that. But my mother, true to form, went along because she saw a job advertised as a matron. And she came out of that interview as the Phys. Ed. teacher, and I went as a staff child within six months. She'd sorted it; she'd seen the solution to the problem and so I went there at thirteen. With the help of another one of her friends with my entrance exam, I skipped a year of school, and I found myself in a school, in a beautiful environment, with absolutely no idea ... and in my first class a teacher was talking to me in French and I had no idea it was a foreign language. I was thinking, this could be a bit tricky! So for my first term I had extra tutoring in all subjects except maths and science.

I found myself at thirteen knowing that I had been given an extraordinary opportunity, and I wasn't going to waste it.

Certainly when I got to the Ackworth Friends School—the Society of Friends School—that really opened my eyes because it really gave me a window into how people from all sorts of different walks of life and all sorts of different philosophies were living. And I thought, Whoa, there's more going on around here. It was a real eye-opener to go there and to have the level of education that I did. It was fantastic. It was just paradise as far as I was concerned. And the ethos ... the school motto was 'Non Sibi Sed Omnibus': not for oneself but for others.

And the engagement in the community from the Quakers in a very different way was something that I was exposed to. I watched, I learnt, and, you know, when you're thirteen to sixteen—I think I'm a bit of a sponge anyway—you absorb different things around you and learn from them and work out where you fit in this whole jigsaw.

Goals

It was very obvious to my mum and dad that if you wanted something you had to go out there and get it. My mother's great line was 'Grasp the nettle with two hands, girl, because if you don't, somebody else will'.

My dad had been in the RAF just after the war, my mum in the WAF, and so they both had travelled. They had this awareness that there was a much bigger world out there and that it was there for us to explore if we chose to do so, and worked hard enough to facilitate that.

But even in this aggressive focus of 'Work hard, do your best', it was always 'but not in isolation from others'—I was one of four—we had it drummed into us. You have to look after the family, and the team in sport, and also in the wider context. Because it was certainly my mother's perception, and certainly as I was learning, that you can never do anything in isolation in life. I learnt that really early on, and if you try to make your achievements on the shoulders of others by pushing them down, it's not sustainable.

A medical career

In 1975 I went to St Thomas' Hospital Medical School and I was one of twelve women. I remember thinking it was very strange that there was no ladies' toilets on certain floors of the block just because there'd not been that many before. I think that a number of people didn't consider it appropriate that I would pursue a surgical career, but I didn't consider it appropriate that they should tell me. I'd sort of ignore that, so my standard line was 'I'm really good at embroidery, so just watch out. Bit of stiff competition because my cross-stitch would outdo yours any day!'

It was something that I never considered in a negative way. I enjoyed medical school enormously. It was a great six years; I travelled, I did research in all sorts of areas. I did research with the plastic surgeons in microsurgery, I did research in East Africa, I worked with the Leakeys, and Professor Michael Day was our anatomy professor, so I was able to go on a field trip with him. And I worked in Hong Kong, did a nutritional research project in India, Bombay. So I had a great time.

I think very early on the first day, I knew I was going to be a surgeon. I thought, Oh, this is where it's at. It was just fascinating. I was fascinated by anatomy and I just thought, This is it. If a surgeon puts this back together then this is where I want to be. And as I went through the various levels of surgery—again I'm a great believer you can learn something from everywhere—I thought burns was a really interesting mix of that initial resuscitation: keeping the person alive with the demands in the intensive care environment, understanding pain measures and all that and the stress responses, and then you have the surgery and the rehabilitation. And those three phases are all merged but they're merged with one thing behind that: the person.

For me surgery wasn't a purely technical exercise, though that is something that stimulates me and it challenges me, that technical exercise, but it was more than that. For a period of time this person's life journey is changed such that they need your help and it's a privilege to help at that point in time. But it's that whole person that you're helping. And to actually bring all that together is the ultimate challenge.

The Guinea Pig Club

My interest in burns really developed out of seeing the scope of plastic surgery, seeing the scope of reconstruction. Initially I was drawn to hand surgery and trauma. Then I met a couple of people who were having reconstructive work post-burns. And so I sought out a job in Queen Victoria Hospital, East Grinstead—by then it was 1985. I'd been around—done general surgery, orthopaedics, I'd done some eyes, I'd done plastic surgery as well, accident and emergency work—and by then I was going into specialist training. I'd got my general surgical fellowship, and I needed specialist training. I went along to Queen Victoria, East Grinstead, south of England. I went there because it was famous for burns, because it had been the home of the Guinea Pig Club and Sir Archibald McIndoe, and that was really where my fate was sealed, I guess.

The Guinea Pig Club was a group of air force personnel who were burn-injured in the Second World War—the majority British but also Australians, Kiwis, Canadians, Polish—and they were collected together. They were young men who had had their lives changed in an instant. They'd been burnt, most in aircraft accidents, they'd survived that, and they'd been collected together by Sir Archibald McIndoe and brought to Queen Victoria Hospital, as a specialist burns centre, where he really took on the challenge of, one, survival from burns and, two, rebuilding and reconstruction. And some of these gentlemen were still there. They were amazing characters, inspiring characters, and very special people. When I saw them at East Grinstead, I thought, There's been so many advances, so much progress; people have been able to survive such massive injuries; but we've got to make it worth it, got to make that survival, the quality of the survival, worth it.

Again, that was 1985 and I thought, We've got to be able to do better than this. So it also married with this whole holistic approach. There's lots of different challenges and I guess that suits my personality, keeping all these different balls in the air. But the bottom line was, Goodness me, we've got to be able to do better than this. The scope and the opportunity to research was huge and still is, and there's an awfully long way for us to go.

Coming to Australia

I came to Australia nineteen years ago. I came because I married a West Australian. And when we met he made it very clear … I think the phrase was 'It's not negotiable: you marry me, we live in Perth'. My mother was a bit distressed it wasn't Scotland—his accent was certainly not a Scottish one—but I remember thinking at the time, I'll decide who I marry, one, and I'll decide where I live, number two. Indeed, it was non-negotiable because when it came to the crunch, and the professor of surgery here was discussing with Tony the timing of his return, it was non-negotiable and we came. But I was intrigued I had visited here once after we were married, when I was pregnant with my first child, and I thought it was a fantastic place. Who would want to live anywhere else?

When we were registrars we would rotate a lot so we would be doing the exchange with the kids, especially on weekends when we were on call in the theatre tearoom. One would go down to the park and then back to the theatre tearoom, exchange and then go in to operate. So, there was always that level of interchange.

I used to practise in my maiden name and Tony used to stir people up, saying, 'Oh, single mother that one, surgeon as well'. So in the hospital he would always put his two-pennyworth in, and it took a long time for people to realise that it was actually his fault, that he was the culprit.

We have a strict hierarchy in order of importance of the surgical procedure, and one day as I rang up to book my theatre case I was asked, have I spoken to the resident admitting surgeon, which just happened to be my husband. I said, 'Spoken to him? I've slept with him!' And so I got my case in.

Spray-on skin

The spray-on skin story ... at one stage it was ten years of my working life and now I think it's nearer fifteen. In many ways it's never going to be completed because we're always going to be looking at how we can improve the technology of healing. Essentially it started for me in 1985, when I saw the burns patients at East Grinstead. And I saw that we needed something radical to actually cover these large areas, that it had to be smarter than traditional split-thickness skin grafting. We had to be able to do this better. And that was, I guess, the gauntlet that I threw down to myself. At that time there was some work being done in Boston, in MIT and at the Shriner Unit in Boston. And they'd grown cultures, parts of skin. They'd made templates of parts of skin, so they were very active in the skin replacement and the regeneration arena.

Growing the surface cells from the skin had been clinically used in 1982 and written up in the United States. And there were the beginnings of a lab in the Blond McIndoe Research Centre at the Queen Victoria Hospital in East Grinstead. So that was my first glimpse of the potential.

Then in 1990 I was a registrar here in Perth and there was a patient who had survived a massive injury but was not healing, as is often the case with massive injuries. There were no donor sites that were adequate, the infection was slowly overwhelming, and I heard on the radio that Joanne Paddle [-Ledinek] had gone to Boston to learn how to grow the skin cells, under Professor Masterton at Monash and the Alfred in Melbourne. So I rang them and, to cut a long story short, we sent skin over, they came back with it, she healed, but she died a few weeks later with a fungal infection of the heart. I'm a great believer that you've got to learn something from everything, and that was a really hard time. But if we had done that five months earlier, would the outcome have been different? I don't know, but I know that subsequently we have achieved different outcomes by ensuring rapid wound closure.

By 1991 I was director of the burns service. By 1993 we had a Telethon grant and that's when I started working with Marie Stoner to explore the technology. We realised that in order to explore it we really needed a lab here, because we wanted to explore the ideas and how we could make it better.

Our patients can be kept alive with resuscitation, and in intensive care they're kept stable for a period of time while the infection risk keeps washing over. It's kind of a race against time, to get the skin sealed and covered before infection sets in. So that's the environment we started working in, and speed was of the essence. I put forward to Marie that unless she could grow the skin cell sheets that we started within ten days, they were not clinically useful I would not delay intervention beyond that time.

Very quickly we realised that if we pushed earlier, with immature cells, the healing was quite different. So we went through a process of investigations of actually putting the cells on the individual cells, so the cells really hung on to the wound, and migrated across and thickened up. Then it was a question of, well, how do you get the fluid onto the wound? Pour it? Dip it? Drip it? Spray it. And that's how the spray was born.

Spray-on skin is skin cells taken from an individual from an area that is not damaged, that is regenerating all the time. And those skin cells have a capacity to keep repairing themselves and replacing themselves. So we use the capacity of the body in a non-injured site and we harvest all those actively growing cells, and we put the cells, the skin cells, into a wounded site to change the balance, to help assist in healing.

This has been a process in evolution, really. The first patients I put skin sheets on were in 1990. The first time we had our own laboratory in Western Australia was 1993. I've been involved in the care of well over 1500 patients with the technology as it's evolved. I think regeneration and this concept that your own body has the knowledge to repair itself is a work in progress—not just in skin but in bone, in cartilage, in liver, in pancreas—and tissue-guided regeneration is medicine of the future. I'm very excited to be part of that.

There's an awful lot more potential. The research that we're looking at now, how we can build the framework to guide the cells with our nano-chemistry, nano-engineering colleagues: can we spray on self-assembling molecules that are intrinsic to the body, such that they assemble in a framework that the cells are familiar with and grow through? I'll probably tell you the answer to that in five years time. Hopefully.

Clinical Cell Culture

[Fiona and Marie Stoner founded the McComb Foundation in 1999 to research skin culture techniques, and Clinical Cell Culture (C3) in 2001 to commercialise the technology.]

My motivation for C3 is not personal gain. My motivation for C3 is for royalties to the McComb Foundation to underpin our research.

We realised that the research funding is limited. And I feel very strongly you should never criticise or whinge about things unless you are prepared to get up and do something about it. The process of commercialising the intellectual property coming from the hospitals into the McComb Research Foundation and then into Clinical Cell Culture was a way of ensuring that we would have a sustainable research income into the future.

So my motivation for Clinical Cell Culture—and Marie Stoner's—was the fact that we would have a royalty stream from the commercial company into the McComb Research Foundation that would give us the security that meant as a researcher we were not so vulnerable to the pressures of the competitive grants, which we are still involved in, to donations which we still have the privilege to enjoy from various individuals and companies.

So it was to underpin that research effort and I think it was a naïve thing in many ways because it's taken a lot of energy and a lot of time, but it's also been very exciting and instructive and educational and I'm learning every day. It's just beginning to bear fruit and I think it is a good model that we can use and can build on in other areas of tissue regeneration or other commercialisation strategies such that we can always maintain that forward progress.

Bali bombings

On the Sunday morning after the Bali bombing I got a call from the registrar. He and his wife, an anaesthetist, had gone on holidays to Bali on Saturday morning. By early Sunday morning they had treated and done escharotomies, which is release of the tight burns to allow blood to flow, on at least thirty patients. That was our first knowledge really of the extent of the injuries, and the extent therefore of our potential response.

Then it was a question of how are we going to get ready? We were full at the time, so we started putting our disaster plan into action in preparation. As the Sunday developed, it became apparent that there was going to be a significant need not just for the Perth Burns Unit, but for the Australian burns community as a whole to provide facilities, to treat fifty-four patients in burns facilities across the country.

Our first patients arrived in the early hours of the morning, on an Indonesian air force flight, and they were the most severe patients, the most severely injured. My overwhelming memory is the relief on their faces as they arrived at Royal Perth and spoke to us just before they were incubated for ventilation and for the treatment to commence. That relief on their faces.

When the Bali bombing situation arose we did in fact deal with 15 per cent of our annual workload in a day, but it's the sort of situation that we had been training for for a long period of time. And when you're involved in it and actually active in doing things, it's a very motivating situation, because you are able to influence those lives—not always to a positive outcome, but we did our best.

Certainly I knew that we were in there for the long haul. It's been said that we worked day and night for five days. But we didn't, we did sleep, we did eat. I was very, very conscious that I needed the people to come back the next day and the next day and the next day. So we did have rosters and we did have enforced downtime. So we were able to sustain this, not through a sprint but it was a marathon.

There were so many people doing so many things that were really positive. My overwhelming feeling was you can never do anything in isolation. It was a real privilege to be leader of the burns team, as it is on a daily basis, but even more so at that period of time.

When I stood back after three weeks—when of the twenty-eight patients we only had four left in the hospital, and we had a bit of a mass exodus as everybody went home and healed—I just thought, Why is it that we only see so much positive energy in response to such a profound negative? And I think that was my overwhelming feeling—that I saw so much good in so many people. And one of my colleagues said at the time, 'We'll never live through anything quite like this, and it's been a real privilege to do so, to be able to help'. And I certainly agree with him but to a point. Why can't we actually lift our game? Why can't all of us actually just give that bit more?

Medical team healing

I think the healing is ongoing. I met a lady last night whose close friend lost a child in Bali. That makes it flood back. That's kind of what we live with on a daily basis. There are certain instances, you close your eyes at night and they are there with you. And Bali is just like one huge episode that you can't forget, and nor should you.

I think in some ways the people that are involved in actually facilitating an outcome—and trying really hard to learn all the time, to make sure that the people get the best possible outcome and quality of scarring, all that—are so focused that in some ways we're not isolated. And certainly, we didn't lose optimism. I say we lost innocence in that period of time. But because we are actually doing things, it is a much more positive situation for us, and therefore we can put it in a framework that protects us. And I think that from a psychological point of view that helps to keep us going.

I face suffering every day but this was just completely off the scale at that period of time. But we still had that framework that we could hold on to in a way, and I don't think others had that privilege.

I think the awareness of burns was very much heightened, but I think the response we saw—and it wasn't just the hospital response, or the surgical response or the burns unit response—it was a community response, and that's what I took away from it. All this good, all this positive energy, being expended by people trying to help, and it was mirrored all the way across this country. We should all be proud that the response was a real, solid community response. It taught us how we can work together, spread our workload across the country, and gave us the opportunity to really develop solid plans for disasters that have helped us in our response to the tsunami and our response to Aceh. So I think the disaster planning has been a very positive benefit.

Motivation

People ask me, 'Why do you keep going?' And I think, Well, because one day we'll be able to do this such that we can reduce that suffering all the time. Reduce it, reduce it. One day maybe we will be able to do it without a whole heap of this suffering happening. So that's the motivation to keep going.

I think people are astonishing and they are inspirational because how an individual can take on that level of suffering and then come back stronger is a mystery to me. Because you see it and you just think, Where did that strength come from? And for that you've got to work damn hard to make sure that even if the person doesn't survive, that every lesson you can learn from that you store away, because you never know when it will help somebody coming behind. I guess my philosophy, my aim, is that nobody ever goes through that kind of suffering for it not to be of use to someone else.

I think my colleagues probably think I'm a little bit mad, really. I am mad, passionate, obsessive ... all sorts of different things, all mixed up, I guess. I think there has to be a level of fight as well, a level of doing something with a level of aggression that you will keep moving forward, that you will not be deflected from your path. That is the focus.

My focus from a professional point of view is scarless healing. We have achieved it in some people, some of the time in my lifetime, and for that I'm eternally grateful. But we haven't sorted out the problems. We have not achieved it in everybody all of the time. We can't deliver that. And that's going to take an enormous amount of energy. I need my energy not only to drive forward and to keep moving, but also to get everybody to come with me. The problem is a big jigsaw and I haven't got the intellectual capacity or the time or energy to actually manufacture all the pieces of the jigsaw. But I know where I can find them. I go and I see amazing science being done. I think, Can we work together? Because that is one of the pieces of the jigsaw. I can see that it will fit and I can see I can help you with a little bit of yours, but you can help me with mine. So to actually use that energy, not just for that forward progress but to say, 'Come on, guys, this is exciting; this wave is building and we can make a difference, not just in skin but beyond skin'.

Professional competition

Maybe I'm naïve. I know I'm a rabid optimist because I think if we could use that energy of ego and change it into the energy of progress, we would be flying to the moon for our holidays. I think actually that level of competition is erosive and we can harness it in a better way, let's put it that way. I think we can harness it in a better way to make more forward progress. And I'm sure I've had enormous support from a vast number of my colleagues and it's fantastic. But not all of them—and that's life, yet I'm not going to engage with that negative because that sucks out energy that I want to use in a positive way. I want to connect with people that are positive. It does not matter which one of us solves this problem, what matters is that we solve the problem. That's what should drive us. Not the ego of 'I am the one that actually found the answer'. And it's never going to be 'the answer' anyway. I'd have to say, I don't spend a lot of time worrying about it because it's by far the minority.

The kind of work we do isn't just done in Western Australia. The particular sprays—certainly we've put that forward and put it on the map, but we're all working around it and trying to get it better. There are other groups around in the world; they're the people I connect with because they are people I can learn more from rather than a minority who say, 'Oh, it doesn't work and we'll prove it doesn't work'. I'm like, 'Well, fine, but then let's give us something that works better. Then come and talk to me'. Because is this about ego? I don't know, but it's not my problem. My problem is the person in front of me, doing the best for them on the day and working out who in the world's going to help me make that better. I really make a conscious effort not to go down a negative route because it takes too much energy. And energy and time are so precious.

I tell my registrars as they go to their exam, 'There is no such thing as surgical fact; it's opinion. And your task here is to demonstrate that your opinion is valid, based on your evidence and logic'. And that's what I've done. I keep repeating the evidence over a period of time and we keep going forward with more clinical trials and more research in basic science in the animal arena, in collaboration with our colleagues in the States.

Family

I was at a med student conference the other day and one of the questions I was asked was, 'Who has to come top of the pile?' because we were talking about careers in medicine. And I thought, It has to be family because you have to keep some of the best of you for those who care most for you.

And you have to believe that there is always somebody who can do your job, and make sure you train them so that they can, so that you've got some of the best of you for those that care most. And family would be my anchor, my shield and my inspiration. From my parents, my brothers and sisters and my husband and kids as well. It's great when I'm with the kids because that's a real change. Because I'm at work and we're talking about things and trying to work out the research plan or the plan for the particular individual, 'What we can do today?' Then I go home, and it's, 'Hello, what's for dinner, Mum?'; 'Should I do this race?' And it's like, 'Who's going to do the washing? Has anyone put the washing on yet?' My kids are all very active, they're all very involved kids. I'm very lucky to be their mum, I reckon.

It's always a mix-match. All the way back when he'd [Tony] bring the kids in so I could breastfeed them when we were both on call, 'til now I'm here with one of the kids, one's travelling back from Europe and Tony is down on the farm with a couple of the others.

We work in the same hospital here and there, but not for that long. In Perth it's terrific because there are enough hospitals close by that we don't work at the same hospital.

I was doing general surgery to begin with so we were working a little bit closer, but there have been very few operations that we've actually been in the same operating theatre. And it's a bit like when I've worked with my brother, my older brother who's a professor in orthopaedics in Perth. And it's interesting because it's quite hard to tell my husband, or my brother, 'Move over, I'll deal with this'. So I think it's much better that they have other surgeons working with them.

Energy and health

We were brought up as kids to understand that being fit and healthy is part of life, and certainly that's the way I brought my kids up. I'll feed you and clothe you, educate you and I'll make sure you're fit and healthy. And so sport has always been an integral part of my life and we love watching sport but much more so participating.

You know that feeling of being fit is very important. And I think it certainly helps you cope. I feel that I'm able to do more because I have energy, because I maintain that energy through exercise.

My bike, I guess, is the one thing that no one else touches or uses. You know what it's like with lots of kids. Probably because I was a runner for many, many years and I find it difficult to find something where you could get that level of exertion but without the joint impact—and certainly cycling does that. When you start to think about sport, I think it teaches you an awful lot of lessons and it teaches you how to win and to lose gracefully, hopefully, which occurs more often. So it teaches life's lessons. But there's no substitute, in my book, for education, because that gives you choice.

I'm not good at doing nothing, something that my family recognises. Not long ago at a birthday I was brought into the house, they blindfolded me and sat me down, chocolates in one hand, wine in the other, video on. And they held me down. It's hard for me to sit through a whole movie. It was *Notting Hill*—they figured that that was suitably tame and would keep me laughing, and they thought it was a funny movie as well.

I'm very lucky. I'm very lucky that I'm in a place and it's exciting and stimulating from a professional point of view and also from a personal point of view. The kids certainly keep you on your toes and keeping up with them is a challenge. Also, there's no doubt in my mind that being fit is part of it because if you are not fit then your energy levels start to fall down and that whole package, to keep it moving forward, hinges on your personal fitness, but also the engagement you have with other people.

Ambitions are interesting. I have personal ambitions as well as professional. On a personal level to see my children have the opportunities so that they get up in the morning and enjoy what they do is really top of the list, and to be in a position to facilitate that wherever I can, wherever is appropriate. In a professional sense there is so much work to do that, I think, really, in terms of regenerative healing, we will not see regeneration in terms of really regrowing a given area, in my surgical lifetime, but we'll make an awful lot of progress towards it. We've started building that jigsaw, with work we do here, but also work around the world. To understand that we will answer questions better in collaboration than in isolation is important. That we will build on that body of knowledge so that maybe our grandchildren will be the beneficiaries, so that they can regenerate, rather than heal by scarring, is I suppose the ultimate goal. So there's an awful lot of work left to do.

> I learnt a long time ago, in fact, around a particular individual that I was treating, that the only thing I can do on any given day is my best. The only thing I can expect or ask of all my colleagues on the team around me is their best. That's all we can do. And the concept of whether our best is good enough is really not a question that we should be asking. What we should be asking is 'How can we make our best better?'

DR KARL KRUSZELNICKI
Scientist

Screened 19 March 2007

Karl Kruszelnicki, or Dr Karl as he is known to the world, has perfected the knack of getting Australians interested in science. He has entertained us for twenty-five years with such zany scientific questions as 'What explains belly button fluff?' For his efforts, he was awarded the Ig Nobel Prize for making people laugh, then think.

> I love explaining the world around me to people around me, and I don't think it takes away from it. Understanding how a rainbow works doesn't make it less beautiful but it means if you're in the right environment, which can even be at the beach on a sunny day, when the wind is blowing right, you know where to look to see a rainbow in the waves, in the spray. And when somebody does that, like my little eight-year-old daughter, Lola, she's happy, and I'm happy.

Childhood

Because I am the first born in the Polish family, my full name is Karl Sven Woytek Suskind Kovitch Matchek Kruszelnicki, and so I've blessed my own son with seven names as well.

Having that many names and being a wog in the early '50s was difficult in Australia, especially when you grew up in a Catholic-Irish background—you didn't fit in. Basically I didn't have that many friends and I think that part of my brain which is set for faces and names never got fully activated, which is why I have a lot of trouble remembering faces and names. So I try to remember how they walk or how they dress. If they change clothes, man, it really messes me around.

My parents loved me, but they had secrets they wouldn't tell me about because they didn't want me to be bitter and twisted and grow up with hate. And they were pretty good at not having hate.

My father would later on let that he'd been in a German concentration camp. My mother would never let it on because it was so horrible. They were both in situations where they should have died. Except ... accidents. My father was lucky because he had a tin of sardines my mother, they ran out of Xyklon B at Auschwitz.

I did not really, really understand why they were how they were. I didn't understand why they had this distrust of people—they were still nice and friendly but there was always a little bit of paranoia—and why they were a little bit protective, and how they would say things like, 'Never have a hammer lying around the house or an axe because a bad person could do things with it if they come into the house'. And they'd seen those things, and I would just mock them and now I don't.

My father was going to be killed, because he was the one who was carrying the dead bodies to put them into the gas ovens. He knew he was going to be killed! And he managed to use a tin of sardines as a bribe to swap identities with somebody who was officially dead. My father was reluctant, but he would tell me some things. He had this big number on his arm—95808. That was his tattoo number ... big ugly thing.

I never found out that my mother was in the concentration camps until she was beginning to dement. It was just so horrible for her. And it began to make me understand why she would say things like, 'You don't know, you shouldn't trust those people, you don't know what people can do'. And I thought she was being silly, and later I would find out she was right. Oh my God, my parents were right. But she was a bit too paranoid because she'd been through horrible things.

I grew up believing that she was a Swedish-born person of the Lutheran religion, rather than a Polish-born person of the Jewish religion. I had no idea that my mother was keeping secrets from me, that she had in fact been in a German concentration camp. But towards the end, when she was demented, she told me stuff, about how, for example, they were all being sent to die. It was getting towards the end of the Second World War and they ran out of Xyklon B gas, and they woke up one morning and the German guards had just all gone; there was nobody there, nobody there to kill them. So they just sat around and waited, and at the end of the day the Americans rolled in. And they started handing out food, and they gave them chocolate. And my mother said to her sister, 'No, don't have it, it's too strong for you'. But my mother's sister ate it and just went into terrible tummy pains and died—couldn't handle the rich food. My father was a bit more sensible. On the first day after the Americans arrived he said, 'I just want only the water that rice has been boiled in'. And on the second day he had rice, and on the third day he had meat.

Mother was a milliner and she won a scholarship to go and work in Paris with Dior, to make hats. But she decided not to and to stay at home and look after me and make hats in Sweden until finally Russia got too aggressive to Finland and so we all went somewhere else. My father had already been in a couple of concentration camps. He didn't want to go into another Russian concentration camp.

Emigrating to Australia

We were all set to go to the USA, on the ship, in Sweden, on the dock. Ready to go! You know, five years after the end of the Second World War. Refugees shunted all over the world. I get a reaction to the vaccine—and by the way, I love vaccines—get a reaction to the vaccine, and the family thinks, Will we go? Ahh, play it safe. Sit there, ship sails away. There we are, on the dock with all of our luggage. Cross out USA, put in Australia, because that's where the next ship is going. The next ship that pulls up at the dock is going to Australia, and that's why we end up in Australia, not the USA.

My very first memory of Australia is growing up in a refugee camp in Bonegilla, which is near Albury on the border of New South Wales and Victoria. And the three of us, my parents and I, lived in this tiny, tiny apartment, roughly the size of a station wagon car. And my very first memory is eating an egg. And only later did I find out that the three of us got one egg per week. And my parents would make the sacrifice and give me, the growing child, that egg. Aren't parents wonderful?

A wog in Wollongong

We could speak a bunch of languages. My father could speak twelve languages; my mother could speak eight. And we had this sort of happy gibberish of mixing Polish and Swedish and Danish and German and Russian. And we were in a shoe shop in the main street of Wollongong. I know exactly where it was, but it's not there anymore. And there was a family from our school, and the parents whispered something to their child, and pushed him forward. And he spoke up, he said, 'Shut up, you wogs. Speak English'. And from that moment forward, I never spoke anything except English, in a desperate attempt to be liked by my fellow classmates. Not that it made any difference at all.

I was sort of different. I would have sandwiches with halva and cabanossi and they would have butter and vegemite ... nothing wrong with butter and vegemite.

I was too geeky. I would wear sandals with socks, still do, and there are good arguments for that—because you have the protection, and you don't sweat. But that sort of separated me from my fellow schoolmates. And the other thing was that I was a wog. And they were all Anglos. And there was just this big gap.

The wogs knew where they were meant to go. They were all pushed out of town (back in those days) to where the streets did not have bitumen on them. We were the only ones who were living in streets with bitumen on them. So, we were sort of living above our class, as it were.

I remember one day in the early '50s there were these terrible floods across the east coast of Australia. It rained every day for a month. Nobody had cars, except for one wealthy family, and they organised, on our street, a little car pool. And they were going to pick up all the kids, and take them to school and back every day—it was only 1 kilometre, 2 kilometres, nothing. Every day I would walk past. I was eight years old and all I knew was that they weren't giving me a lift. And there was room. I mean, nobody had seat belts and there was lots of room in the car for me, but they wouldn't give me a lift. Every day, backwards and forwards for the whole month, they didn't give me a lift.

Lucky I didn't become bitter and twisted. I don't know how, but I've developed this philosophy that most people are not malevolent; they're just ignorant. They just have not walked in your shoes. And all you've got to do is give them a chance, and they'll be understanding. And I guess it pushed me that way. But, irrationally, I'm an optimist. My father was an optimist. You know, somebody dumps a tonne of manure on my front lawn, I don't think, Oh, what's this crap? I think, Gee, the roses will grow really well this year.

There was one case of my father, who ran into one of the guards at his concentration camp in Wollongong. My father was involved as a very low-level bureaucrat on the Water Board, helping employ people. And he gave him a job. And later he said to the guy, 'You were my guard at the concentration camp'. And he'd done bad things to my father. He said, 'Well, why'd you give me a job?' He said, 'It's not for you. I don't mind, I forgive you, but it's for your children'. And that was really nice because there are some parts of the world where they keep grudges from generation to grandparents to centuries. And my father was prepared to forgive a grudge directly against somebody who had done bad things not to a relative, but to him personally, who'd beaten him. And he forgave him and gave him a new life.

Learning

I started reading when I was about seven or eight. And then I started devouring all the books in the Wollongong library. And by the time I was about twelve to fourteen I started on my quest of reading one science-fiction book a day, which I did until I was thirty-two and I started studying medicine—because the body of knowledge that you had to put into your brain is so huge I couldn't possibly waste a whole hour a day reading a book so I just had to stop.

The first moment of consciousness was reading a book on astronomy. And I thought, Wow! Isn't the earth big, the solar system big, the galaxy big? Oh my heavens, there's other galaxies! Oh, we'll never get to the end of it. And that's … I was about seven or eight, and I suddenly had this immense feeling of awe and wonder, and it's never gone.

I remember, when I was sixteen trying to read Plato's *Republic* and I couldn't; it was way too hard, it just didn't seem to make sense, all these contradictions and big words in it. But I remember one phrase, 'The unexplored life is not worth living'. And I thought, Yes, I'm living now but that second that just went past, it will never come back again. I should live that second to the fullest. So I'm always trying to learn, trying to understand the world around me.

I'm just filled with this sense of awe and wonder of the universe around me.

At high school, they had a very limited number of courses available: physics, maths, chemistry—that was sort of it. If you were really artsy you might do French.

And I went to Wollongong University because it was nearby, and I did science, because that's what you did, and I just drifted through doing science. I was just drifting along, as Norman Gunston says, like a paddle-pop stick in the gutter of life on a rainy day. I did not quite fit in with anybody else, but I had a few friends, and I loved the intellectual freedom.

Immediately I graduated I started working at the local metalworks as a physicist. And so here I am at the age of nineteen doing metallurgy, because if you're trained as a physicist, you can do anything; you just need a little bit of background knowledge. Being a physicist teaches you how to think and to understand the universe in terms of the basic forces that run the universe. And so that's how I ended up drifting into metallurgy.

I had a broken heart in Wollongong and left to go to New Guinea because there was a job advertised and I wanted to go far away. Found myself doing research into hair and wool, as related to nutrition in New Guinea ... '72 or '74, or something like that, I saw this advertisement in the paper: 'Become a film-maker'. I thought, Hey, I could be a film-maker! I always liked taking photos, and so I applied. And I got one of the first grants, and ended up making one of the first music videos in Australia of a band that later became Air Supply in the USA.

Movies were a wonderful way to be both technological, which I loved, and creative, which I loved. You could do both at the same time, so I drifted into making music videos, and unfortunately dropped out of it when I presented my finished product, which I'd shot, bought the film and processed and edited and neg-matched and added all the sound effects and everything, and go up to the hotel room—they're drinking bottles of champagne, 'Here's forty bucks; go away'. Boo hoo, maybe this film business will never make any money, so I became a hospital scientific officer.

In love with science

I just suddenly pulled myself together and thought, I'm not going to have a life out of this, and I want to have a life where I'm in control of a little tiny bit of the world. And so the idea of using my film-processing skills in the hospital system, taking pictures of hearts, and also learning about hearts, was just a wonderful opportunity.

I think I began to fall in love with science again when I started reading *New Scientist* during the long hours in the operating theatre when I was working in the hospital system as a scientific officer. And there were times when you just had to be there, alert, ready to go, but you couldn't leave, so I started reading the *New Scientist* and *Scientific America*. And I thought, Wow! There is so much in that universe that I don't even know about. I started reading the popular science literature, and I started telling these stories, and people liked them, and that's how it began. Science is really weird. There's lots of boring stuff. Don't tell people those stories; tell them the interesting stuff.

A hippy taxi driver

The hippy phase lasted for about five, six, seven years. And during that phase, I really opened myself up to all sorts of things. So I became a taxi driver, drove 250,000 kilometres, labourer, car mechanic. I thought it was ridiculous: Here I am, I've got a degree in physics, I know how the universe began, I can't fix up a handbrake on a car. And so I taught myself to become a car mechanic, then became apprenticed, and then repaired cars for money. And did all sorts of different jobs, just to try and experience life.

I was a taxi driver for many years and on the one hand I loved it to pieces, because I was a bit shy, you know, growing up the wog in

Wollongong, and suddenly here I am driving around at night, facing forward, so I don't have to make eye contact. And they're coming into my lounge. 'So, you guys been going out long? You married? Why not?' You know, asking really outrageous questions like that. And they'd say, 'Oh, well, I don't know why we're not married'. 'Yeah, why aren't you married? Why? What about?' But on the other hand, it was a little bit scary. A few of my friends got killed.

On one occasion I got beaten unconscious; on another occasion a guy literally put a knife to my neck and said, 'Just pull over here, give me all your money, and it'll be okay'. And this was the end of a weekend; it was Sunday night and I had a lot of money and I thought, Bugger you for a joke. And I knew that wearing seatbelts in Sweden, in a Volvo, you couldn't die if you had an accident under 60 miles per hour. It wasn't a Volvo; it was a Falcon, but it was the same sort of thing, so I figured, I'm wearing a seatbelt, he's not ... Parramatta Road, jumped the median strip, wrong side of the road, Sunday night about nine o'clock, and we're going head-on against the other traffic, weaving around them. He said, 'What the hell are you doing?' And I said, 'Hey, *swear word*! Throw the knife out of the window or I will drive head-on into that car. And I will survive because I've got a safety belt and you will die because you haven't'. And to my surprise he threw the knife straight out of the car. I was so happy. And then just drove as fast as I could on the wrong side of the road to a police station, and he just ran off into the night.

Back to university

After taxi driving, I firstly drifted off into doing a little bit of non-degree science at university. And, blow me down, I got reasonable marks.

And then I went on a holiday with my parents and I taught myself to swim. I mean, I went and got lessons, had a swim, and then practised up and down this beach in New Caledonia. And one day I had this terrible cramp from swimming a kilometre, which I'd never done before. And while I'm lying on my bed in agony I thought, I'm going to university. I'm doing non-degree subjects. Why don't I get a degree?

And when I came back to Sydney, they were doing a degree in biomedical engineering. And I had no idea about this thing called the human body. As far as I knew, it was just this sort of slush inside. And so I started, and I ended up designing and building a machine, with Jackie Joy, for Fred Hollows, to pick up electrical signals off the human eyeball, and diagnose certain types of diseases.

And I was just astonished by this universe inside the body. And so the next step, you know, when I'd finished my master's degree in biomedical engineering, was either do a PhD or do medicine. And I decided to do medicine, purely because you get a more hands-on thing, and I was feeling more comfortable with people, less shy with people. I wanted to be able to help liberate them.

A children's doctor

It was the best job that I ever had in my whole life. In fact, I realised as a doctor that the reason I went into medicine was to liberate people from what held them back. I knew I wanted to do it for some reason, but I couldn't say what it was.

There was one time I was working in emergency and this family came in and they were just crying like crazy, and the three-year-old kid had these rolling fevers. And I looked at the kid and he's breathing like a little cyclone, and I just looked at him and he's got pneumonia, it's obvious: he's sweating, he's got pneumonia. But the family was distressed, so I put them through the whole 'Let's have a cup of tea', asked the nurse to get a cup of tea, then get the history. I didn't need the history, I didn't need to go through the full examination; all I needed was an X-ray but the family needed to think that somebody was paying attention to them. 'What do you think it's going to be?' And I said, 'It could be a million things', but I knew what it was going to be.

It was so satisfying being a doctor in the hospital system, but on the other hand, the hours are so long, you know, the 100-hour shifts and the extra overtime and all that sort of stuff. Being a medical doctor takes a huge amount out of you.

Being a kids' doctor—in terms of satisfaction—was the best job I ever had in my life. But I can do more good for the community by going into the media. As a doctor in a kids' hospital, one family at a time: in the media, thousands, tens of thousands of people. And so I say, 'Get your kids vaccinated. It's a really good thing. It's not perfect; nothing made by humans is perfect'. And that's why I'm doing it, because I can do more good that way.

Radio

I've been with Triple J, even 2JJ, for yonks. It all began when I applied to go on a space shuttle, because I thought, I've got a degree in science, I've got a degree in engineering, soon I'll have a degree in medicine and surgery—I'd be useful on a space shuttle. So, I sent a letter saying, 'Dear NASA, I want in on a space shuttle. Yours truly, Karl'. And they sent me a letter back, saying, 'Sorry, we're all full up. And we wouldn't employ you anyway because you're not American! Yours truly, NASA'.

And then Triple J, as part of the year of transport, was running something on the launch of the space shuttle. And so I rang them up and said, 'Look, I know a bit about the space shuttle. Can I talk about it?' And they said, 'Okay'. And it just never stopped. And I've just been with Triple J ever since, and still there's new questions coming up.

Quantum

I had been doing this stuff on Triple J—and also doing these prerecorded little stories, which were going out on the radio—and one day a book publisher rang me up and said, 'Hey, do you want to turn it into a book?' And I said, 'Okay'. And he released the book, and sent it out to various places including the ABC TV

Science Unit. And then one day the ABC TV Science Unit rang me up and said ... 'Hey, we're starting up a new TV science show on the ABC. Do you want to come along and be interviewed?' And I said, 'Yes', went along, and then I went back to my fellow fourth-year medical students and said, 'Hey, I've been offered this job, $40,000 a year, travel around the world, talk about science, and be on TV every week. And I said No'. And they said, 'You're crazy!' So, I dropped out of fourth-year uni, and took up the job, and helped start up *Quantum*.

Communicating science

At the time I didn't know but now I realise that I'm trying to fight the forces of evil and darkness who say, 'Things are bad and if you sacrifice a goat, it will get better'. What I'm trying to do is bring little islands of sanity. And somebody gave me some very good advice in the early days. They said, 'Keep away from opinions; everybody's got opinions—they're not worth anything. Keep away from the opinions and stick to the facts'. So I just tell little stories of sanity and understanding, where you can follow a logical process through and you end up with a good outcome, a happy story.

I don't know what it is about my radio programs or my books that inspire people to use their brain, but I'm really happy that I can help liberate people from what holds them back. And so people will say, 'I heard your story on blah, blah, and so I decided to become a nurse'; 'I heard the same story but I've decided to go back and become a carpenter'—same story, completely different result. The only common thing is it involves using your mind. So people say, 'I want to go back to high school'; 'I want to finish my PhD that I dropped'; 'I want to take up a career as a sparkie'. On my various science and radio talkback shows we have huge audiences amongst people who actually do stuff and make stuff—technical people, tradies, shippies, sparkies, fridgies—all those people and the female domestic engineers, as we call housewives nowadays.

The Ig Nobel Prize

Somebody rang in and said, 'Why is belly button fluff blue, and why do you get it?' And I said, 'I have no idea; I'll go looking'. And I finally found an article in a *Lancet* which said that in the same way that all roads lead to Rome, all hair on your belly leads to your belly button. But it didn't quite make sense. Then a guy rang in, and he said, 'I've got a hairy belly, and I shaved a 10-centimetre circle around my belly button, and that stopped the production of belly button lint'. And suddenly I thought, We're getting closer here. We started up a survey on the ABC; we asked a couple of dozen questions, then asked people to send us samples of belly button fluff from around Australia. We had 5000 people in our survey and we got samples from overseas. And we found, when we looked at it under an electron microscope, that belly button fluff is made up of fibres of clothing, mostly, a few fibres of hair, held together by sticky dead skin cells. And for that, I won the Ig Nobel Prize, given to me by Harvard University. And they showed me so much respect that they flew me to Harvard at my own expense.

There's a Nobel Prize, which everybody knows about. The Ig Nobel Prize is sort of comedy science given for research that cannot, or should not, be done. But on the other hand, it makes you laugh and then it makes you think. And so a winner recently was a paper called 'An Estimation of the Force required to Drag Sheep Across Surfaces'. And you think, Oh, that's so stupid. But what about the sheep-shearers who have to do this all the time, and having a slightly sloped floor is better for them, and better for the sheep. So you laugh, and then you think.

The Julius Sumner Miller Fellow

I ended up at Sydney University almost by accident. I had stopped being a doctor, gone travelling around Australia with the family, doing four-wheel driving, came back to civilisation, ended up being a TV weatherman for Channel Ten and doing their science stuff, and then somehow I thought, Well, it's time for a break. And I successfully dropped my salary down to under $10,000 a year, and all my mates who were doctors were thinking, Hey, mate, you're a bit of a loser. So I'm doing all this science stuff and getting paid peanuts for it.

A fax squirts out of the fax machine, saying, 'Hi, this is the University of Sydney. Do you know anybody who wants to apply for the Julius Sumner Miller Fellowship? Could you recommend anybody?' And I thought, Oh, Julius Sumner Miller, he's a heavy dude. Um, but no, I don't know anybody. And about a week later, I got, 'Do you want to apply for this job or not?' And so I applied for it. And there were a whole bunch of people, and I got the position. And so I've been here for the last ten years at the University of Sydney as the Julius Sumner Miller Fellow.

I never thought I'd end up inside a university, which some people regard as a rest home for slightly dysfunctional people. But, I have ended up here, and it is because they value learning. They value skills. And so there are some people who, quite frankly, don't have many personal skills and if you met them in a pub you'd want to punch them, but boy, can they give something to society in terms of their knowledge. And there are other people who are so perfectly balanced and handsome and beautiful and who win the world frisbee competition that you would have no idea that they had a PhD in something and won the university medal. So universities are real mixes of people, and I just love it here.

Marrying Mary

We've been together for a couple of decades, and have three children. I proposed by phone, from the Himalayas. And Mary said, 'Why do you want to get married now? Why didn't you marry me when I was pregnant and barefoot?' And I said, 'I don't know, I just want to get married. I don't know'. And she said, 'You have to give me a better reason than that'. And eventually I did.

I wanted to get married because of bad things that happened in the Himalayas.

On a school group with my son we were travelling through the Himalayas and one of the party gets sick and almost dies. And I've got to both reduce her pain and get her to the only MRI unit—you know, imaging unit—in the entire Himalayas ... Just got her through, and she's okay. And I'm thinking, My God! Just like that. You can die. And so I thought, Gee, life is really fragile. Why haven't I got married? I'm a fool! I love Mary, I love my family. Why haven't I married them?

And so, I ended up getting married, taking the kids, taking the grandparents—so three generations of us—get into planes, fly for thirty-six hours, go deep into the Arctic Circle, go to bed, wake up the next morning, have a coffee, go down the nursery, because we suddenly realised we didn't have any flowers, buy three freesias for $75 and get married, on the longest day of the year. So, in the same way that the sun doesn't set in the Arctic Circle, so too will the love never set on our marriage ... A scientific metaphor, see? Marrying science and love together.

I always wanted to get married. After we had our first child and we were living together I thought, Well, this is it. This woman is the best woman in the whole world for me; there can't be any better. And our children have turned out absolutely wonderful. But I needed something to kick me and it was that near-death experience and realising that I could have been the one almost dying in the Himalayas, not my colleague, that made me think, Hey I will die one day. Let's get married before I die rather than after.

Family relationships

Eleanor Roosevelt said, 'Small people talk about people; medium people talk about events; and great people talk about ideas'. And that's okay if you want to run the world, but if you want to run a family you have to reverse it and talk about people and their ideas and what they're feeling. I found it so much easier to always talk about things, cars and electronic things, rather than people.

I talk about things, not ideas, not concepts, not feelings. They're the important things. I'm evolving. Women are really good at it; guys have to learn. And I think I'll keep on learning for a while.

Driving with the family

I test drive four-wheel drives, and have been through ten of the twelve deserts in Australia. I love four-wheel drives out of town. Hate them in town, because they're so high, so one person has good vision, but twenty people suffer, and have to look around them.

But Australia's got a million kilometres of road, and half of them are unsealed, and they're really rough roads. And so out of town you need a four-wheel drive to get anywhere, both for the toughness of the vehicle and also sometimes you need the ground clearance and the lower range.

Four-wheel driving is lovely because we have such a good family time. And I'm going to take the kids out this September and check out the five central deserts, and re-baptise the kids in the red dirt of Australia, because they've forgotten—it's been about five years since we've done it. And the life is lovely. You have an early dinner and then as the sun sets you wash up and you lay down the ground sheet. You lie on the ground sheet, all of us, with our heads pointing towards the centre and the little laser pointers. And then you watch. 'There's a satellite!' And you point towards the satellite. So, in the first hour after sunset you see the satellites; the second hour after sunset you watch for the meteors. When we've seen about twenty meteors, we go to bed. It's a good life, and we're there together and we're talking, and we're not being force-fed music or television or radio—although television's a fine thing, especially if it's government television! And we're just being a family. I love it.

My kids have gone away from the heavy science-maths thing that I've been involved in. And so my son is doing economics and maths.

And so I've told him commerce, economics, maths—that's fine. You just have to reinvent the world economic order so the environment has some economic value rather than zero. And my daughter is going off into a different direction, and I think I'll see her as the editor of *Vogue* one day. But that's okay; my mother got a scholarship to go and make hats with Dior in France, and didn't take it up because she was busy having me as a baby in Sweden.

Those loud shirts

Our family's been in showbiz for a couple of centuries. So, this is called stage clothing. Early on I was introduced to the concept of stage clothing and even the stage autograph. So you have a special autograph, which is not the same as your credit card autograph. I love wearing bright clothing. Why should women have all the fun and get to wear the bright clothing? There's this thing where you've got a mass of all the colours at one end of the spectrum. Forget that! I'm into the rainbow theory of colour dressing. You wear every colour at once.

My wife makes them. I help a little bit ... cutting, actually—buttonholes. We had to send them out to Mary's mum, because she's got the machine that does the buttonholes. So we find the material that ranges anything from $8 a metre to $40 a metre, has to be cotton, then make up the pattern, then we have two pockets, and long sleeves ... two pockets so you can store stuff, and long sleeves so you can wear them long or short. And usually we have a little pen holder on one side because I'm obsessive. For 2 metres of cloth and three hours' work, you get a shirt, but you've got to have an overlocker—differential feed, four-thread overlocker.

Role of science

I've written twenty-six books, and the latest book ... just yesterday I got an email saying, 'This thing you said is wrong'. And blow me down, they're right and I'm wrong, so we're always correcting it.

That's what I like about writing books: you're always ... Science is not a process where you say, 'We have the answer, and this is the way it is'. For example, if you read any science journal, every issue they've got a little section: corrections, *errata corrigenda*, where they point out the mistakes they made in the previous issue. When was the last time you heard a politician or a businessman or a management consultant say, 'I was wrong'? Never! Scientists say it all the time. So it's five steps forward, one step back, five steps forward, always trying to explore the boundaries of the universe around us.

I usually check everything with the scientists who have worked in that field, but scientists are only human, and there is that sort of pettiness of: you didn't do this research; therefore, you're not entitled to talk about it. But on the other hand, often the people who can do it can't talk about it, and the people who can talk about it can't do it. But in general scientists are just fine, and by the way, 80 per cent of physicists can brew beer and play a musical instrument. A doctor told me this and I realised it was true: scientists don't make a lot of money but they know how to have a good time, and they know how to enjoy life, and they're really well rounded. The ones you see in the movies—two tufts of hair, lab coat, certifiably insane, want to overtake the world, no friends—they're microscopic, maybe one in 100,000.

> I guess I am really passionate about science, as are my fellow colleagues, and I think it's because science gives you a little bit of sanity; it tells you something that's fairly close to being absolute total and undeniable truth, rather than opinions. And from that truth you can make opinions rather than going the other way round.

DR JAMES WRIGHT
Celebrity GP

Screened 12 September 2005

Dr James Wright is the energetic GP who became known to millions of Australians through his writing and his television and radio appearances. Some call him the 'Merry Medic'. These days one of his passions is caring for the elderly.

> In life, you've got to do something. And the medical journals keep on saying if you've got a goal or some passion in life, you'll outlive all the other guys. Take the bank manager that retired. They gave him a rocking chair and he rocked himself to death. So you've got to have a passion, whatever it happens to be. Whether it's this or something else, it doesn't matter, as long as it's a reason to get out of bed every morning, as my accountant of fifty years keeps on saying.

What's in a name?

My real name is John Knight [AM], born, bred. It's on my birth certificate. But a few years ago, a long time ago, I was given the name of Dr James Wright. It was a legal necessity at the time. The law said you have to have another name; otherwise, you're considered to be advertising and you could be deregistered.

I was born in Brisbane in 1927, the twelfth of the twelfth 1927. And when I was six months old, my parents thought they saw the light and left Brisbane and came to Sydney. I don't remember much about it, but I do remember vaguely that I had my nappies changed so I've got a pretty good memory for way back. I think that was in Sydney.

I have two brothers, one is twenty-two months older, and one is seven years older; he was a bit like a father figure and very good to me. Being the youngest, you got a little bit of love and tender care from your parents specially, but also from your brothers. They regarded me as the baby, and they still do, I might add.

A strict upbringing

My dad was a clergyman. He was the chaplain of a large hospital in Sydney. So we had a very strict, very strict, disciplinarian upbringing. A bit too strict, I think. We used to get a hiding pretty regularly, once or twice a week. Dad had a strap and Mum had a cane. We'd get it around the legs. When we knew a beating was coming up, a flogging; as we called it, we'd go to the bush next door and get bracken fern and stuff it down our pants so when they gave us a whacking it wouldn't hurt. But one day, the short pants revealed the bracken fern sticking out, so they made us take the bracken fern out, which was not really fair.

We grew up during the Depression years. I was brought up in Fox Valley Road, Wahroonga, as a child ... a lovely place, very busy now. Then, horse and carts brought the bread and milk, and Dad had a cow and chooks, and we were self-sustaining, with vegetables and fruit trees ... a marvellous place to be brought up as a child.

We had a large house on a very deep block of land. Being a clergyman, of course, the funds were absolutely dreadful, like two quid a week to bring up a family of three. So Dad had a lovely flower garden in the front; he had a vegetable garden behind, fruit trees everywhere. We had a cow called Susie; we had to milk her, the rotten thing—we hated her. I had chooks when I was at high school, and the chooks were my project. But we really were fairly self-sustaining, which in that era was pretty good.

Mum and Dad just believed, they were before their time, that good simple living was a good way of life, so they were vegetarians, by choice, and we had the cow so we had our own milk and cream—lovely thick cream, which of course you don't eat now—it was beautiful. And the chooks had the eggs, and I used to feed the chooks all the lawn clippings, so the eggs were lovely and yellow, they were beautiful eggs. And Dad's vegetables ... Mum would pick all the stuff at five o'clock and you'd be eating at six o'clock, so it was really nice and simple. She'd do the cooking, make cakes, bikkies, scones, all that sort of stuff ... really simple living. But Mum lived to 100, so it wasn't a bad recipe. Dad lived to nearly ninety. I didn't eat meat until I was eighteen. I thought, What's this dreadful stuff?

There was no money. Christmas time you would get one present, wrapped up in brown paper, that was something pretty simple and Mum probably made it. Mum made all our clothes, and I got my first suit when I was in late high school, which was twenty-five shillings, and that was a major event, getting a suit for yourself, didn't happen very often. We used to get a penny a week for play money, to buy an ice cream or something, but that was all. If you wanted money you had to go and earn it. I had a little vegetable garden, plus the eggs, at high school, and I had a bit of money and that was fine.

My parents were extremely strict. They taught us good manners. You don't put your elbows on the table, for example. That was typical of the era, of course. And education was paramount. Mum's mother was a school teacher. Mum was mad on education, punctuation, correct spelling, all that sort of stuff. And they were very enthusiastic. You make goals you set goals and you reached the goals.

My mum had an absolute rod-of-iron character. She said, 'Education's essential. So I only have three boys; they're going to go to university; they're going to become doctors, and that is that'. Right from the time we could hear Mum talk. No discussion.

So we did the same thing when our kids grew up: school, university, become a something or other with a minimum of two degrees.

Medicine, I thought, how boring. But Mum said, 'You go to kindergarten, you go to primary school, to high school, then you do medicine, go to university, become a doctor and then you do whatever you want to do'. And she was right. Doctoring was great, but most good ideas I inadvertently learnt from patients and a little red light would suddenly flash on.

If you didn't do what Mum said, she'd say God would strike you dead. How was that? She used to use these dreadful terms. But it really stuck in and indicated parental discipline. I don't think it did any harm, in the overall total pattern of life.

When you're brought up with this sort of stuff from when you're still in your mum's arms and this is drummed into you, that's just part of life but nothing special. Just that's the way you live and that's what everybody does. You have the Christian ethic, which I believe in and follow. Whether people think it's good or not, I don't know, I don't care.

I went to North Sydney Boys High School during the war years. It was dreadfully competitive. You either worked very hard, got a good pass and went to university, or you went to the army and probably got your head blown off. Why wouldn't you work like the devil? So the choice was made for you. I didn't want to go to the war. I just hated the thought of it. So I studied like crazy, won a university exhibition, only 100 awarded, and a Commonwealth scholarship, and went to uni to do medicine. I was lucky, but it really was a good incentive to study hard.

Money-making ventures

When I was a little boy at school, I found that people liked fresh vegetables, so I had my garden. I also used to make coconut ice, which I'd bag, and one of my mates would sell it. Mum wouldn't let us sell; that was for the 'lower class'. Mind you, we were already there but that's what Mum thought. And I had chooks; I was able to buy the chooks, buy the feed, and I'd sell the eggs to the neighbours. We had all these childhood things ... At school I'd buy textbooks and sell them to my mates, and make a little bit of a profit.

I was eight when I wrote my first story that was actually printed in the *Sunday Sun* children's page, as it was back then, which I got five shillings for, which for a little boy of eight was a huge windfall. We couldn't afford the Sunday paper, so the neighbours saw it with my picture and everything in it. They came running over—'There's your story' ... it was about eighty or 100 words about a picnic we'd been to.

I used to write stories at high school for the Sydney newspapers. *The Daily Mirror* used to run a short story, dreadful thing, every day and they paid £2. So I'd often write these stories and got into the way of writing stories. Then I thought, When you're writing something, if you sell it once, that's good, but if you sell the same thing a few times, that's even better. So I dreamt up syndication, and I wrote a little short, 150-word column, question-and-answer type column, and three newspapers bought it—*The Hobart Mercury*, *Brisbane Telegraph* and *Evening News* in South Africa—so I had a good income. I was well off compared to a lot of the other kids, so I really wrote myself through uni.

I'd spend the holidays in the public library in town, getting all my information. I'd write a year's supply of stuff in the holidays, and put it out week by week. And my girlfriend, later my wife, used to type it up for me, so I had a few bob. When I say a few bob, I had not a car, but a pushbike.

In first-year med, I went to the lectures, took the notes down, published them next year and sold them to all my mates. It was ten shillings each. That went on for years. So, you'd turn your hand at whatever you could make a few bob doing, because it was nice having a few bob in your pocket. But I did it because I enjoyed it.

A country GP

My first job after university, I had a hospital posting, after which I went to the central west of New South Wales to a place called Tottenham, where I was the local GP, and also I was the chemist as there was no chemist in town. I was also the government medical officer and the guy who had to perform post-mortems, and that sort of stuff. For a young guy in his early twenties it was a pretty daunting sort of job.

I remember one night, a guy, he was madly in love with a girl, he was actually a labourer on this farm, and she didn't return his affection. So one night he was out at his little quarters, and he rigged up a gun, pointing to his chest. So the girl, after the pictures one night, came home, opened his door to say good night to him and boom, he killed himself. So I, as the local government medical officer, had to go and see all this horrible mess. These weird things happened, I mean, they were happening all the time, but in a tiny country town, it was sort of unbelievable. You're the new bloke who has to go and clean up the mess. The coroner came too but fainted.

The nearest doctor neighbour was 60 miles away. And next to him was another 50 miles. You're really on your own; you had to learn the hard way, the quick way; it was good. I was the local vet as well because there was no vet in town. And I found very quickly if you treated the animals like humans, they'd get better. If a cow or a sheep was very sick, with a shot of penicillin, next thing they were up and running around, perfectly okay.

I was mad on writing. I thought it was great; I really liked doing it. And I became the local ABC rep. out there. I was also the stringer for the *Herald*. Many funny little stories would happen, so I would knock up these, and I'd take the story down to the local post office. It sounds archaic but this is the early '50s, and it was sent by morse code, I'm not kidding, down to Sydney. It was unbelievable. That was only fifty years ago, and I tell my kids about this and they say, 'Oh, that was the dark ages'. And yes, it was the dark ages. This poor bloke would probably send three telegrams a week, then he had this dirty big page of newspaper copy, and he had to tap it all out ... I think he got arthritis in his hand to finish up with.

I worked in the country for a few years, then my mum came out and saw me one day and said, 'I think it's time you moved back to Sydney'. So, okay, whatever Mum says, Mum's always right. So she actually ran around Sydney finding suitable places for a young doctor to set up practice. And she found this place, so back I came, and under Mum's eagle eye, did what Mum said. Mum, as always, was right, and I've been here ever since.

A practice in North Ryde

When I came back to Sydney I came to a suburb called North Ryde, which was just a stone's throw, quarter of an hour, from the centre of Sydney. At the time it was part of Sydney's food bowl, largely made up of 5-acre blocks which were mainly worked by Italians, who had come out a generation before, chopped the trees down and established their market gardens. So I bought this little house that was half completed, with these beautiful market gardens, dairies and poultry yards all around.

If you were called to an Italian family, the sick kid would be in the best bed in the house, with chairs all around. They'd all sit in the chairs watching you diagnose the child. And then you'd talk to the parents, who'd go through various translations, so the older parents could understand. And when it was all over you would have coffee. They'd want you to have home-made vino. I don't drink, but it was lovely in retrospect. But then that changed overnight. All of a sudden, with a stroke of a government pen, the so-called 'green belt' of Sydney vanished and suburbia took over. I was the only doctor there.

In those days, sounds a long time ago, but it isn't really ... It was a new area, so young folk came, young couples, not much else pre-television, so there were heaps of babies. And the GP would take the lady through pregnancy, through labour ... and they all became part of your family, in a sense. I had all these lovely people and their little babies, with the nappies fluttering in the breeze. That was my life for many, many years.

Marriage and family

I married in 1955 to Noreen Weslake, and we've been good friends ever since. I met my wife-to-be at a church social. In those days most of the churches had a social club activity on a Saturday night, every two or three weeks, and all the locals would go along for a bit of fun, and it was a great meeting place. Dad being a clergyman, of course we were involved. And he was hooked up with the hospital, which meant that the nurses from the hospital would tend to attend regularly. So we caught up, and caught up and caught up ... and after about a ten-year engagement, we got married.

I got married slightly later in life compared to a lot of folk at the time. Most of them got married at eighteen or twenty. But when you're at university and own very little, you didn't marry. I've been married for fifty years, and in fifty years have never had any major blow-up; that's how tolerant my wife is. We don't fight; we get on extremely well. Four children—at one stage, their ages were two, four, six, eight. So we'd have a holiday every two years and go somewhere and have a nice time. They're all fairly close together, which means we've been a very close knit, happy, really united family.

When I first set up my surgery, Noreen, who had a business training, worked in an office for a few years, and then, seeing I was doing med, she decided to do nursing at the hospital where my dad was. And in the early stages she used to help me a great deal in the surgery. In those days nursing sisters used to wear the big long veil and nice uniform and everything, very imposing. So she used to look after my patients, and helped me an enormous amount in those early years, until she became pregnant. Then she spent the rest of her days looking after the children and now the nine grandchildren.

Her job was to stay home, look after the kids and run that side of life, and I ran all the other professional and business side of life. There was no 'ifs or buts', no arguing. Never had a fight ever. And we just did our own job. So she looked after the kids and brought them up, which was fine.

Writing

I love writing. I love the smell of newspapers—that smell of the printers' ink I just used to love—so I started writing, and had my first article published at eight, which was pretty young, and from then on I've been writing ever since, really.

When I was at high school I wrote for various magazines and papers and I had my little column, and did ad hoc freelance pieces. But in 1968 *Woman's Day* magazine was coming through the ranks and just getting off the blocks. And they decided to build their circulation on weight-reducing diets. They'd have the double-page spread, and the poster, and all the television coverage, and the lovely girls in bikinis, and palm trees and whatnot. There was a bit in the middle where the diet was. So my job was to regularly, month after month, provide that diet. You know, the 'bikini diet', the 'heatwave diet', the 'him and hers' diet, the 'sex diet', whatever.

They claimed a good diet on the posters and the front cover would sell another 100,000 copies. But after two weeks, people soon forgot and were after the next diet. Whatever diet you're on, you'll lose 2 pounds first week, come what may, as it is only fluid loss, so it had to work. But after the next fortnight, they want the next diet after that. So this went on for years, these jolly weight-reducing, dreadful diets. They were basically all the same, low carb, but they all worked ... for a week.

And that led, inevitably, to *The Mike Walsh Show*, which was just getting off the blocks in 1973. It had only been going for three or four weeks. One of the researchers rang up, so we went along and discussed one of these awful diets. The next week they rang up again, and twenty-five years later, they were still phoning. 'Can you come back tomorrow?' So it went on and on and on. It took over your life, actually. It really did.

They would ring up as late as one o'clock, when some guest from somewhere had lost their way from Mascot to the studio, and I'd get there probably about quarter past one, trying to think up a topic to talk about. This happened frequently, especially in the earlier days. Usually it was fairly scripted and you knew in advance. But sometimes these emergencies cropped up. I was the nearest regular who could jump up and do something immediately.

I'd say to my patient, 'Just stay here for a little while. I've got to go away for a short period of time. I'll be back, though'.

A resident television doctor

I was the resident doctor on *The Midday Show* roughly the whole life of the show.

During the *Midday* period, I often would illustrate the topic of the day with a little blackboard. We tried to keep up to date and show viewers simple illustrations. At that particular time, or up until then, you weren't revealing parts of the body. So we did a lot of operations, Caesarean sections, normal births, gall bladders, tonsils, appendixes. Weird things that just were not done. So even though it's commonplace now, at the time, it was cutting-edge stuff.

I used simple words that I thought most of our viewers used and I didn't get into all the scientific jargon. A lot of my peer group looked down and thought, 'Oh, well, he's babbling on about all this stuff'. And they tended to ignore it for quite a long time, until they realised that I wasn't upstaging them; I was trying to say, 'Look, if you get crook, go and see your doctor and have a talk'. I was trying to make a nice, happy relationship rather than anything else. They eventually realised that, but it took quite a few years.

Around about the same time as the television, I got approached by Macquarie Radio syndicated events, who said, 'Look, we'd like a little capsule, a little health capsule', which at the time was five minutes; it later became a ninety seconder. So we did this for thirteen weeks, as it was supposed to be. Anyhow it seemed to go okay, on about eighty different stations syndicated right around Australia. And would you believe that it is still broadcast today—it's in its twenty-sixth or twenty-seventh year. We prerecord a month's supply, forty of them. It's up to six or seven or eight thousand this year. We're still doing those regularly. It's a lot of fun; I enjoy doing them.

A KC is a Kerbside Consultation. My attitude was, if someone was nice enough to come up and say, 'G'day, how are you? Liked the show', or whatever ... If they were kind enough to do that, I think you've got to stop, and say, 'Nice to see you'. And in thirty seconds, you can diagnose their minor ailment, you can treat them, and they go off happy and you've made another friend. That's how I used to regard it. Never knock them, always have a bit of a smile, a bit of a laugh.

The letters

When I was writing for the newspapers and on television and on radio, a lot of folk would write in letters asking about various topics. So we got the idea of preparing a little booklet, about twenty pages, just a short thing, the size of an envelope, and people were invited to write in for the booklet. They had to enclose a stamped, addressed envelope, and name the book. These were on posters, on the front page, on television, on radio, and got huge saturation. And the response was absolutely enormous. And all the mail eventually arrived at my place. A mailbag contains 2500 letters, and we'd get up to twenty or thirty mailbags. Our biggest response to a weight-reducing book was 120,000 letters.

And I'd think, Why do people write these tens of thousands …? We processed over a million letters. We got huge volume. And it took a long time to realise into my thick skull the majority of folk didn't understand what their doctor said or couldn't remember it or didn't understand the technical jargon. So they'd go home, say, 'What the hell was he talking about?' So they'd ring muggins up on radio, or write to try and get some nice, simple explanation. So it was a plus, not a minus; we weren't upstaging anybody.

So the general mail would pile up, so often I would go away to a little farm I had and type an answer to all these letters on great sheafs of paper. Most were three- or four-line answers, which were all numbered, and that had to link up with the number on the letter. So the family went away with literally thousands of letters … This particular holidays, my kids were growing up and they said, 'Daddy, can we help you?' So Daddy said, 'Yeah, what a good idea'.

So their job was to chop the answer up from each A4 sheet and stick it on the bottom of a rote letter, and put it in the envelope, and they were ready to post.

But at the end of one day, after these thousands of letters, my seven year old said, 'Dad, I've got one left over'. This of course meant the last 100, probably 1000 letters, were all wrong! And we got these funny letters, 'Doctor, I wrote in about my tinea, and now have this great answer on contraception. Thank you very much'.

In the early 1970s I was approached by a publishing company in Melbourne, who said, 'We want a book for girls, titled *Everything a Teenage Girl Should Know* … we want a very high moral standard', because at the time, all the new sleazy type magazines were taking over. They took the very smart view that a lot of parents mightn't want their kids knowing all the sleazy side, and they wanted this very high-standard book. I wrote it, and they printed it and the girls' book went very well ... it was sold by mail order. Then they said, 'We want a boys' book'. That was fine; I did the boys' book ... *Everything a Teenage Boy Should Know*. And then, *Everything a Married Couple Should Know* and *Everything a Growing Child Should Know*. And then eventually they said, 'We want a *Family Medical Guide*'. And we produced a four- and later a five-volume *Family Medical Guide*. Now, after all these years, these books are updated and partly rewritten every year, and they're still sold all over the world in all sorts of translation, even braille and discs for the sight-impaired.

Family time

During the peak years, which went on for over five decades, I was running a surgery, which was a very busy one. Because I was the only doctor in this area for quite a few years and the local population exploded, often the surgery would go till ten or twelve o'clock at night. I was doing all my media stuff—television, radio, newspapers, magazines—so you had to really set your time out and try and work to a really strict program. Well, I saw my four children, but my wife really brought them up, so her job was to look after them; my job was to do all my stuff. So we had a clearcut demarcation of activities.

Because I had a very strict upbringing, I said, 'I'll never ever lay hands on my children', and I only hit one of them ever, with the back of my hand on their rump for something they shouldn't have done. My wife used her feather slipper, because that made a huge amount of noise but didn't hurt at all. My parents were lovely and caring but it was too stringent. It was not right, looking back. It was quite wrong but pretty typical of the time.

Radio

It's funny how things happen: you just get a phone call out of the blue. One day I got a phone call from John Brennan, producer at 2UE, and he said, 'Could you come down and fill in for a few weeks for us?' And that was fine. I went and filled in for three or four weeks, then he rang back and said, 'Oh, could you fill in for a few more weeks?' So the show went on and on and on. And, would you believe it, eighteen years later I was still doing my own weekly show on 2UE and just finished it recently when the station changed hands.

It was an exciting time. I loved doing the show; there was a big talkback component and that kept your brain working reasonably well. So whatever happened, no matter how crook you felt or tired you were, you had to be bright and cheery and get the answer right first time. There was a huge amount of backup work. Every day I read a new medical journal just to keep up to date with current medicine.

Folk rang about all manner of things. They liked to ring because they felt they knew you, they were too shy to ask their own doctor or felt embarrassed. But also a lot of listeners were lonely, with nobody to talk to, and a lot of people didn't understand what their doctor told them. They heard the words, went home feeling ill, and just forgot what he said, so they just rang up me, of all people, to ask simple advice.

It's very emotional because talkback radio has a very emotional component. And you're trying to listen to what the person's saying and work out an answer, and you get involved with the person, and become part of a jolly family.

Housing the elderly

The great passion of my life is the Medi-Aid Centre Foundation. This was established in 1971 largely because my dad saw the need for older people who weren't being looked after very well. And so he said, 'When you guys grow up, do something for the elderly'. Medi-Aid was established in 1971 by my wife, Noreen, and myself, and the prime aim is to provide nice housing for the community when they get older, across all socio-economic levels. So we provide housing across the board and we currently accommodate about 600 people in Sydney and in Queensland.

We funded it ourselves from a variety of commercial ventures over the years. And about 99 per cent of income went straight back into Medi-Aid just because we like doing it. We get a lot of internal enjoyment and satisfaction out of doing it. Nearly all projects were real estate based. The majority of my builders, three or four over the years, were Italian guys who I just seemed to get on well with. In the overall pattern they were very honest guys, and for years we did a lot of commercial building. And we'd say, 'Okay, we'll do this building', and we'd shake our hands and that was it. He'd bring the bills along every month and we'd pay them and then we'd go on to another project, then another project. And this went on for year after year after year, and most of the money went to Medi-Aid.

At the present time, in Sydney, we have several villages. Our flagship is 'Vimiera Village', on 6 acres of land at Eastwood ... 150 units, caters for about 200 people living on site. We provide meals and domestic services for a lot of them. With the village, we've tried to make it as nice and roomy and friendly as possible. 'Vimiera Village' is mainly for those who do have some financial resources. It's run similarly to most community and church groups, the so-called 'resident-funded' system.

There are a lot of folk who are financially disadvantaged, so we also have units for them—one- or two-bedroom units—and some of these are as low as $70 per week, which in today's economic climate is very, very small. Others, depends on where they are, are a little bit more than that, but the overall pattern: we try and look after everybody.

About forty-five years ago I bought a block of land right in the centre of the Gold Coast to build a holiday house. Forty years later it was still there, so we had a look at it one day and realised property on the Gold Coast was much cheaper than in Sydney. So in 1999 we started buying ad hoc units, one here and one there, and after about four or five years we had acquired about 150 individual home units in the various high-rise apartments, most of which are on the beach, right next to the surf. Now these are made available 100 per cent to elderly folk who are having a tough time, such as old age, poverty, illness, or just finding life too difficult. They have a really nice unit at a greatly reduced rental, and there's no ongoing charges whatsoever.

In the overall total pattern, parents are very good to their children. But many children really don't care about their parents. A lot want to put their parents somewhere, get rid of them, see them once a year and that's that.

So if we're there, if they've got a few bob and can afford to go into one of our nicer places, that's fine. If they haven't got much money, just the pension, they can also live quite well, in our 'low rental' units.

All of a sudden, you have a place in Sydney or at Surfers Paradise overlooking the surf. Not real bad, is it?

Over a period of many years, Medi-Aid has built up a series of commercial ventures, which fund the organisation. We also give most of our spare cash, so we are self-funded and haven't made any calling on the government whatsoever over the many, many years.

We never ever asked the government for any funding. I thought, If you get government money, there's a sting in the tail somewhere down the line.

We registered, at the time, to take donations. And after a while the government people rang up and said, 'You haven't made any appeals'. I said, 'No'. They said, 'Well, give us the certificate back', which we did.

[The 'Gift Fund' was re-started as it is now a statutory requirement for Public Benevolent Institutions to seek public gifts and donations.]

Making money

Yeah, well ... chooks and eggs, when I was a little boy. Later on, real estate, that's the only way you can really make money in

Australia. To start with, one horrible old block of land, get rid of all the blackberries and fill up the dirt holes and put a fence around it and mow the grass. And in the '50s, you could make substantial money by reselling it, so it was originally blocks of land and subdivisions, then houses ... then blocks of home units. And then every now and then you could actually keep one, and you'd buy and sell, and wheel and deal, and build another one and keep that.

We built and operated a motel for forty years. It was going to be a block of shops, but motels were just starting ... then a printing company ... Every doctor has a funeral director who he deals with, mainly. This guy came along one day, said, 'Oh, I've got the sack'. And he said, 'We ought to start up a funeral director's place'. I thought, What a great idea. So we found a block of land in what proved to be a good spot, and got it up and running, and that went for forty years.

All these projects produced money; they had to. And all this money went to the foundation. They all added up every year, and we'd buy and sell and rent. It mainly comes from rental now.

Life today

Today I'm still living in the same home I moved into roughly fifty years ago. It was only a tiny modest home when we bought it; it wasn't even completed. Then when a new arrival would come we'd build another bedroom on here, another there, so it's like a jolly rabbit warren now, offices replacing bedrooms now as they've all moved out.

We're a happy family, very seldom have any disagreements. If we do, we sit down and negotiate it. And we all help each other, try and share everything. And we're determined it'll be that way. So, that's life, and make the most of it. You only get one hit at this racetrack, as they keep on saying, and you've got to make every step a winner. Every day, you've got to make every day win.

The things I don't like in life are great big, flash, expensive houses, the 'right' suburb, an expensive car: I just discount them.

It doesn't mean anything to me. I just enjoy sleeping in the same old bed for the last fifty years. I enjoy life as it is. The simple things are what I personally like. I mean that seriously.

What kept me going? Well, you must earn a living doing something. But also, I just loved my work. Enjoyed doing it, plus all the other projects which I did, which I probably enjoyed as much as, or maybe more, than looking down sore throats and prodding tummies.

Secret of life

When you're in medical practice it doesn't matter how crook you felt, at nine o'clock you had to be there smiling. And if you had a headache, bad luck. After ten minutes of listening to people complaining, mate, your headache went. You were just so involved. Same with [Medi-Aid] Foundation. After a couple of phone calls, doesn't matter how you feel, you're out there worrying about their problem, whatever it happens to be, 'My shower's not working', 'My toilet's leaking' or whatever.

Mum lived to a great age and so did Dad. So, I think I got the right genes. But you've got to make an effort to keep healthy through life. If you do that, you get the most out of every day. I think it helps a great deal. In my whole professional life I've only taken two weeks' off ever—I got the flu in 1971 … plenty of water, good sleep at night, positive attitude. And I really believe that the Christian ethic is good for us. I just believe it is. Whether others believe in it or not, I do. If it's right or wrong, it doesn't really matter.

> The most important things in life are jumping out of bed every day, knowing you're going to have a great day, seeing my family, looking after my elderly people and just getting on with life, getting on with people. I love it. I look forward to every day.

GENERAL PETER COSGROVE
Soldier

Screened 2 July 2007

General Peter Cosgrove is hailed as one of Australia's greatest soldiers, with an outstanding military career that has spanned forty years. He scraped in to Duntroon, served in Vietnam, led our troops in East Timor and was made Chief of the Defence Force. In 2001, he became Australian of the Year and also led the effort to clean up in the aftermath of Cyclone Larry. These days, Peter Cosgrove describes himself as a 'corporate warrior', sitting on the boards of Qantas and the Australian Rugby Union.

> I hope I'm a people person. I hope I really empathise and identify with the people I work with. I hope that's the case. And I think it is. I think over the years that's been noted as something I'm good at. My weakness is I've actually got a pretty short fuse. I've managed to keep a real lid on flying off the handle, so to speak, over the years, but I know that I've got an Irish temper which I've really always got to grab on to.

Early years

I was a post–World War II kid born in Sydney with khaki in my veins. Grandfather on Mum's side and my dad were both in the army. My father served through World War II and stayed on in the permanent army after the war, and he was a mighty guy. He was just a popular fellow, professional soldier, warrant officer, no pushover, but just an all-round nice guy. And in the family there are sundry relatives who have also been in the army and the air force, so we have a great tradition of service in uniform.

Mum was a feisty woman. She grew up initially in the country, then moved to the city. Irish sort of background, red-headed, really a wonderfully loving mum but could be fierce. We adored her and she ruled the roost at home. She had to take on the mantle of being mother and father for much of the time, until Dad would come home on breaks, on leave, on a weekend off. And then he would go away again and Mum and all of us were sad to see him head off to wherever he was posted.

My eldest sister, Stephanie, a wonderful girl—really just a tremendously creative person. And in growing up, that four years of distance between Stephanie and myself didn't really make any difference. We still used to fight and then get back together in the usual brother and sister way.

We were a volatile family. We used to have great joy, sometimes big arguments, but it was very much a kiss and make up family; there were never any estrangements.

The family lived, and I grew up in Paddington. That was a working-class suburb full of wonderful people. These days it's changed its character, but then it was decidedly blue collar. We lived in Underwood Street and just across the road was a pub, the Grand National. It's still there, and in those days it was a lively place and there were some rolled gold stoushes out there from time to time. Our bedroom fronted onto Underwood Street and though we were put to bed at the usual time for young kids we would often sneak a look out the window to see the goings-on at the pub, just across the road.

It was a very close family in Paddington. Dad sometimes would be away for weeks and weeks, but when we all got back together, with him home from his job, it would be party time.

Mum ferociously devoured public affairs. She followed politics very closely and she had a view on everything, and that used to rub off on us kids, and we had some of the best talks around the kitchen table about current events that you could ever imagine.

They wanted me to make the best for myself. They knew I was pretty bright and if I could harness my energy and intellectual opportunities I could do a lot of things. So my whole education and their love and upbringing were designed to give me a good start.

We went to the parish school, St Francis, at Paddington, and it was a nun's school for the junior kids, and it seemed to me it was an enormous place. These days when I see it it's quite small, but it was a place where we got our educational grounding and I loved St Francis. Of course, education in those days was of a piece, I mean, tough discipline, learning by rote; yet, nonetheless, we got a good foundation in the three Rs.

[Peter was dux of St Francis in 1958.]

St Francis Church is right alongside the school. I was training to be an altar boy and I was doing all right on the Latin. I thought I was the next cab off the rank to be a proper altar boy. But I was caught one day in the vestry by the parish priest wearing his vestments and doing the mass in Latin to the vast amusement of the other trainee altar boys, so I got the sack.

Having finished at primary school at St Francis, Mum and Dad sent me out to Waverley College, a Christian Brothers' school not far away, but a very big high school. After a little bit of an orientation period there I came to love that school, and I was there for the rest of my schooling. Although I'd been a reasonable student at primary school, in the big time there, lots of other bright kids, I was a bit lazy as well, so I was really middle of the road there. I just got into high school, and things like sport and new circles of friends. All of the social milieu of school gave me an opportunity to just glide along. And gliding along in a more competitive environment wasn't good enough. I did the Leaving Certificate twice—'63 I passed but just barely. It wasn't a very satisfactory pass and I was also pretty immature, so I had another go in '64 and did much better and was obviously more mature and ready to move on to the next part of my life.

That immaturity, I think, was probably behind some of the indifferent results, because you find so many other distractions at school, and you're a bit lazy. And really, I feel bad now that I didn't optimise my school time a bit better. I was always a lively bloke at school, especially towards the latter part and we used to play practical jokes on each other and, of course, on the teachers fairly often—and probably drove them mad.

We were always getting up to scrapes, especially near the end of school when you get into that muck up period, and we would get gorilla suits delivered to the headmaster in full gaze of the boys during one of the lunchtime breaks, and watch the head brother take the gorilla suit out of the cardboard box and then sort of go off his head.

When I left school the mix of careers that I might have chosen were teaching, the law, journalism, army. And of course, I chose the army. There's no doubt that seeing what a fine man my father was, and my grandfather, and both had been in uniform, that I understood it to be a very honourable and necessary profession. And I think when I was weighing up all the career options in the final year of school, I just kept coming back to the army. And Dad said, 'If you're going to do it, son, knowing all the pros and cons, have a go at being an officer'.

I knew the absences and the separations of having a dad that kept moving around—army postings—while the family stayed put, that was a decision they took. I knew that was going to be part of my life. But on the other hand, I also saw that it was where great Australians became great soldiers.

Duntroon

Of course, in going to the army, I went to the Royal Military College, Duntroon, to train to be an officer, and from the first day, I was under the gun, unfit, untidy, lazy and unpunctual. I mean, I had the lot. In those days, Duntroon was sort of a closed and monastic society. It was preparing officers in a traditional way, with about fifty years of history, for service in the army—an army which had been at war for a goodly part of its time.

You are shown that while you might be intellectually capable and physically talented, nonetheless you do need to be imbued with the notions of selflessness and focus and interminable hard work to become the officer that your men and women deserve. So in that sense, there were no false impressions of your own God-given gifts. You had to understand that you've got a long learning process which you are now undertaking with total focus on your accountability as a young officer.

I loved everything about it, but I hated being in trouble. And why was I in trouble? Because I was chronically a little bit untidy, a little bit unpunctual, sometimes a little irreverent, a little bit rebellious. Those last two weren't bad qualities because they showed, I guess, a spark. But the first two, that of not being totally reliable or organised, those had to be worked on. So, I understood why I was in trouble. I just didn't like it.

When I graduated, I did some early duty in Malaysia with an infantry battalion and then off to Vietnam as a reinforcement officer.

Vietnam

I joined the 9th Battalion of the Royal Australian Regiment on operations in Vietnam and this was the most exhilarating time of my young life, because it was dangerous yet very, very important for me to get it right. It's where the training wheels are taken away: there is no longer somebody to say, 'Now, we got that wrong; let's go back and do it again'. This was the real thing. This was on war service, with an infantry battalion, commanding men in combat in a really, really high-intensity and dangerous war—Vietnam. And no second prizes: you had to get it right every time. You had to be positive, confident, professional and lucky for that whole period if you were all to come back in one piece.

Subsequently I received the Military Cross for an action involving fighting against the Viet Cong in the bunker system, and my fellows did amazingly well, and I was recognised pretty much on their behalf. Being recognised in such a way is always a thrill, but it's also humbling because you know that many other people did so well and weren't recognised.

It's interesting that after I received it, I had to change from being a sort of larrikin into a much more responsible and upright officer, in that the army had expectations of me from that point on. It was the halo effect, if you like, but it changed my life.

I found out I could do it, that I could function when we were in the midst of combat. I found that I could analyse the situation, give orders and lead the troops—my men—when we were under fire. And you don't know that before it happens, and you don't say, 'Well, that's it. I'm forever after able to do this'. You treat it as the gift that you needed to have to find out at that precise moment. There's a lot of adrenalin pumping.

People will tell you things slow down. When you're involved the seconds seem to draw out. Later on someone might opine that it was only a minute or so of life, of time, but in that minute everything is so crystal clear. You see things through the jungle which, if you were just gazing calmly before action erupted, you wouldn't have noticed. You smell things, you hear things even in the roar of combat.

Taking a life is something for which maybe you can talk to people about how they might feel, but it is every individual's dilemma and challenge when it must be done to save your own life or that of your comrades. I think one of the starkest moments is when you look upon a fallen enemy, dead or badly wounded, and if your feeling is one of some level of regret, that is, if you like, a token of the respect in which you hold human life and what they were doing just a few moments before. All their hopes and aspirations have become naught. And if you understand that, you shouldn't go into a deep stage of mourning because you have a job to do. But you're not only allowed, but I'd think it was reasonable, to have a moment of regret.

Ataturk, I think, showed the greatness of spirit which a fierce warrior and a great and sometimes even ruthless national leader was nonetheless able to broadcast to previous enemies, when he said, 'Your sons from foreign countries lying in our soil, weep not for them, because now they're our sons as well'.

Vietnam vets

I think perhaps there was a sense of alienation when they returned home to Australia. A lot of regular soldiers, those who were serving on, came home and, apart from perhaps feeling a little bit of bewilderment at the level of opposition to the war, after their leave, disappeared back into their army family, into the care of their army family.

A lot of the national servicemen and not a few of the regular soldiers who took discharge when they got home were back in a community where the war was disapproved of, and their own experiences and needs were not front-of-mind issues for other people. Also, I think our services, our veteran services' caring facilities, were not as well developed then as they are now, so people just disappeared back out into the community and tried to get on with their lives. Over time, this sense of rejection became an important issue for veterans, and perhaps played on those who, with a bit more care, and a bit more debriefing and a bit more counselling, may have been more robust. So we had vulnerable people stewing on a level of alienation and rejection.

I would always say that in my regular army family, both my real family and in my broad army family, there were so many like-minded souls, we just, perhaps unconsciously, used to go through a debriefing session where we endlessly canvassed what we'd been doing for a year in Vietnam to a point where it was almost mundane discussion stuff. And you would run a mile from your mate who wanted to recount a story and he would run a mile from you as you trotted out the same old yarns.

It was only when I became older and I looked back on it, and I saw that we'd gone in there for about a ten-year period, and Australia alone lost 500 and the United States lost something like 50,000 and then we left; we just threw up our hands and walked out. And I thought, Well, we didn't appear to finish the job we went there to do. So that was the reason why I thought if politicians are going to send people in harm's way for good and valid reasons, we need to stick the course and not walk away and say, 'Well, there you go, those 500 are basically written off'.

Marriage and family

In 1975 I met this lady on a blind date and it was Lynne, a wonderful woman, the love of my life, and I was smitten from the first moment. A rough diamond got a bit polished on that day. I certainly think my friends thought I'd done rather better than I deserved. I'm not sure what her friends thought but they were very kind to me.

In late 1976, December, we got married in the church I used to go to as a schoolboy out at Waverley College—Mary Immaculate Church in Waverley.

From beautiful bride to mother-to-be … I can remember when Lynne said she was expecting, and then of course when our boys started to arrive, suddenly a new dimension took hold of my life. I was no longer an officer and a husband; I was a dad as well.

I discovered, like most people, that being a dad is the greatest experience of your time on earth. We had three sons—Steven, the oldest, Philip and David—and they're now in their twenties and being their dad is just one of the greatest things I could ever experience.

It was another step up in maturity and responsibility. I mean, I'd always been technically, professionally and emotionally responsible for my men, and then later as I got more senior, men and women, but, fatherhood has a very humanising effect on a bloke like me in the military, where you're dealing with tough missions and the need to ask people to do dangerous things. As a dad you become absolutely aware of your own human frailty and a need to be nurturing and, compassionate and fatherly. 'Fatherly' being softening and, I think, in this case, a very good softening.

East Timor

Looking back I've had over forty years in the military, from being a young cadet through to Chief of the Defence Force, but there's no doubt that what most people would remember me for is my time commanding the force in East Timor.

There were so many good commanders around but I happened to be in the right place at the right time, and it was an honour. In 1999 when Australia led a major international operation in East Timor, I was commander of INTERFET, the force put in place. In East Timor my role was to command a major international force which was making sure the militia could no longer interfere with East Timorese people.

There was the obvious security challenge that there were evil people operating, with murderous criminality against their countrymen, and they were ranging free, and we had to get them under control and protect the people. We had to get people back. We had to allow the UN back in. And we had to make sure that speedy aid was delivered to people who were without homes and without a job and without food. That was a big challenge. And then we had to knit together a force that turned out to be about twenty-two nations, and operate in a very organised way until a follow-on UN force could come in. And we knew that might take months and months.

You use all of that stored up experience and energy and you get it right. You so regulate, so organise, so direct what's happening that confidence imbues the whole of the community both in East Timor, in twenty-two separate nations, the international audience watching on, and you get the job done.

Command at that level is always a question of making sure that your logistics function well, that your people who are at the sharp end taking the risks know what they're doing, are properly trained and equipped, and have got all the backup behind them, and that the job that you've sent them to do is a worthwhile job they're capable of doing. I was always confident that we'd hold up our end; and the risks that did ensue from further afield, I always felt that they could be dealt with.

Before you start such an operation you wonder how your people will go, but they were magnificent. They had old heads on young shoulders and performed magnificently.

As a leader I think the most satisfying thing was to see the way that the parts of the big military machine meshed together and worked so well. Our people and all of our allies all meshed in together and did a wonderful job.

There are so many high points in such an operation, but the thing I was most proud of was that when we finished we were cheered by the people and they thought we'd done well by them. You can't have highs without there being some lows, and there were occasional battles there was a lad who died from a disease while we were there, unpreventable but a very sad loss.

It was initially a bit of a surprise, but then subsequently I understand why I had to have a public profile there. It was to explain the operation to the Australian people and to others, and I came to terms with it, and I had to become comfortable with it.

When I came home, though, I was a little surprised about the high level of public recognition. This had apparently been on every screen and on every newspaper, front page, at some stage—and so had I. In a lot of ways it's a bit of a culture shock because we're not used, in the military, to having such a public profile—and suddenly I was identified at every turn. It was initially a little embarrassing but you come to terms with it and I always am very gratified with people's good wishes and almost invariably they're wishing you well.

You sometimes worry about a downside to this, but I think it's inevitable with modern military operations that the media will put you in the spotlight, so you just get on with it.

I have got a couple of great mementoes from East Timor. When Xanana Gusmao made his triumphant return to the country, he wore the uniform of the commander of the resistance movement and, just before I left, he handed me the uniform shirt. He literally gave me the shirt off his back. The other one is ... there's only one of these, the only one that exists ... it's the INTERFET flag which flew outside my headquarters. I've got that now and I guess one day I'll send it to the War Memorial.

I felt that the whole force, not least our Aussies, had this affection for the people of East Timor. And as I was about to leave, my last public words were to say to their beloved leader, 'Long live', and to this country we'd had so much affection for, 'Long live'.

Chief of Army

In July 2000 I was made the Chief of Army—a great honour and very unexpected but the pinnacle of my career in my own service. When I was a little fella, the last thing I would have thought of was to actually head up the whole army, and I wouldn't have thought that, even up until I was a brigadier, I had any show of being the chief. I used to reflect on the luck involved. From Vietnam, not getting shot, through to the serendipity of various promotions along the way until finally Timor, Chief of Army. Reflecting on Timor, I have to think that was a major factor in me having the profile and the reputation to become the Chief of Army.

I knew that I was an experienced warrior, if I can use that word, that I had great experience in command, and a really good grasp of how you successfully execute operations. And we were coming into a period ... you could see, through the war on terror, that there would be ongoing operations of all natures—not least disaster relief, and not least the war on terror, but other things such as the Solomon Islands, the resurgence of unrest in East Timor, all of these things were in play—and that the defence force should be doing all this. I thought, I have high confidence in my ability to do that and to take care of the ADF in other ways for the period I had, which was my three-year contract.

I suppose the outstanding thing that occurred when I was Chief of Army was the 9/11 attacks in the United States. That really knocked us for six but we had to get back up and adjust for that immediately. And that dominated the rest of my time as Chief of Army. Not only did those 9/11 attacks have a worldwide implication, but for a military force you suddenly started to have to protect your population in ways you never thought you'd need to do. And while you're making a professional response to that, personally you start to think about these people are taking away our liberties, they're not to be allowed.

Chief of Defence Force

In the middle of 2002 I was made the Chief of Defence Force and promoted to the rank of general—and that again was a great thrill, an honour and a tremendous challenge. The Chief of the Defence Force is actually the operational commander of all the forces, military forces, at the government's disposal—navy, army and air force. I'm greatly honoured by my selection as Chief of the Defence Force.

Taking over as CDF in the middle of 2002 meant I inherited our operations on the war on terror. I remember when Bali occurred, that really created for us a new threshold of activity in the war on terror. We had to make some organisational and operational responses to that. And things just seemed to accelerate, because we found ourselves deploying troops to the Solomon Islands. We found the Iraq operations on our doorstep. We found there were other terrorist actions that took place. The Asian tsunami came along to devastate the region and kill almost a quarter of a million people. All of these things were enormous challenges for the defence force.

When you're the chief and these things occur, you sometimes reflect on how you're going. And I found myself full of energy and exhilarated by the challenge—not looking for problems, but when they arrived I thought, I'm into this, and this is my job, and I found myself really exhilarated. If you were to stand back you might start to become overwhelmed, but if you immerse yourself in those issues you find yourself coping with them, bits at a time, until you get them solved. And at the end you think, Yes, that went all right.

I suppose one of the things I dwell on is the enormity of that natural disaster, the Asian tsunami. A quarter of a million people killed in the region. In a few minutes, a great natural disaster put in context a lot of the wars, and the present war on terror, and just showed us that nature still has a way of emphatically underscoring the frailty of our existence.

I think the way in which the defence force responded to the Asia tsunami showed people just throwing themselves into the problem and accepting any hardship in order to render aid to desperately needy people. I was so proud of them. It called for every operational skill, less that of actual combat, from the ADF. We had to organise extremely quickly, mobilise people as if we were heading off to a war, except this was a war against need. And we had to get there so rapidly and save people from their own injuries or the deprivation of every reasonable service, from the outbreak of disease, and simply to minister to the sick and the starving and the homeless.

Just as in any other job there are high points and the low points: I was always sad about Abu Ghraib. It slipped under our guard. We didn't ever consider that our ally would have people involved in that terrible set of events, and we got caught out, and I regret that. I wish we'd known more about that. Another low point is, of course, the Sea King disaster, where we lost nine of our very finest, dead in that crash.

The high points? Just legion. Let's just say they come to the surface in the wonderful performance, over and over again, by very young soldiers and sailors and airmen and women doing their job and doing it magnificently.

As CDF I suppose the thing I hold dearest, the thing I cherish, is the way in which our people performed under my leadership and the fact that we were able to do the jobs with very little by way of casualties. I'm very relieved about that.

On the matter of public profile, it was not something I sought but it was necessary to accept it—and once it's there, you've got it forever, so best learn to live with it.

Retirement

I wanted it to be private simply so it was a moment confined to my family and my immediate staff and didn't become a public event. But it was something ... I thought, just as I was getting close to retirement, what a proud duty it would be to go and present yourself symbolically at the foot of the resting place for all of those men and women who, having served Australia, have passed on—and that was at the foot of the tomb of the Unknown Soldier in the War Memorial in Canberra—and to basically pay respects. And I was going to have some words I might utter internally, think, if you like. I stood at the foot of the tomb and I placed a wreath and stood back and gave a salute, which is traditional, and then the only words that occurred to me at that moment, and I just sort of thought them, was, 'I did my best, mate'.

I was never going to say anything out loud, in that place—that's a place of silence—but standing back I thought, Well, I haven't got anything particularly clever to say or think, so I just thought what I really meant after forty years.

Life since I retired has been anything other than sedentary and nostalgic ... No time. It's exhilarating and really busy. Early after I retired I was invited onto the Qantas board and I jumped out of my skin. I thought, What a great board, and I've really enjoyed it, and that's been a centrepiece, if you like, of my retired life.

I've really been a 'corporate warrior' since I retired, both on businesses and not-for-profit boards, and as a consultant to one or two companies. And that's good fun and I like it. There're always some oddities and I was honoured to help out after the cyclone in far north Queensland. And now I'm on the Eminent Persons Group looking for a way forward in Fiji.

I didn't know what to expect; it's really busy but it is nice to matter and to still have something to contribute.

Cyclone Larry

Reporter: We've got winds around 250 kilometres per hour or more. Everything is snapping in half. Coconut trees are bending in half. You can probably hear the roar in the background. You can't see a lot now because of the debris.

I was sitting with my wife doing a bit of a diary update when the phone rang after the cyclone on 20 March [2006], and it was the premier of Queensland asking me to go up and help. So naturally the answer was yes. A lot of things that you might normally worry about would be put on hold for a while. As soon as I saw the devastation, I knew I'd have to live up there, and I lived up there for three months. It was all to do with coordinating the relief and recovery effort to put people back on their feet. One of the great things about having a public profile was when you first meet people in any circumstance, after a cyclone, they say, 'I know who you are, I'm glad you're here to help, let's work together'. For me it was reminiscent of Darwin as I flew in. You get used to seeing inspiring things in the military, but to see civilian people helping their neighbours when their own place is wrecked is uplifting. That's great Aussie selflessness.

Although my formal role is now completed in the cyclone recovery, I'm still involved with support functions to get funds to assist with the further recovery, and I'll keep doing that.

Biography

Although in the last couple of years I toyed with the idea of writing some kind of biography, I really zeroed in on that when I retired—and I thought, A boy from Paddo becomes the CDF; there's a story in that.

Particularly over the last number of years when there were important events with quite complex issues involved, I was lucky to have extensive notes available, so that part was relatively well researched. And of course my own life was the subject of family folk lore.

I'm a rotten typist, two fingers; thank heavens for voice-recognition technology—that's how I wrote 134,000 words of the book, and I'm using it now to reply to a very lovely letter that I've got from a lady concerning the book.

I gave my publisher the panics because we only had a few months in which to write it. And I said, 'Oh yes, no problem', and then got stuck into it—and they were surprised and delighted when I met the deadline. As somebody who'd never written a major piece of that nature before I was a bit unclear about how it would go, but it actually, for me, was quite easy in the end.

Although I enjoyed writing the whole book, I had the greatest fun with that from boyhood through to mature age. Writing that early part of my life was just a joy. Part of the enjoyment is you go back to your youth when you did funny things or you saw funny things and remember characters, and it's like you shed the years and you're reliving it. I think that part's great. I'd like to say that I was a bit of a saint growing up, but that's not the case. I was just a normal sort of urchin, a bit of a larrikin and probably a great trial to my parents. It's probable a lot of people who've seen my last number of years, in particular, in the public eye might be a bit taken aback to know that I was that way at Waverley College and then for a few years at Duntroon before I woke up to myself. But it's a fact of life and my mates from that era, they know it.

There was never any doubt when I finished the book about the dedication of it. I was always going to dedicate it to the two families I love so much, obviously my own I love with all my heart, and that great family, the men and women of the Australian Defence Force and their families.

Out of the public eye

I might have retired from the military but I haven't retired from the love of sport. I still love to watch sport, and whenever I can I love to play golf. I'm lousy at it but it's a great way to get out and do something. How would I sum up my playing skills? Untutored, unfortunate, untalented, disastrous!

I'm passionate about books and music, because with those you can step into a beautiful space, which is your imagination. I've always been a reader. I devour the media but for enjoyment I'm into military history and fictional works. I've often got four or five books on the go at once. The fiction I like is adventure yarns which are both probably fantastic and yet with an edge of credibility, and I also will go back into Napoleonic naval affairs; I like that. There's a whole raft of modern authors who write really good fiction where there's adventure, heroes and heroines, villains—Dale

Brown, Matthew Reilly, who writes escapist Australian literature; I find him a very entertaining author.

Music—I like anything from the Dixie Chicks through to classical music and opera. My musical tastes are probably like types of athletes—fast twitch and slow twitch. My slow twitch stuff is to just disappear into some of the symphonies and operas, particularly lyrical operas, and the fast twitch is the ballad stuff which is from my youth and really takes the years away and makes me feel young again.

It's not an escape, because you're always part of the here and now, but it is an opening of a door into the imagination. You join the composer and the artist in the case of music and you join the author and his or her characters in the case of literature, whether it's a history or something fictional, and your imagination is a marvellous space in which you can roam without the constraints of time or place.

When I was CDF and then when I wrote the book, I always felt young, but, you know, you do notice you slow down a bit, and in that regard you've got to try and keep yourself fit so you can postpone when you become decrepit. Even though you work on your fitness you're still going to notice when you jump up quick or you have to kneel down for a long time, but the idea is to be as fit as you can be, and enjoy your latter years.

Faith and family

Being a person of faith has always been a very important component of who I am.

I know that God's plan for all of us doesn't include a guarantee that we will not have pressures in our lives. Each human being will go through all kinds of sadness and challenges in life, and it's part of the design for our existence that we will suffer, against the expectation of a hereafter.

I'm an ordinary frail human being but I don't suppose I've spent a lot of time saying, 'Well, I don't know about there being a God'.

I've accepted this human condition involves a lot of things that appear overwhelming and for which we will suffer, but I don't suppose I've ever gone through a paroxysm of doubt about there being a higher being.

Thinking back over thirty years of Lynne's and my time together and with the kids, I wouldn't have been able to do any of the latter part of my military service without their love and support. It's just been absolutely fundamental. There have been a lot of demands on the family over the years to shift around all the time. I can't tell you how lucky I've been that they're healthy, happy, loving and supportive. I'm a very lucky man.

I've found that, while I was fairly stone-faced as a younger man, that really, as I got older, you especially—through being a family man—you need to empathise. You need to show people how you're feeling about a particular issue. I think it was being a husband, and then a father, and feeling fatherly towards all the men and women in the defence force, that allowed me to have the confidence to show that I was overjoyed or sad or praising of them ... sometimes angry but not very often.

I like the idea of just observing these great young men of ours going into their further adulthood and being excited by what they will do. I like the idea of friends who now, as we get older, have more time available to be as friends and can enjoy endlessly our experiences of the past. I like the idea of continuing to work because work can be fun. And I really like the idea of watching Australia be safe. We are safe, could be safer. But one of the things that I'm always concerned about, you can't be any other way if you've spent a lifetime in uniform, is to think to all of those who make us safe—good luck, keep it going, do more.

> I'd like to think I'm remembered as someone who gave it a go, and who loved what he was doing and in particular loved the people with whom he was dealing. Did my best, mate.

LILLIAN FRANK
Hair stylist and fundraiser

Screened 27 March 2006

Lillian Frank is much more than a hairdresser. As one of the most socially connected women in the country, she has used her access to high-fliers to raise millions of dollars for charity. Yet behind her image as a trendsetter and social butterfly is a woman who still drives a much-loved, 27-year-old car. Despite her fame as a fundraiser, Lillian says people never turn away when they see her coming.

> No, never. In fact, my phone calls are, 'What do you want, darling?' Never, I promise you! I thought about that a long time ago, and I give them value back, much value. People want to be known. People want to be advertised, publicised. People want to have a good time. People want to know that what they are connected to is the best—the best hospital, the best charity lady, the best of everything. They give. I promise you, nobody says no to me—not one.

Early days in Burma

We were all born in Burma, six of us. My mother came from Baghdad my father comes from Turkey. My mother was very strong—it's the genes that come through the family: we are a strong women's family. My mother's grandfather left Iraq about 120 years ago. Before Saddam, before the royals, there was another tyrant. We weren't brought up to be religious—we're not religious people—but we do belong: we're Jewish, and it was just that there was no life there for Jews.

My father ... my mother always told us whenever she had fights with him, 'He's a deserter in the army'. They were fighting the Greeks; he didn't want to go into the army, so he left. He went roaming the world teaching children, private tuition, any language. When my father was a young man he spoke and wrote seven languages. He was a tutor and my mother had private tuition with four of her girlfriends. Even the Queen didn't have that; Prince Charles didn't have that. He was teaching her, and he fell in love with her. And my mother fell in love with him. And her hand in marriage was given to another merchant's son, so they eloped. That's why I say my mother's so strong. Anyway, in the end my father ran my grandfather's business, so everything was forgotten, forgiven.

My aunt, who had sixteen children, she was my namesake, and my mother always said, 'You will never have those sixteen children, will you? You will never have them'. 'No, I won't have them mother.' She said, 'I didn't think you would'.

We had eleven brothers and sisters from my mother's side ... all their children. And we had a hockey team, a netball team, a football team, every team: everybody had to choose a team. And we all played all sports; I mean, what do you do there? Read books and play sports as kids. All that, and we had a wonderful time, and when we sat for dinner or lunch it was at big wooden, timber beautifully done, long tables, with thirty, forty kids, like in a school. And we had a lovely, lovely time. My childhood was precious, precious.

I could speak more languages than I do now. I've forgotten a few. But I still speak Arabic, Hindustani ... I've shocked the daylights out of taxi drivers in Europe or here. They turn around and I say, 'Don't leave the wheel, don't leave the wheel; look at me in the mirror, don't turn'. I speak Arabic, Hindustani, I speak a bit of Burmese, I speak Polish now because of Richard—my grammar's not so good—and English.

A naughty child

When I was little, I used to answer my mother in French when she spoke to me in English. When she spoke to me in French I spoke to her in Arabic, always spoke in the other language. I used to annoy my mother, just for fun. I was naughty, I was the naughtiest child in the world. If I didn't get my way, I would go and sit in the tree, if I didn't get enough swimming time, or whatever. They would be looking for me; my clothes would be put underneath the tree, and they would think I had drowned, and they would be looking. Once I was too frightened to come down because my father had a belt in his hand and I thought, I'm not coming down. But the fire brigade, the police, everything came, and they were just going to start searching and I thought, I'd better come down. I came down and I faced it. I got three on my legs with the belt. Never did that again.

But one day, it was so petty and I didn't have my way and I was so naughty, and I went and lay in front of a tram coming along. My mother said, 'Oohh!' And I got up and she let me do what I wanted to do. I went to extremes to get my way. I was so focused and I didn't let anybody not let me do something. That was really extreme because my mother was very generous: she let us experiment with anything we wanted to do and helped us and helped us. And if we couldn't get it right she would say, 'Maybe this way', without saying, 'No, don't do it this way; do it this way', by putting doubts in a child's mind—she never did.

I know I became the person I am because my parents were very strong,. They wanted us to be independent; they wanted us to have a view, to ask questions; they were very wise people.

The Japanese invasion

In 1941, the Japanese invaded Burma and we were all frightened. My grandfather, they were very wealthy, they were in the coffee business, so we had a house at the Cochin Lakes, and we had disappeared to the lakes. But we still had the Japanese war, Japanese flying over and bombing everything, so he built a 9-foot, big steel bunker going nearly to the river, and covered it and covered it and covered it.

Every time the air-raid warning went, we all ran into the air-raid shelter. And when it was New Year's Eve there was a bombing on Burma and we sang 'Auld Lang Syne'. And we all went in there, and I remember it was the last time we all were together, from grandmother to parents to children, and we sang 'Auld Lang Syne'—and I don't like 'Auld Lang Syne'.

We had been shattered, not the air-raid shelter, but we came out and everybody went to a different country. And I've got family all over the world, all over the world.

And still I can't hear it, I honestly can't hear 'Auld Lang Syne'. If I hear it on the radio, I turn it off. If I go anywhere for New Year's Eve, they know I leave at 11.30. I can't cope with that. Even not listening to it I cry. I know it's there in the back of my mind. And that was the last time I saw everybody together. Now they are all over the world.

Escape

From there we were on a boat, and the Japanese came on board and we were hidden in the cargo, and they said they would blow us up if there were any white people on board. So at the next port they threw us out in the jungle and we didn't know where we were. And my mother played games with us and said, 'We have to follow footsteps. Whoever finds the first footsteps will get the biggest ice cream when we get to the end, like something at the end of a tunnel', and I found the first step. My mother was so bright, so clever, and we walked and we walked.

I remember trees and pulling at mangoes and fruit and things like that. I remember having feet that were hurting like hell, frightened like hell. We were three—my sister, my brother and myself. We were all under ten. We had holes in our shoes; we didn't want to walk. She never let us sleep … She looked for footsteps, footsteps, footsteps. And she said, 'We are going to be there. Now, I'm telling you, children, we are going to find someone. Somebody's going to find us'. She never gave up hope, no. She never gave up hope. She never, ever told us, 'We'll never come out of it'. She said, 'We're going to get there. They're going to find us, they're going to find us'. We were found.

We saw fire and we knew we came to a camp. They did the fire to attract the attention of army, navy, air force, whoever, and also because of the tigers—Burma had a lot of tigers—and we went there and we moved with them. We were rescued by the Americans and then flown to Calcutta.

A mother's influence

My mum has influenced each one of us. And one of the ways she influenced me really, into this kind of helping other people, was she was a very rich girl, from a rich family which left Iraq and came to Burma, and they made a lot of money. And she and her friends, all of them had money. They got up from bed and showered, and got themselves dressed and then the servants came in and they gave them orders for the food. Everything was in hundreds, you know; we fed everybody in the village, I think.

We used to have a man who was a bit 'sad' and he came for lunch every day, and the servants wouldn't wash his plate. My mother used to wash his plate.

My mother, when she had her card games—she played cards five days a week—and I saw always servants coming behind these women with parcels, big parcels, trolleys full of stuff, and they went through the house to the back of the house, a big room, and I never saw anything coming out of there, always something going in. And I was never home. Always my mother's famous expression, 'Little children should be seen and not heard, and not be seen at all', that was her famous saying. And that's how she got rid of us; she never said, 'You can't do this, you can't be here, you must go there' ... never.

So I was sick one day and she forgot I was there, and I came right down, I sat on the step and I saw all these things going ... the door's open and I'm looking from the top and when they went away I came down. I jumped on my mother. I said, 'Pandora's Box was here'. Parcel after parcel, things were hanging, and drawers were full of underwear. This was the dowries for poor girls who, when they got married, if she didn't have a good dowry, there was an indictment on her. So the mothers whose daughters were getting married, they would come to my mother and she would give them everything from slippers to combs for their hair. And that would be their dowry; the girl would never know it didn't come from her mother ... the mother wouldn't know where it came from. And the people who gave helped my mother put this together, with her own stuff as well, never knew where it went, so that is really one of the best ways of doing it. I say it's helping others; it's not charity. I hate that word, charity. I think it's terrible. It's an overused word, it's a dreadful word. I hate it.

Early hairdressing

I was always a girl that was looking in the mirror and putting bows in the hair, and then at school I used to take girls and cut their hair. I was punished for cutting hair. I cut a girl's long hair and I couldn't match the two sides, and I cut one side, the other side, one side, the other side, with kitchen scissors from the house. And then she went home crying. Her mother came to school the next day. I was put out in front of the whole assembly, whole school, with my hand out. I got the cane and I was punished. I had to go with a placard on my back saying that I was a naughty girl and I shouldn't do things to little children.

Abroad to Aunt Clare

My days in India ... I went to school, made friends and things, and then again an upheaval in my life. My mother came one day and said, 'India's no place for you anymore. You are a young girl, fifteen. You've got a life ahead of you. You are going to Aunt Clare in London'.

And she said, 'You will be all right, you will find your way. I am telling you, I have no worries, you will always remember my words, you will do exactly very well. You will do it yourself. Aunt Clare will keep an eye on you'. I cried my eyes out and I said, 'Mummy, I don't know Aunt Clare. I've only met her once, when she came visiting. I don't want to go. You don't love me, that's why you are sending me. You love the boys'. She said, 'No, it's not that. The boys need me; you don't need me anymore, you just go'. And I cried all the way, six weeks on the boat to England. And after that I lived with the guilt, because my mother was right. I felt that my mother loved my brothers and had to protect them, and she said to me, 'No, they are stupid. They have to have somebody—a woman—telling them things to do. You are on your own feet. You are very clever. You will cope'.

At Elizabeth Arden

Once I got to England, Aunt Clare said to me, 'I can get you a job at Elizabeth Arden'. And I said, 'Oh, I'd love to work at Elizabeth Arden'. I was thinking I wanted to be a hairdresser. And then I went there, found out that Elizabeth Arden doesn't train hairdressers, but they will train me as a manicurist and a beautician, so I took the job.

I had a different agenda to Elizabeth Arden. I broke the ice there. In that place, at Elizabeth Arden, they were all baronesses' daughters and the Honourable this and that; they were from very nobility families. They had two-and-a-half-hour lunches, so I took two-hour lunches, too. But I was in the salon with the men, and I kept saying, 'Do you want me to sweep the salon?' 'Oh yes, sweep the hair.' 'Do you want me to wash the client?' I stood on a box because I was not tall enough, and washed the hair, and I cleaned the trolleys and did all sorts of things and I learnt hairdressing. I went home and practised, practised, practised, and I made myself a hairdresser in my own lunchtime.

So do you know what they did? Every time Miss Arden came to London, she didn't come that often, they would hide me. They used to put me on a stool; they were frightened she would find out there was a woman. I broke the taboo.

I was in the scene there too, because the girls that came to Elizabeth Arden were training to do manicures, pedicures—these were the girls that I mixed with. Then I went to the derby with them, and I spent my whole year's money and I bought a Mugler suit, a black one with white frills, and I bought a big Conessa hat, white one, and we all went to the derby. They took pictures of all of us, and suddenly you open the paper the next day, *The Times*: there you were, and I thought, Oh, that's easy.

Coming to Australia

My sister kept saying to me, 'You're having a good time in London, but it's not home for you. Come to Australia—you will love it. I've got everything under the sun here but I haven't got anybody to share it with'. She said, 'All I want is somebody of my family. And you are so close to me, come and visit'. I had no intentions to stay. I came in October. The first Melbourne Cup was in November; I was home and hosed. I wore what I wore to the English derby and got photographed—a picture, full length in the *Herald*.

I was having a ball in London, I was running to this and that fancy thing, and going to the races, getting photographed from top to toe, and all of this nonsense, but I thought, All right, I'll just go for a month, and I stayed. I went and said, 'Listen, I'm going to take a job'. I went to the government and told them what I wanted; they let me stay. I took a job at Ardens.

Elizabeth Arden's niece came to Australia when they opened, and I did her hair for her here, and she said, 'Oh, wonderful, a woman doing hair'. And she went back and told Miss Arden, 'There's a very good hairdresser in Australia, and she's a girl'. And then Miss Arden, she was running a horse in the Kentucky Derby and she had a big house there, and she had house guests from all over the world, and she didn't know what to do for hair, and she said, 'Oh, I'll bring this girl from Australia'. And she flew me there, and I did all her guests and even her hair. Oh my god, I was walking on cushions, floating.

Meeting Richard

My sister and my brother-in-law wanted me to marry money. I was not in for money, I was in for a good time. I was in to satisfy my curiosity, my love for the person. None of them I could have fallen in love with. So one day we went to a party. In those days we used to have house parties, where the girls in the community all went, they had roulette tables and things, they raised money. And Richard was a gambler and he was putting his money, you know, very nonchalantly on, and then he would come and dance. He danced with a redhead and me, two of us, like one dance here and one dance there. I think he was dancing to see which one he wanted to take home. So in the end he asked me, 'How did you get here?' I said, 'In a taxi'. So he said, 'Can I take you home?' I said, 'Yes, of course, if you take my sister'. And he said, 'Oh, all right'. He thought I was just having him on, then we had to go and look for my sister, so four of us went for coffee, and then he dropped me home. The next day he rang me, and he said, 'What are you doing next Saturday? I'd like to take you out'. So I said to him, 'Next Saturday? Oh no, I'm busy next Saturday, but I can come with you on Sunday'. And he said, 'No, no, that's all right, I'll ring you again'. Never rang for six weeks. He was put off, so I should have known he was a chauvinist then. Didn't get his way the first time, then six weeks later he rang me out of the blue. I said, 'Oh, you decided to talk to me?' And I said, 'When do you want to go out?' He laughed, and that's history now. And when I married him, I stopped him from gambling. I hated gambling!

We had a lot in common. He lost his whole family. His father and his mother took all three children and they were going through the snow. Two people were paid a lot of money to bring them to Lithuania, or one of the eastern countries, to get out of Poland, and this woman looked at his sister and brother and said, 'No, I can't take three of you. We'll get caught. So we'll come back and get them'. So they left them with a Swiss aunt, and the children didn't know her, so they went to the grandmother. So when the people went back, everyone was gone. He never talked about it. Richard never discussed it with me; his mother never discussed it with me. His aunt told me about it. And I never discussed it with my children, because it was too hurtful for them to talk about these things.

My family never approved of Richard, because he wasn't rich like the other boys they lined up for me. My sister and brother-in-law didn't think he had enough money for me. After we were married he started restaurants. He was working with his father making silk handkerchiefs when I married him.

Two years after I was married, that was Michelle, and then I had a skiing accident and because of that I waited to have Jackie, and now I have two beautiful grandchildren.

A working mother

I went to Elizabeth Arden to start with, and I was working there, and I had a baby, I had Michelle already, while I was working at Elizabeth Arden, and they really were shocked. First of all a woman, second of all that I'm having a baby, then third of all I'm going back. So I went back and Antonio, a very good hairdresser, said, 'Lillian, you and I are wasting time here. We are the only two people working. Come on, we'll open our own salon'. Michelle was just not even a few months old, and I opened my first salon.

I didn't have a disease, I had a child. I was not sick. My mother-in-law said, 'You are like a cat, you can spit them out and get up and go'. Now the difference was I never had them wanting anything. I was always home when they came back from kindergarten, or school. When they were little, each one had their own nanny; they had the housekeeper, they had the gardener, they had everybody, they had plenty of people. Today you can't afford all the things you could afford then, because for the same money you had the whole lot.

An exotic in Melbourne

They took to me very well, because I was invited to a party as, 'This is my friend, the hairdresser, Lillian Frank. She is ...'. You know? They thought they were getting royalty because they were bored with each other's company. Every time there was a party I was invited as a showpiece. I was accepted very easily because I came from a good background. I wasn't just a hairdresser ... I had my manners, I knew all about life, I went through life. And I was very successful.

Now it became so, if I don't go somewhere, they ring me on the night and say, 'Listen, we're sending a car. You must have forgotten'. And I say, 'No, I'm in bed, I'm not coming'. 'Oh, can't do a party without you.' That happens all the time.

When I came to Australia, made myself the social butterfly, was the best hairdresser, the men were chasing me, wanting to get married. My sister was in the right position, I had to go back to my mother. I went back five times to India. I kept saying to her, 'Mum, you were right, you were right, you were right'. I'd kiss her, kiss her. And when she was dying—she died in India—I wanted to go back, but she was in a coma and my family wouldn't let me. I would like to have done that.

Franchises and fundraising

I was going to start to franchise, open one in Sydney, one in Frankston, one in Toorak—and I was in the city—and one in Cheltenham, I think it was, and I was going to franchise. And I was just about to do that, and I thought, I'm sitting in a car and I'm doing hair wherever they want me, and I'm not happy. I want to do what my mother did, to help other people. I've got enough if I stay in one salon and do it.

So I gave those salons to them at a pittance, and I went back to one salon and stayed there, and made my name, made my money. Then I joined the Lady Mayoress's committee and I was on the executive, the youngest girl. I made the most money and I did their PR for them, all that, and I went through a few Lady Mayoresses, and the Children's Hospital wanted me to do something. So we started a door knock for cancer; I remember that was one of the first things I did. And there again all the ladies come to the party thinking they're having a wonderful time, and when they were told what they were there for, they put their hands up. 'I'll do Toorak, I'll do this, I'll do Malvern.' And there was nothing left for Richard and me. There was St Kilda, and at that time—must have been in the early '60s, I'm not sure—St Kilda was infested with ladies of the night and old pensioners in flats. So I went straight from that meeting. I thought, I'll beat them, pull the rug from under them. I went to each school, St Catherine's, Mandeville, all the schools, boys' schools, all of them. I went to the principal, and said, 'I'm doing this ... Can I have your top two, three classes?' And I had a pyramid system. And they said, 'How will you look after them?' And I said, 'We'll have fifty or sixty older people and they'll be in control. One will be in charge of one floor ...' And we went on and on, and we had 500 people in St Kilda and we raised £9000. That was a challenge. But I knew I would pull it off; I wouldn't have started otherwise.

The hats

I was always mad about clothes and hats. I spent all my fortune on my back. When I went to the races we were all photographed and then the next morning we opened the paper and I was there from top to toe by myself, the lead picture. I thought, 'Oh, this is easy, so I'm going to do it'. And that's what inspired me to wear those funny hats.

I don't take long to do things: I'm very impulsive and my mind works fast. One month before the races, I get my clothes made; everybody else is thinking all year for it. One month before the races, I get my two, three outfits done and three hats. Melbourne Cup is the main thing; they wait for me to see how mad I am. I don't mind; they call me mad, mad, mad hatter; that doesn't worry me.

Talking about hats, I had a pink and purple hat, and the girl from an agency came in and she saw that hat, and she said, 'We are just going to launch a toothbrush, a new toothbrush, all colours of this. Will you put them in your hat?'

I said, 'Yes, for $10,000 for the Children's Hospital'. They said, 'Yes!'

Once I wore phones in my hat. I was in the Emirates marquee; I met the sheik and he said, 'Why have you got that in your hat?'

And I said, 'They dared me to wear it, and they are paying the Children's Hospital a big fee'.

Charity work

I hate that word, charity; it is an overused word, dreadful word. I hate it. It is 'helping others'. I've been working with the Royal Children's Hospital for a very long time, raising a lot of money. I only work with the children, and I work for children because I was a refugee child, and that does … you know, obsesses you. My husband tells me, 'You're possessed with this. You give up everything, you wouldn't give this up. Isn't that right?' I said, 'Yes, you're right'. I wouldn't give up making money for children, raising money for children.

Burma, coming through there, it left a scar on me. Everybody has scars some see them, some push them aside, and that's my scar. I feel children don't want to be born. They don't ask to be born. They don't say, 'Hey, I want to come in'. We bring them for our own needs. You want a son to take your name, you want a daughter to pretty up, you want your children. I mean, nobody gets married for the sake of being two alone, you know.

I don't go into the hospital hardly. Once a year I take the girls into the hospital and we have our first meeting. And I thought it's a good thing, because they should see the equipment that I bought. The middle of the year we gave them $310,000, and they bought this ear equipment; they showed us how it worked and everything else. We had our lunch, we had our meeting. I don't like to go to the hospital; I don't want anyone to patronise me. I'm doing it because I want to, because I love to and I want to, that's why I do it. And I stay away from there.

With charity I always look for things that nobody else wants to touch. A prime example was Odyssey House, because nobody wanted to touch children on drugs because they were stealing and snatching bags. People said, 'Oh, you should give it to the police'. And I said, 'No, I'm not giving it to the government; I'm giving it to the children'. Because kids want to take drugs to obliterate their pain; they come from behind the eight ball.

I say, 'I'm sent for this reason'. And people think I'm mad when I say that, you know, priests get 'called' but I feel I will be doing that, I was called for that.

Fundraising tactics

I go straight to people. I say, 'Look, you have it, they don't. Come on, part with some'. And they say, 'Oh, what can I do?' I say, 'You can do more, but if you think you haven't got time for more, then give me more money. Support us, support us so we can support other people'.

I work on their guilty conscience and they think, Let's get rid of this woman. That was the early times. Now I just pick up the phone. They say, 'Hi, Lillian, what do you want?' I say, 'I just want to say hello to you sometime'. There are times that I am inviting them to something. They say, 'Yes, Lillian, how are you? What do you want?'. I say, 'This time I want nothing. I want you to come'.

Business does give, but I am saying they are the ones, when we get the reputation for Australians are not generous. The average Australian person, they've got precious little, but they give you their precious little. They are very good. Look at the example of the Telethon: last year raised $10 million. This comes from small money, and some women who are in committees and auxiliaries, and big business gives $500 or something. Yes, now they are starting to realise that they have to give.

Friends

The friendship group is very close. I have plenty of friends. They're all European and they've been through wars; they've been this, that. We have a lot in common. I haven't got a lot of Australian girlfriends. I haven't got a lot of model girlfriends. And my husband said to me, my mother-in-law said to me, when I have a party—I'm going back a few years when my mother-in-law was alive then—and she said, 'Why are you bringing such beautiful women for encouragement, your husband and young men around?' I said, 'Look, if my husband wants to play, he doesn't need my friends. He can play without them'. So I was never jealous of anybody, never envious of anybody. I never had a problem in my life that I couldn't solve. I solve everybody else's problem. And that's why I'm happy with myself.

My sister was my best friend, but Richard, I go to Richard for help. I go to him, I talk to my daughters; there's a lot of friends around me that I talk to. If something irritates me or something annoys me or something hurts me, I talk and talk and talk and talk about it till I get it out of my system, and then I've forgotten.

On the speaking circuit

I'm very ready for talking to corporates, trying to influence them, change their thinking, not only for themselves, but for others. I'm not going to tell them for any one person, they can do what they like, but at least to motivate them into that. I mean ... it's not enough to have money and to give to your grandchildren. What the first generation makes, the second generation pilfers, so they might as well get names, do things.

If every country did that twenty-five years ago they wouldn't be in such a position, all the poverty in the world, no water in the world, all those tyrants in the world. I mean, we are being selfish, only looking at ourselves, our inner side, but there is an outer world that needs people ... Try and make other people as successful as yourself. There are so many people who are very clever but can't get on that first rung of the ladder. Motivate people, because motivation is what really put my life together: my mother saying that, 'You will do it'.

In love with Richard

Yes, I am. Actually, I admire Richard for knowing me. Knowing me is hard. Not everybody knows the depth of me; he knows the depth of me. And he knows what I need. I need space; I need to do what I want to do. I don't need to be put in a box or in a bottle or in something. I need to be free. I am a free agent. I was born to be free, and I do what I want. And I do much more: I do four people's jobs in one week. But I don't feel that I'm doing that; when they tell me I do, I know I did it. I know I have to do this. I stay up every Wednesday night and do my *Herald* column. And I'm there till one.

Richard had a career, and so did I. So we gave each other space. But Richard worked at night at his restaurants, so I was alone at night. I had the children; I bathed with them. Richard chooses where he wants to go. Otherwise he's working in the restaurant. He had a restaurant until one year ago. We do a lot of fighting. But we're still together for a long, long time. We fight a lot, we fight over nothing. It's a noisy house, my household.

Strong women

We have a very strong gene in our women's side of the family: my mother, my grandmother, my daughter and even my granddaughter Ella.

But one daughter says I love them dearly, dearly, dearly, 'but she's not a nurturer'. She said that to me. She said that on television. She said it to somebody on television, I remember. I don't know what it means to nurture, but I gave them a lot of advice. When they were little, I brought them up to be very independent. That was the first thing I tell every young mother. And you asked me what I regret in my life. Two things: not enough education because of the war, and I've got only two daughters. I should have had four children. I would like to have had four children, and I would have begged them to have had four children. Look, I have nobody at home now. At least I would have children at home.

A health scare

I had a scare not so long ago: I went to an opening night, and I felt bad in the cinema. And I said to Richard, 'I just feel pain like mad and it's shooting up'. And we were sitting in the front row, and I said, 'You go out first and I'll come after you, because people will notice us getting up, they think we don't like the film'. So we went out, and I was walking down the stairs, and I got worse and worse—my heart was going like that. And we went straight to the hospital. And I said, 'Could one of your doctors please look at me? I feel quite agitated; you know, my heart's beating fast'. Two men came with a chair and they put me in, and I said, 'I can walk!' They said, 'No, no, no, you can't walk; you're in a hospital; you've got 180 heartbeat; we're going'. Five minutes later I was in an emergency—oh, doctors galore. And they gave me, I don't know what kind, four different treatments, and took my heart back to its regular beat. But I have an irregular heartbeat, I have always known.

You come back with 'Here but for the grace of God go I' to live longer.

Loyalty

I'm not tough. No, I'm not tough. I'm friendly with my staff. They are very happy to do things for me. When they do something wrong, I do give it to them. I am hard to please but I know the difficulties of people. If you do something that I know you can't do, I will not aggravate you. But if I know you're capable of doing something more and you're lazy, or you're not doing because, you know, oopsy daisy, close enough is good enough, then I will take you to task. But I am a person who can not take you to task behind the scenes. I come straight to the point, and that is my downfall. My worst asset is I come out if I am angry to the person.

Richard and I fight sometimes—people have told us that we're divorcing. We're married nearly forty years. People have made us divorce five, six, seven times in our life, saying, 'Oh, they are going to divorce'. The rumours going around, they had a big fight. We fight. He has a difference of opinion, and if he doesn't like it he tells me right in front of everyone. Everyone! Out it comes. I don't keep anything inside, and that's the secret too, you know, nothing stays there.

The Herald column

What does it do? People want to be in it; they kill themselves to get there. The *Herald* tells me, I take the *Herald* to places they've never been before. I stayed with my ex-*Herald* editor last night and she brought out pictures and pictures—we were up to all hours—and she said to me, 'You took the *Herald* to many more places than the *Herald* took you'. I opened the doors that the other people at the *Herald* don't get invited to.

I don't need people telling me all the time, 'Why do you do it? Why don't you retire?' I get that all the time. I get so angry with them. I said, 'You are worried about me? All right, worry about yourself; don't worry about me, because I will retire when I want to'. But I will never retire.

I still do hairdressing in the salon, but I want to cut down a few hours at my salon. I want a few days of doing my research on my book. For every one story that I wrote in the paper, there'll be another two or three that I couldn't write, and it'll be a pretty good story.

> I'll keep on living the way I do. I'll do that till I push daisies. I'll not stop anything of my life, nothing at all. A lot of people would love me to stop—you know, tall poppies, cut, cut—but they can't cut me; no one can cut me.
>
> What are my obstacles? People who are ignorant and people who hate tall poppies. I hear about myself such things; you would have to be a wonderful writer to write such things.
>
> Take every opportunity that comes your way. You should never, never see an opportunity in the eye and pass by. Never! I've told that to my daughters.

RENEE GEYER
Singer

Screened 27 August 2007

Renee Geyer is the soulful diva of rhythm and blues, with twenty-two albums and a career now in its fourth decade. With that trademark husky voice, Renee says there was never any doubt: it had to be rhythm and blues.

I think since I was a very young girl ... I've always been musical and wanted to sing ... never thought I'd actually do it for a living. I've always known I had an ear, but I've always had a very husky voice, and I remember my singing teachers or music teachers at school saying, 'Too much chest, too much chest'—the 'too much chest' is paying my bills now. So, obviously, I've found my voice. I love R&B music—that just happens to be intrinsic, that just goes hand in hand with my life—and ever since I was a child I've loved black music. So my chesty sound seems to suit it, and I've just kind of evolved into my own sort of sound.

When I worked in America it was a lot of, 'Dang ... where you come from? What church you go to, huh? Wow, how do you sound like that?' I'm like, 'I don't know. Just ... you know, I don't know'. I'm a white Hungarian Jew from Australia sounding like a 65-year-old black man from Alabama. I've lasted so long and it's become, 'Well, this is what she is'. But in those days it was really hard.

Mother

My parents came out to Melbourne in 1948 and then got a job with the Sydney Jewish Welfare Society, running the hostel in Sydney for immigrants that were coming out still from the Holocaust, but coming later, in the '50s, to Australia.

My mother is a Holocaust survivor. She was liberated in 1945 from a camp in Mauthausen, after having been through many camps, one of which was Auschwitz, where her parents perished and her eldest sister and her eldest sister's children also perished.

My mother talks about arriving at Auschwitz and she remembers seeing Mengele. My mother was separated from my grandmother, and my grandmother screamed, 'Give me back my daughter, give me back my child'. And Mengele picked my mother up and threw her into the line that lived just because he didn't want to see mother and child together. It was more out of that than saving my mother's life. And there was a woman that lived in the village in Bratislava with my mother's family, and her name was Renee; she was a little bit older than my mother. My mother would have been fifteen, sixteen, and the last thing my grandmother said, as their line went, was, 'Stay with Renee, just stay with Renee', and that's how I got my name.

A white bandana

Steven Spielberg when he did *Schlinder's List* sent film crews all around the world to get the survivors' stories for the Washington archives, because he wanted the people who were left, he wanted their stories to be forever in the archives. They hadn't had that happen until then. And he would give each family or person who did an interview a gift. My mother got a gift, a book of the liberation of all the camps, and there was one page of Mauthausen. And my mother always talked about how in the group of five or six girls that she was always stuck with in this little sort of box ... she had this white bandanna that they used. She used to cover her head with it, because they shaved their heads, so she was always embarrassed by that. She tried to cover her head or it would be used by someone if they were sick, then they would wash with it; it would be used for everything. It saved everybody, this white bandanna.

Whenever my mother would see pictures, gatherings of people at Mauthausen, she would almost half look, half not look, because she'd know she'd see this white bandanna. There was a picture of people gathering at Mauthausen; she had it blown up about 100 times, and there she is, my mother with her white bandanna standing in this group of a couple hundred people. Skinny—because my mother's always been since I've been born, a more portly lady—skinny, sixteen-year-old girl with this white bandanna. And she has it framed.

Hungary was the last place that was invaded, and my father had an inkling early on that Jewish people were actually being killed. A lot of people couldn't believe that this could be so, so their life went on as normal. My dad wanted to get out very quickly and ended up going to Palestine. After the war, when all the people were liberated—because it wasn't just Jews, all sorts of minority people—they were all on ships that took them to Palestine. My mother met my father in Palestine after she was liberated.

Australia

My parents came to Melbourne. Within a year or so they got an offer from the Jewish Welfare Society to manage a migrant hostel in Sydney. When I was little it seemed like this huge place. I've been back since and it's just a really big kind of boarding house. There were always about five or six families living in this place, and there were always kids, and it was a wonderful place to grow up, from the age of three to twelve or thirteen years old.

Got kicked in the shins a lot by my brothers—two older brothers, one, one year older than me and one, six, seven years older than me. Soccer nuts and, of course, I always wanted to join in and, of course, I was not wanted. I was just generally a pain in the neck when I was growing up and always wanting to play with my brothers who did things that girls weren't meant to do.

It was just a wonderful place to grow up with kids from Poland, Russia, Hungary; there were even mid-east Jews, all sorts of Jewish families, but always lots of children. And me and my brothers had a ball. All the holidays were upheld and my parents still go to synagogue on all the holidays—Yom Kippur, Rosh Hashanah, Passover—they were all upheld in the hostel. So there would be feasts and Passover, and the feast the night before Yom Kippur, and it was a very, very Jewish upbringing.

Back in the '50s there weren't any great Jewish, private, good education schools, so they sent us to the next best thing, which was Methodist. I went to a Methodist ladies' college and my brothers went to the brother school, which was Newington Methodist College, and we were just told, when we have that one lesson a week in the church, 'Just go and sit there …' They just said, 'Just do what you're told; you know who you are, you're Jewish'. But it's the education part and it would have been very expensive for them to have sent all three of us to Methodist college.

Father

My father is a strict no-nonsense, very, very clever, academically minded Hungarian with a love of Mahler and inventions. He used to go on the old *Inventors* and win, back in the '60s. He invented something before the guy that actually did it got the real money, because he never trusted anyone with any of his inventions so he never made any money from them. But he was always inventing something. He invented a spray can of oxygen for people who need oxygen quickly. He invented lots of things and they were always in the lounge room. There was always trouble because my mother said, 'They're always in the living room, always in the lounge room'. We called it 'the big room' in the hostel we lived in—the room where my parents lived and slept was called 'the big room'. And off the big room was my room and then down the hall was the boys' room. And Daddy always had his inventions in the big room and he had a thing that made vinyl records. Why did anybody want to make vinyl records if they're not a record company? Who knows? But he knew how to do it, so he did it.

The thing is, he was into the inventing. The minute it was done he was out and it was gone. It was making the thing that was great for him.

Not getting on

We didn't get on and we sort of still don't get on, but I'm more like my father than either of my brothers. I just think he's found me—as my mother and my brothers have—a strange, odd person in the family, that's all of a sudden a showbiz person and really good at her job, and the only one that's actually stayed with the same career for thirty-six years. But, we're similar in temper and temperament. My father doesn't suffer fools gladly and neither do I; I think we're alike on that level. My mother's always trying to smooth things over: 'Oh, he's only joking, he's making a joke'. His delivery is deadpan and right on, right on the money.

My father, I think, wanted another boy. I remember my mother saying, I think my father's first words were, 'Oh, it's only a girl'. So there it started, but it's a strange thing, because of all the children I am most like my father, very much like my father, very set in my ways, stubborn and, of course, growing up it caused a lot of problems. And he had quite a bad temper, typically Hungarian and with a bad temper on top of it, so that makes for a sort of scary concoction when you have a problem child, an unusual child who was always wanting to be the 100 per cent centre of attention ... and now I get paid for being the centre of attention.

When I decided singing was my life, I had to leave home; there was no way I could stay in that house. You know, gigs, shows in the early '70s to his generation ... to them Shirley Bassey in a glittering gown is someone singing contemporary shows. 'What do you mean? You're in a pair of jeans, thongs and a T-shirt and you come home with money in your pocket and you say you've been singing?' I mean, I think he thought I was hookering.

And I was probably a problem to raise because I didn't want to walk the road that they wanted me to walk down, which really ... in those days Jewish girls would go to university to meet a nice husband. They would call it that they would go to study whatever, whatever, but they would meet a nice Jewish boy and then they would get married. The boy would finish his university and the girl was basically at university to meet the guy. So I wasn't going to walk down that path.

Of course, they're very proud now. And everyone, myself included, is stumped how I am the only one in the family who is doing what I am doing, although I do have relatives who are cantors in synagogues. So there must be something of what I do comes from that. And I think the R&B wailing is not unlike what Hebrews and what a cantor wails in a synagogue. I think they're not that dissimilar.

A transistor radio

At home there were certain parts of the house I was not to be in. You know, my father would be sitting quietly listening to Mahler, the most depressing music on the earth ... I've actually grown to love it now but in those days, when you're a young kid running around on the weekend, and you have to be very quiet, and it's very dark ... And so I used to be in my room a lot plotting my revenge—'Wait until I get out of here; I'll show you', which has all gone by the wayside.

So there was a lot of me in my room with my transistor radio, which was my saviour, and in those days there was a new, modern, plastic, round transistor radio that you could twist and it would open up. Or you could put it together and it would be like a little bag. I used to have that under my pillow and that was my saviour growing up from the age of about ten onwards.

Any time something came on the radio, like Sam and Dave or Aretha Franklin, something was stirred up in me and, I still don't understand why, it just hit a nerve. I never entertained the thought of being in show business, because there was no avenue for me to go down and be in show business, and my parents didn't know show business people. So that was all a happy accident, but my transistor radio in my room was my saviour. It saved me.

Ten is when I knew I could sing. I'd watch *Bandstand* and go, 'I'm better than them', but never thinking I would have a chance to be out there. I always thought I would just be singing in the shower, and singing at home into a hairbrush in the mirror. But I got an inkling that I might actually be good and get into this business when I was about sixteen, when I sang with a friend's school band. And that was it: they just all went, 'Oh!' And I went, 'Oh, oh! I must be really good. I really am good'.

May I help you?

When I knew that singing was going to be what I wanted to do, I was in my last year of school, and I wanted out. And I really, really wanted out, so my mother said the only way I could leave school was if I went to study something somewhere, so they sent me to typing school. So I can type well! And I went to typing school so I could get a job, and my mother took me to my first job and I remember it was $28 a week, as a clerk at the Law Society in Sydney.

I found out while I was there that the girl on the switchboard, who operated one of those Sylvester switchboards—the ones that Lily Tomlin does when she does that character, the big plugs and everything, the hardest switchboard on the planet—I found out that

that job got you $60 a week. And it was also the show person in me, thought I'd be great at, 'Good morning, Australian Law Society; may I help you?' You know, the whole idea of me being the first person they speak to when they first ring.

It wasn't long between leaving school, getting a job, and then leaving home, to then being able to live on money from singing. It was all within a year.

A band singer

I've always been a band singer. I called myself a band singer because the best part of what I do is when I collaborate with musicians, and throw the ball around with them musically. That's what I started doing, that's what I still am; it's just that my name draws people in, but I still am a band singer.

My very, very first band was a band called Dry Red, and we played in wine bars ... Eric McCusker, who ended up being in Mondo Rock. And my MO in those days was pretty ruthless. I would figure out who the best musician in whatever band was and hook up and suggest we leave and join the next best band. So I sort of ruthlessly moved my way up the ladder of band success by grabbing the greatest musician of each band I was in and moving to the next best band.

So after Dry Red there was Sun, which was an incredible learning curve for me and it helped me with my inhibition, because I was inhibited. But joining a band whose heroes were John Coltrane, Thelonious Monk, avant-garde jazz musicians ... My thing was to scat and make sounds, as opposed to words, and whenever I'd see a band that had real songs I longed for a day when I'd be in a band where I get to sing, and I'll know where 'one' is on the beat.

An entertainer

Well, when you're born with a gift, you get the gift, but you don't always get the knowledge of the fact that you have been given this gift. So I could sing but I didn't know that I was an entertainer. I could sing, and hearing myself with the band, and coming out of the speaker, and we're creating something really great here, but the audience part was always very nerve-racking to me. Becoming an entertainer evolved after about twenty to twenty-five years.

I look at these kids on *Australian Idol* today and go, 'Wow, how did you do that?' It took me ages to be able to be comfortable on TV, on a TV set, on those Don Lane shows. It was a really unusual thing for a band singer to have to perform like a Shirley Bassey–type pop star.

Then it became evident that showbiz is in my blood and I am born to this, because the audience fed me, and what I was doing with the band was our treat for them. But the audience fed me and I can walk on to a stage with a migraine or have laryngitis or be very ill, and finish the show healed. That's when you know you're born to it. And I think Barry Humphries calls it 'Doctor Footlights'. Doctor Footlights, that's what it is: you're born to it, if you can get through. The show must go on, no matter what, and you're healed.

Rhythm and blues

From that band I joined Mother Earth, and Mother Earth is the beginning of the rhythm and blues ... of actually performing it and knowing that that's my life.

Rhythm and blues is just soul. It's just soul, and it's just from the heart. I mean, even Celtic music can be kind of soulful. Rhythm and blues is just soul, and that was all that was required of the musicians, that they had a yen for that sort of music and that they were open to 'throw the ball around' and let it go where it fell. And happy mistakes are something I love very much.

The *Man's World* record took me to Melbourne, and it's when Michael Gudinski and his partner at the time, Ray Evans, from

Mushroom records, found me and saved me from what was a potentially really dreadful record deal.

I was lucky to be with guys who were genuinely interested in the music. A lot of people asked me back in the early '70s, 'When you were singing "Man's World" people must have been quite shocked'. And I think for an Australian woman to be strong and singing in a man's style ... I just didn't know any better and I loved it, and if I pleased the musicians, and we all were cohesive, then my job was done.

Ready to Deal was the first album that I made completely from scratch with my band on Mushroom records, where we created, wrote, did everything, all in a six-week period. That album to this day is a classic. It's been sampled by people all over the world and the playing on it is extraordinary. And it is in the days before click tracks, so the things that those musicians did on that record are awe-inspiring, and we were a white Australian group sounding so soulful and it was a really great piece of music worldwide.

Difficult

It wasn't musically that I was ever told what to do, because what I did musically was what they wanted, so never have I done anything on a record that I haven't wanted to do. So any of the records of mine that are dogs are my dogs, no one else's fault; no one ever made me sing anything I didn't want to sing. But the press and the promotion surrounding anything was always like a job, and I was always told where to go, and you have to be here then, and do this then. And that was a chore for me because I never saw benefits of anything. It didn't occur to me that all this PR brings attention, therefore record sales, therefore money. I never saw money, so everything building up to all of this was a chore for me—and a boring chore because most people that interviewed me in those days were mental midgets, just morons.

The questions were so idiotic sometimes and I wasn't very good at hiding my disgust, and so therefore comes this reputation of this difficult person. Yes, I'm complicated, but I'm not really hard to get on with; it's only if they want to do something that I don't want to do that I become difficult. And so there was a lot of that in those days.

The Liberal Party ad

As part of the chore of doing promotions and things, my manager said, 'We'll do something for the Liberal Party and they're paying so and so money'. And I thought, Oh, that's good, I'll get more clothes and shoes and bags, and it didn't occur to me at that point ... my life was so filled up with music and 'Me, me, me, enough about me, let's talk about you: what do you think about me?' But anyway I didn't think about politics and all that sort of stuff, and most people who know me know that I am a little more left of centre ... very left of centre, especially with what's going on nowadays, but in those days I didn't really know the difference. All I knew is that my manager said, 'The Labor Party wouldn't pay any money: the Liberal Party are paying money'.

And it was the worst year I could've done something like that because it was that year that Fraser got in and Gough got the sack, and it was the 'turn on the lights' year. We realised when we went on our next tour, at a time when I was at a peak in my career, the houses were half if not a quarter full. It occurred then to my manager and to me, it became hugely clear, that my audience were not Liberal Party supporters.

First of all it was a learning thing for me that never again would I do anything, whether it's political or anywhere where I have personal opinions. I don't think I would ever do anything publicly about that because my music is there for itself, and if people like my music they should buy it because they like the music.

Blue-eyed soul

About '76 we were in America and I made an album. 'Heading in the Right Direction' was the actual single off that record. The whole of the east coast of America, 'black radio' picked that song up and was thrashing it. And this was in the days where black radio didn't play white music—'blue-eyed soul' hadn't come into being yet. There was no George Michael. I think Hall and Oates had just arrived on the scene.

So the record company suggested to me that we don't put my face on the cover and just let it seep into the consciousness enough so that at least when the penny dropped, people would have already fallen in love with the music and it doesn't matter what colour she is, it's okay. This is my cross that I bear, I insisted, out of anti-racial ... sort of like the other way around, but I'm white and I'm proud of being white, and I can't help it if I sound like a black woman. But I'm white, and why shouldn't my face be on the cover? Idiot! Id-i-ot. Because as soon as they saw the big pink head on the cover they just yanked the song and it hadn't been on long enough for people to really ... 'Well, it doesn't matter anymore; we just love her, you know', so that's all my stubbornness, that's my fault.

After going back and forth from America and living there quite a bit in the '70s, I ended up making an album in '80, *So Lucky*, on which was an Eddie Grant tune called 'Say I Love You', which I loved, and still love the record of—not crazy about it live, because it doesn't do much, but it's a great piece of music.

And that was probably the biggest single I ever had. I think it went to number two—never had a number one, but it went to two. And I remember being in America and I'd buy *Billboard* over there and I'd look at the Aussie charts and ... 'Oh, look!' So that brought me home until I left again in the mid '80s.

The '80s was musically horrible in Australia. It was a drought for rhythm and blues. So I packed up, I fibbed to my mother and said I had a job, got the money from the last two weeks of gigs, got on a plane, and went straight to New York and stayed two years in NY and about eight years in Los Angeles.

Working in America

Very tough! It's like, you know, taking coals to Newcastle. But, in the end, what propels anybody anywhere is great songs. No matter whether you sound like a Chinaman or a Celtic person or a person that sounds like a rhythm and blues person, if you are singing a great song and it touches people in some shape or form ... and, you know, some of the worst songs in the world, 'The Wind Beneath My Wings', for instance—I'm sorry to people out there who love that song. It was a huge hit. Certain things grab audiences and latch on. Great songs, and great performances are what it's about. And the way you get to that is by collaborating with musicians and then being very, very astute at looking, at listening and to new talent and listening to great new material.

Financially, it was really hard because I was unknown in America. But I would always come back to Australia to tour every seven or eight months.

I got signed to A&M and they moved me to Los Angeles, and I joined up with the boys who are my idols, the Average White Band. We ended up doing an album called *Easy Pieces*, which never saw the light of day because A&M ended up getting sold to someone. So it's a great album and a great trivial pursuit question, 'What do these people have in common?'

So, what I ended up getting going in Los Angeles was ... because I'm pretty good with background vocals, and because I had a very good low level to good mid to high range, and a pretty good ear for harmony, producers would hire me and they'd get one girl to do the job of fifteen girls. And I could make things up ... they'd have a little spot and go, 'We don't know what ...?' And I'd go, 'I know. I know exactly what you should put in there'. It culminated with probably the most well known thing I did … I sang on that solo record of Sting's, 'Together Tonight'.

Paul Kelly

Collaborating with Paul Kelly just enhanced my musical knowledge, in that I was always aware of the lyrics of a song, but having met Paul they became so much more important, and the actual beauty of the poetry in a song became so much more important to me. And so I've improved as an artist for knowing Paul.

I met Paul because of a record which was the soundtrack of an ABC mini-series called *Seven Deadly Sins*. Paul wrote a lot of the songs, and one of them was a song called 'Foggy Highway', which I sang and then went back to America. And I remember getting a phone call from Paul telling me how much he loved it and he was coming to America—this was about 1991. We've been friends ever since and he's been writing songs for me. Well … I had to squeeze the first one out of him. He'd written stuff for Kate Ceberano and all sorts of people, and I said, 'What about writing me a song?' And Paul tells the story better than anyone, that it was more like a command than a request. Then when he finally wrote the song, 'Difficult Woman', he called me to tell me about the song and wanted to come over and play it. And I said, 'No, tell me over the phone. What's it called? What's it called?' And he really wanted to explain it to me in person, and I insisted, and he said, "Difficult Woman". It's called "Difficult Woman"'. And Paul tells the story that it was probably the longest twenty seconds of his life. I was, 'Mmmmm …'

Of course, when I heard it, it's such a beautiful song and it's more about being complicated, and as he will agree, I'm sure I don't know a difficult woman that I don't like—there's no such thing as a non-difficult woman; it's just that you don't call men difficult; it's just that a woman that knows what she wants to do, they call them difficult.

He's a great writer. I think some of the best things that he's ever written have been when he's written for somebody else. And he's a great interpreter of anything to do with love, sex, death ... weather. He's got an uncanny way of putting things that a billion people have said a million times, but he has a way of making it sound like it's the first time you've heard it.

Time to come home

There was a big earthquake in early '94. I'd been through the one in '87 and there'd been a couple of others, but this one was seriously bad, and I remember standing there as the ground's rolling underneath me, thinking, Well, we're going to die, I just wonder how. Does the roof cave in, does the floor go, or do the walls come in? Then it stopped, and then the aftershock, and then darkness. And after five minutes faint sirens getting louder and louder and louder, but for that five minutes, black, silence. And my pussy cat, who was so freaked out that he wanted to be somewhere solid, squeezed himself between the cistern of the toilet and the wall, and I had to get a guy to come and help me get him out. Mr Big was his name.

So me and Mr Big, within one week we were out of there and in New York City. So I spent my last year back in New York and it was during that last year that Mr Big died, Jackie O died—and I loved Jackie O. I used to love every now and then going uptown, where you might see her on the street. I made a record with Paul Kelly and it was about to come out in Australia, and I thought, Time to go home.

ARIA Hall of Fame

[Renee was inducted into the ARIA Hall of Fame in 2005.]

Never received an ARIA. I've been nominated about a billion times. But I made mention of that, I have to say, because the whole ARIA board were in that room, so I had to say, 'Considering I've never gotten an ARIA in my life, it's nice to actually get one of these, for actually just living'.

You'd be a liar to say that you wouldn't be moved by the very people who are your peers putting you in the Hall of Fame. I mean, that's the greatest, highest level that you could be at.

A great moment

I sang with the Melbourne Symphony Orchestra a couple of years ago and my parents were in the audience. That was a great moment for me.

It was basically a musical autobiography of my career, with seventy human beings, including my rhythm section. So we sort of had this juxtaposition of guys that don't really read, with seventy people who only read, and then a conductor who had to deal with the two and me in between going … There's an Italian word that means 'Wait till ready, till ready'; there was a lot of that word going around, 'Till ready, wait till ready', because there's a lot of bits where we just let things just hang.

The wonderful Richard Mills, who is an incredible conductor, highly renowned with the MSO, was my conductor. And he came out in his dicky suit and his tuxedo, the whole thing, bowed, and it was like, you know, we ain't doing Mozart; we are doing 'Shaggy Ground'. And my parents were there; they flew down from Sydney. It's just very bizarre to me that it was all so formal. I mean … they make you go out and bow. Now rock'n'roll, you only go out if you're doing an encore, and you do another song and then seemingly you walk out in a huff—that's how I end my shows. I'm not actually walking off in a huff but the band plays me out, and I go, 'So long, get lost', you know, seemingly walking off in a huff. But with the MSO, they kept pushing me back on. I said, 'But I don't have another song'. 'No, no no, you bow.'

But my parents seeing … the second time I went out, the whole orchestra stood up, and the conductor, and bowed to me, and that for my father to see would have been ... It was bittersweet because I would have loved my parents to have lived through all of it with me and been on the journey with me. They kind of wanted to suppress it because they didn't think it would lead to anything good, so they don't really approve of my being in the music business and they didn't encourage it when I was young. So it was a bittersweet feeling, seeing them sitting in the audience, thinking to themselves; they must have just been floored. My father must have been, 'Wow, she's singing with the MSO, and they're bowing to her. Oh, ... she's good'. I don't know. All he could say when he saw me after the show was, 'You sound very good with violins'. And I think he told my mother, 'If I wasn't a man I would cry'. That's about as far as we got.

Latest album

I did an album a few years back called *Tenderland*, which consisted of existing soul classics that my audience have asked for over many years. And finally I turned fifty, 2003, and it just seemed the right time to do it. So I did it and it became probably my most successful record.

I thought, Well, there are a few that didn't fit on the last record that I could have a go at, but I would love to do that and have some original music as well that fits with the genre. As with *Tenderland* I produced it myself with the engineer, and the original songs ended up being two of Paul Kelly's. In the last fifteen years there's always been a Paul Kelly song somewhere in my music. And it comes out early October or late September [2007].

And then I'm going to tour everywhere. The packing of suitcases and catching planes ... I'm over that. But the reward is that at the end of each day there is an hour and a half of collaborating with musicians and that's the reason I'm still here. When the love of that is gone, I'll be gone.

Sleeping Beauty

With *Sleeping Beauty*, the play/musical at the Malthouse, Michael Kantor, in his wisdom, approached my manager, and my initial reaction was, 'No, I'm not a natural actor'. Then I was told, 'Look, it's the script of *Sleeping Beauty* all done in song'. To enter into that world after 35-odd years of just having my world—and when I walk onstage they're already there to see me—to step into a world where most of the people haven't heard me or seen me before, there was a lot of me having to prove myself all over again.

Discipline has been the big learning curve, and working with people that are actors … Somebody actually referred to me as an actor the other day and I thought, 'Wow, I'm an actor. Oh, that's nice'.

Nobody told me about the dancing … something tells me they did it on purpose halfway through rehearsals so that it was too late to get out of it. Having said that, as a child I always wanted to be a ballerina, so I have to say, considering I've never danced before, I've taken to it very well.

So I acted and sang and danced, and one of the reviews said, 'She acted, sang and danced very well', and I liked that. One of the reviews said that they thought the director was very clever in having the twist be that the parents were very elderly. I thought it was fantastic, because I've always, you know, been the ADD-type person, always act more like a child than a grown-up. So I liked being referred to as 'elderly'; it means people have to respect me and be nicer to me.

There is no price tag you could put on what I have picked up from being in that show. Eight shows a week, learning how to shut up when it's time to rest. Learning how to rest. Learning to reserve. When we go onstage in my world, rock'n'roll, I call the shots, so I can tailor. I can do two hours of singing, but I tailor it around me so by the end I'm bellowing. With theatre, you're on, then off, then on, then off, then on, then off … And it's just so much discipline involved. Never in all my thirty-five years in this business had I ever been in anything like it.

Today

I'm only getting good at what I'm doing. I'm good at delegating and getting really great musicians and passing the ball around. Any business where you're visually needed to be pleasing, it's ageist, and a lot of people get counted out. I was on a *Sydney Morning Herald* magazine in 1985 and it said 'Survivor' then, so what am I now? That's the kind of business we are in. But I'm still doing records and I'm with a major record label, and thank God for people like the guy that runs my record label, that he has faith in people that just make good music, no matter what their age.

In the last couple of years I've started tutoring young singers. I don't read and write music, so the people that I do tutor need to already be at performance level. My tutoring involves helping with interpreting a song in order to touch an audience.

I think I've been in this business a long time because I've been a really honest performer, as a musician. So if I've paid my dues on that level, then I've earned the right to come across like I want to come across, like I am. And so the only time I knock heads with people is when I'm asked to do things that are just not me.

I've had a couple of marriages that are finished. I'm on my own at the moment and very happy to be at the moment. Although, the door is always open. I always have hope. But, you know, I'm a kind of nutty person. I think you're lonelier if you're with the wrong person then if you're on your own. So I just choose to have a lot of male friends, and a lot of female friends. And I'm happy where I am at the moment.

I like to live alone, especially with my job. If there's a human being within any eye distance, I'm yapping. So, for my own good, for my throat, I need to live alone. And I also think that you would really have to be majorly in love in your fifties to then all of a sudden share your abode with somebody else, because you get your own way about you.

You do come to a point in time when it doesn't become like, 'Oh, I'm single and alone. Oh, woe is me'. You go, 'There's a reason I'm alone'. I'm a nightmare unless there is someone that is very special that can put up with what it is that I can dish out. But I'm worth it too. A lot of people that know me well enough always know that I might be a handful, but I'm worth it in the end.

DICK SMITH
Businessman and adventurer

Screened 7 May 2007

Adventurer and businessman Dick Smith has the real scouting spirit, with an attitude in life of throwing his whole heart into things ... 'dyb dyb dyb, do your best', as the Scouts used to say. Dick became a Cub Scout as an eight year old and credits the movement with encouraging a life-long sense of adventure.

> It allowed me to be involved in what I call responsible risk taking, and it was wonderful in those days. The Scoutmaster would come down with his truck; we'd all climb in the back with these great big patrol boxes and the huge tent poles and then go off 50 miles to the Blue Mountains, all just sitting in the back of the truck ... never be allowed today, but they were wonderful days. You learnt to take risks and to do it responsibly, and to be accountable for what you did.

Childhood

I was born Richard Harold Smith in 1944 in Roseville, which is a northern Sydney suburb. When I was born, my dad, Herb, was away at the war, so I lived with my mum, Joan, and my sister, Barbara, and I think I was eighteen months old before I saw my father.

My mum used to say to me, 'Dick, you march to the beat of a different drum', and I would disappear into the bush. But I remember saying to her, 'Don't worry, I will always turn up'. And I always did. I've sort of always been a loner, which some people would be amazed at, considering I'm in the media and that, but I just loved disappearing into the bush and I never understood what she meant. But I've never been any good in a group. I was never any good at sport. I don't even know the rules of cricket at the moment. Now don't tell anyone that because how can you be an Australian? I just developed ways of nicking off from sport, so I could go down the bush without anyone knowing. I really hated school in the early days. Sometimes my mum would take me to school, and I'd run home and get home before she got back. So I just liked being by myself.

In those days, in the 1950s, if you lived in Roseville ... I was allowed just to disappear into the bush when I got home from school, and it's amazing—you couldn't do that today. But my parents let me and it was just wonderful.

I think the influence was a loving family. My dad was quite strict, but my mum was really kind. I remember I used to have to do the washing up at night and I found out later she used to hide some of the dishes in the oven so I didn't have to do them. What a kind mother. Dad and Mum were always involved in the community—they were in the garden club, the Progress Association—and they taught me by example. They didn't have much money, but you put something back in, you rolled up your sleeves, and that was wonderful.

School years

I hated school. I had a speech defect until the age of about eight. I couldn't say the letter S, so I used to say my name was Dick Miff, and the kids used to laugh at me. Once a teacher took me out in front of a class and sent me to the principal, which really affected me. Luckily, the principal rang my mother. She said, 'Well, he can't say S'. I was hopeless at school. I left at fifteen and got a job in a factory and found that was even worse than school. And I went back and, it's interesting, I must have matured late, because in my fourth and fifth year, the last two years at school, I did quite well, and I ended up topping North Sydney Tech High in maths, and it was unbelievable.

When I was about five years of age, I looked quite Chinese and kids used to call me 'Ching Chong Chinaman'. And I remember I went home to my mum and said, 'I didn't like that'. And she said, 'You tell them that the Chinese had the first civilisation in the world'. It didn't help much. They were nasty to me, and I think it was because I was a bit different, a bit weird. I used to come to school with lizards and snakes and then bits of radio. And I think if you're different, well, you're sort of picked on a bit. Maybe I deserved it.

They just didn't understand, and I was too silly to communicate that it was hurting me. In these days it couldn't happen, I'm sure, but in those days it was just life and maybe it made me a better person because of it. It's made me a kinder person, I hope.

One year I even used to make up that I had a headache and one or two days a week I'd stay at home because I was scared to go to school, and no one's known that until now.

Scouts

I joined the Cubs at about eight years of age and I went right through scouting, became a Rover Scout, even won my Baden Powell award—the only qualification I've ever had, and it encouraged my adventurous spirit. And I used to read the *Famous Five* and *Biggles*.

Scouts 'made me', sort of thing, because it allows you to be an individual. People think, Oh, Dick must have been a patrol leader. No, in those days I was never a patrol leader; I was always just this loner there. But I did well in Scouts and I got my Queen Scout and the Baden Powell Award, and that was something which was quite fantastic.

The radio room

As a young boy I used to live opposite my maternal grandfather. My grandfather was Harold Cazneaux, the famous pictorial photographer. I used to go over and hold on to my mum's knee as she was retouching the photographs for Harold Cazneaux, and, of course, in those days, as a little five, six, seven year old, I didn't realise what a famous person he was. Now people know me as Harold Cazneaux's grandson. It makes me very proud.

Harold Cazneaux had a son, Harold Cazneaux Junior, who was killed in the Second World War. And occasionally I'd be given the key to Harold's room. I'd open up this room with the key and it was full of radio equipment. Harold was a radio enthusiast. When he died in the Second World War they'd locked the room up. So in the early '50s, five years later, I was allowed to go into the room, and it gave me my love for radio. Seeing the old speakers, the valves, I used to occasionally be allowed to take something or actually fiddle with the soldering iron. It gave me a love for radio, and that, coupled with my love for the out-of-doors, stayed with me for the rest of my life.

It had a great effect on me, and how lucky am I—if I hadn't had an uncle who was into radio, I probably would have never got into radio myself. But I always remember turning that key and seeing Harold's room and seeing this radio equipment. And from that day on, I started building things. I built my first crystal set when I was about eight, and then I built extra radios and even little basic computers when I was very young. I've never been any good academically, but I'm good practically, if I can understand something. And radio, of course, was what I turned into making my fortune.

My grandfather Harold Cazneaux was a businessman who made money out of pictorial photography. And [when I was] a kid, in the '50s he had this silver anniversary Buick that we'd go to the beach in. I think some people would have said he was wealthy from his own business, so maybe the genes came that way to let me be a businessman.

Business beginnings

I've always had a work ethic. My mum and dad, Joan and Herb, really didn't have any money. Dad worked in a publishing place, and then for Angus and Robertson, and Mum was a homemaker. I used to sell newspapers from the age of about eight, and one day I hit upon the idea of making money by selling white mice. I got a pair of white mice, and they bred very quickly, and I ran a little advertisement at school—I think it said, 'White mice at the Railway Station Pet Shop, ten and sixpence, but two and sixpence from Dick Smith'—and in the end I was selling lots of white mice. It was my first business.

I was working in a factory doing process work and all my friends had gone off to university. I went to one lecture at university and thought, I'll never get through that, and so I ended up in a factory. I was going to do electrical engineering. I realised that I just didn't have those academic abilities. And I thought I was a failure.

Some people would say that gave me the drive to prove myself, but I must admit I didn't really think that I was ever going to be able to do that. I thought they were different, they were better, and I was sort of inferior, and I would be running a small business for the rest of my life, and that was my lot in life. I was more surprised than anyone when one day my accountant said, 'Look, you're doing really well; you've made more money than the prime minister of Australia'. And I remember saying to him, 'Well, how come I don't have any money?' And he said, 'Because you've got more stock, and you've paid your tax and you've done this and that'. And I thought, Wow, that sounds fantastic.

I've always been a really hard worker. My dad worked hard and I've always worked hard. Where did I change from being a process worker to being a successful businessman? Somewhere along the way between the age of seventeen and twenty-five. I haven't worked for anyone since 1968, when I was twenty-four years of age. I've always had my own business.

In starting a business, I thought, Oh, having two or three people working for me would be great. I never thought it could be any different. So it wasn't as if I dreamt of becoming a millionaire or dreamt of becoming a pilot and flying round the world. It was beyond comprehension.

Meeting Pip

I was twenty-two when I came back from overseas after a backpacking holiday, and at one of the Scout functions I met Pip, who was a Girl Guide. She was an identical twin—sometimes you had a problem in picking whether it was Pip or Susie.

In 1969 Pip and I got married. She was only nineteen. But even before we got married, when we were still engaged, we started Dick Smith Car Radio. I had $600 and Pip had $10. We put it in together. I'd been working for Weston Electronics and they decided to stop fixing the Manly Cab radios and I thought, Well, who's going to fix them? And so for some reason I said, 'I'll fix them, I'll start a business doing it'. And I had no idea; I thought, I'll work in a small business, two or three people if I'm successful, and that will be my lot, because all my friends have gone off to university and they're going to be successful. We started at the Big Bear at Neutral Bay paying $15 a week rent. And that was the start of the Dick Smith empire.

Pip and I were goal orientated. We really worked hard right from the beginning, but we were incredibly naïve. We thought from the start that if we worked really hard that we'd do well in business and we thought 'doing well' was having three or four people working for us. And within a few years we had fifty people working for us and then 100, and within a few years the business was doing millions of dollars turnover. We were more surprised than anyone.

Pip has always run the finances, and in the early days she worked in town for about two years. She's a very competent secretary but then she came and worked with me. We've basically worked together ever since and it's been a fantastic combination.

Business lessons

When I was thirteen years of age, a very impressionable age, my dad opened a printing business. He had worked in a bookshop and then decided to start his own business. Within four or five months it went broke and he had a nervous breakdown, and ended up in bed. I used to come home from school and for six months my dad was lying in bed. So it's amazing to me that I ever wanted to start my own business. But my dad really wasn't a businessman. He was a lovely person, compassionate, very honest, but he really wasn't a businessman.

At one stage my business was in receivership, $18,000 of stock was stolen, and I was the lowest of the low. And in fact, it was only because we decided to trade the business out of its problems that I ended up making the money, because that Dick Smith Wholesale turned into Dick Smith Electronics, selling components.

I learnt two things. First of all, don't extend yourself too much, and by deciding to trade the business out of its problems and pay back the debt ... there was one accountant who said, 'Oh, just liquidate it'. And I said, 'But how would I live if Dick Smith owed money to people?' So I thought I'd pay back the debt and then close it down. But in paying back the debt, I realised that there was a lot of money in selling components, and that was the business which I ended up selling to Woolworths for over $20 million.

It showed me that if you do the right thing ... I'm not a religious person, but I believe in karma, that if you do the right thing, the right thing happens to you.

The face of Dick Smith

That was an accident. I never would have thought of doing that, and one day I was installing a car radio and I always asked the people, 'What do you do?' And this man said, 'I'm an advertising agent'. And I didn't even know what that was. I said, 'What's that?' and he told me what it was and I said, 'Well, look, I want to become famous around Sydney installing car radios, but I only have $50 a week to spend. And so he took a photograph of me, and came back with that famous bromide. We call it 'the famous Dick head', which now does $1 billion turnover a year, Dick Smith Electronics with that horrible head of mine.

He took that photograph and we started running little $50 ads, 'Dick Smith, the Car Radio Nut', and I suddenly saw by exploiting my name that I'd become famous. Originally, I was going to call the business 'Alltronics', and a relative of mine, Peter Garrett, who's in advertising, said, 'That's crazy, use your own name'. And I was so self-conscious, I said, 'Oh no, that wouldn't work. Can you imagine someone with a Mercedes coming into a place like "Dick Smith" to get his Mercedes radio fixed? They'll never do it'. Luckily, he said, 'Yes, they will; use your own name', and it was the best thing I could have done.

Success and ambition

Yes, I've had ambition. I've also never had a problem in asking advice. Because I haven't got any qualifications I've never had problems in copying the success of others and asking advice, and every bit of my success has come basically from that—copying other people, asking advice.

I wasn't ambitious with the aim of becoming a millionaire. I used to see millionaires and I thought, Oh, I don't like that; if ever I made that type of money I would never be a millionaire—I'd give it all to my staff. Well, that didn't happen, because I tried to bring in bonus systems and it failed. Some people work with incentive, other people don't; they just want a steady job. And I can understand that. So ambition ... always worked hard, and was more surprised than anyone that I did well.

Success

Dick Smith Car Radio expanded into electronic components and we ended up with fifty shops right round Australia, $50 million turnover. But I didn't really like the business when it was big. And I thought, If I'm not careful all I'm going to become is a Rupert Murdoch or a Kerry Packer and just be working all the time, making more and more money. So I decided to sell out.

One of the success forces that I always talk about is to surround yourself with capable people, and I was really lucky: a young nineteen-year-old Canadian came to work for me, Ike Bain, and we expanded the business together and ended up selling it to Woolworths in about 1982 for $25 million. It was just amazing; no one could believe it. But it allowed me to go out and go adventuring, and to do some of the things I wanted to do, and to put something back into society.

Lots of people say to me, 'How could you sell Dick Smith Electronics?' Well, I never thought that Dick Smith with the Dick head was actually me. I worked there and it was this wonderful adventure. And here I was, thirty-eight years of age, and I was going to sell my business for over $20 million. Now, it's a lot of money today; back then it was a tremendous amount of money. I couldn't believe it, and I thought, Well, I'll be able to go adventuring, I'll be able to donate money to charity. I used to hear about philanthropists—I can't even say the word—and I asked my mum what was that. And she said, 'Oh, that's a person who's done well and who gives money back to the community'. And I remember thinking, Oh, I'd love to be a philanthropist. So this allowed me to do that, and the best thing I ever did was selling Dick Smith's, moving on to something new.

An adventurer

By selling out the business, it gave me the freedom to do what I've always wanted to do and that's be an adventurer. I mean, as a little kid I was an adventurer, I used to disappear into the bush. And so at thirty-nine years of age, I had the money and I had the time to be able to go adventuring. In 1983 I attempted the first solo flight around the world in a helicopter. I couldn't have believed if someone ten years before had told me 'this is what you'll be doing'—it would have just been unbelievable. And here I was on the most wonderful magic carpet, flying around the world by myself, scared half the time. And I actually completed the flight, which was fantastic.

Fear is a big thing with my adventures. When I plan them I don't think I'm going to be frightened, but often when I'm on them, I'm scared. There have been numerous times on the flight around the world where I've thought, How can I put the helicopter into a container and ship it home? I'd sleep the night and the next morning I'd think, That wasn't so bad. Fear is part of the excitement. Some people get onto drugs, some people support the racehorses; my adrenalin is from testing myself. I'm a risk manager. I've flown five times around the world as a pilot, never been late or put a mark on an aircraft, never caused any search and rescue. I'm meticulously organised and I ask advice. I'm not saying that will happen forever. I'm more surprised than anyone when I end an adventure and I'm successful.

It's experience and it's instinctive and it's being careful, but knowing that you have to have risk to give the excitement. And that's the same in my greatest adventure—Dick Smith Electronics—

because it was a lot of risk. It was unknown, but it was successful in the end. It was very exciting. But once I'd finished that adventure, I sold it and wanted to move on to something else, like with every adventure.

Australian Geographic

In 1986 Pip and I founded *Australian Geographic*. We wanted to do a magazine that was positive about Australia and an equivalent to a magazine called *Canadian Geographic*. And it was very successful, which was great, and we were able to donate even more money to the environment plus couple the adventure with it, so it was just an ideal business.

I never thought *Australian Geographic* would get big. It ended up with, I think, 500 staff, and I thought, It's too big. I don't know anyone. I'm not good at running a big business; let's sell it. So I'm really a small businessman at heart. I like to know my staff and talk to them. That's what I'm good at.

Formula for success

There's a formula for being successful in business, and that's a very simple formula. Copy the success of others, ask advice, and work damn hard. Keep the overheads low, of course, but it's so easy. I've never had any problems in making money.

In those days [of Dick Smith Electronics] if you went to buy electronic components you'd stand behind a counter and it'd take an hour to get served. I went off overseas and found there were self-serve shops. So I just copied it. I also found that the businesses in America and England had a catalogue, so I copied those catalogues and brought one out here. We just copied the success and we did incredibly well. With *Australian Geographic*, people think I copied *National Geographic*, but I didn't. *National Geographic* is about the world. I copied *Canadian Geographic*, which was about Canada. I went and saw them and I said, 'Look, I'm thinking of doing something like this in Australia. Would you give me some advice?' And they said, 'We'd love to, it's a great idea'. And so they gave me advice. For my mail orders with Dick Smith Electronics, I was told *Reader's Digest* were the best with mail orders, so I went and asked them advice and they gave it to me. People love to be asked. Most of my Australian peers don't like to ask advice. I don't know what it is. I don't know why they don't, but that's how you can become successful.

Once it's big, the challenge is gone. I don't need the money; I'm comfortable. I've never been greedy in that way. And I want to have a life, I want to be with my family. I hear stories of these successful business people who have never had a family life. Well, I never allowed that to happen. I spent my time with my family because that's more important than anything. People say, 'Oh, my family's more important than anything, but I had to work eighty hours at the business'. That's ridiculous! Once you've got a certain amount of money and you have one bed to sleep in, one car, dare I say it, one aeroplane, you can't do much more.

I thought, I should go into politics, because I've done well and I have an obligation to put something back in. I didn't, basically, because I'm selfish. I would have lost my freedom to say what I want to say. And, hopefully, by being outside I can get into causes which are important, that are probably politically unpopular. And that can give me some satisfaction, from the outside.

I always thought I should have the responsibility to put something back into society. My mum and dad had no money but they were always involved in the Progress Association or the mothers' club— they rolled up their sleeves and helped. So that was the spirit, and suddenly I had more money than we could ever believe, and Pip and I decided, Well, we should use that money to do worthwhile things. And some of them were the drug education centre with Ted Noffs, which was incredibly satisfying. Putting money into the environment, so important, and then there's the social causes like the Salvation

Army ... All of them done because it's given us immense satisfaction, not only to have done well in Australia, but to be able to put something back in, makes you feel good.

A love of flying

I think it was reading *Biggles* books, and can you imagine, as a kid I'd see the vampire jets flying over. And then one day I had enough money in my business to actually learn to fly. That wasn't big money, it used to cost $22 an hour, and I'd go out about 5 am in the morning, all the way out to Bankstown before work, and do an hour flying, and I flew fixed-wing. I always found that boring because there was always a wing below you if you were trying to look out, and you could never land if you saw something interesting. And one day I got into helicopters, and it just changed my life, and I've been flying helicopters for over twenty years—keep them under my bedroom at home, and fly off around the world, or around the town, and it's just a wonderful way to travel.

My first flight ever, I think, was when my dad and mum had taken me with my sister, Barbara, to Forresters Beach, north of Sydney, and we saw a little joy-flight plane parked there. And I was taken on a flight with it, and I just couldn't believe it. And then when I started the business, one day I went to Melbourne and you could pay so many dollars and go in Reg Ansett's helicopter from Melbourne city to the airport, and I did that once, and I thought, That's fantastic. But I didn't think I'd ever be able to afford a helicopter.

A flying business? Look, I've said to Pip, you'd have to certify me if I ever tried to make money out of aviation. It's so interfered with by government, which is probably right, because there's the emotive issue of safety. But it would be very difficult to make any money out of it, because there are such high expenses, and they won't allow regulatory reform—most of these businesses can't make any money. And what's the use of being in a business if you can't make money?

I've been wise enough never to get into a business unless I know there's a good chance of success. In fact, I've never been on an adventure unless there's a good chance of success. And so far I've succeeded at all these things, because I'm realistic. Now to actually get into aviation, which would be great, and run a business, the chance of making it successful would be almost impossible, so I'm not going to do that.

A full-time adventurer

In 1993 Pip and I set off in a big Sikorksy helicopter, from our front lawn, to fly around the world. Now, when I'd done the solo flight, Pip was at home minding the kids and I'd always promised, 'I'll take you one day'.

So in our Sikorsky helicopter we flew right around the world—it took about eleven months—back to our front lawn. Pip took the most amazing photographs on the way and we published a beautiful book. So actually the book paid for the trip, so it was a working holiday around the world in a magic carpet.

During the trip we wore uniforms, because when we'd land at an airport, especially in the Middle East and places like that, people just wouldn't believe you were pilots, so I had my pilot's uniform, and Pip had to have a pilot's uniform or they wouldn't let her back out into the airport to get on the plane. They couldn't believe it was our aircraft.

For most of my forties and fifties I became almost a full-time adventurer—everything from ballooning to solar vehicle races to searching for lost aircraft—and it was the most wonderful adventurous life. I was incredibly spoilt.

Dick Smith Foods

One of my most exciting adventures—and some people mightn't call it an adventure—was opening Dick Smith Foods. Because, I just couldn't get over that Aussie farmers couldn't get their products onto supermarkets shelves—and I love the outback. I'm like most Australians: I live close to the coast but identify with the outback; and that's where our farmers are. And even though I'd imported electronics from overseas, that's because I thought the Japanese made the best electronics, but we grow the best food. So I started Dick Smith Foods and it was to sell Australian-grown produce produced by Australian factories, and it's been exciting. I think we have done over $200 million worth of business selling food. But it's very difficult and right at this time it's diminishing in its sales because the big supermarkets don't want to support small suppliers, and also, so many of our suppliers are being taken over by foreigners, we end up running out of people to get our products from.

It wasn't all smooth sailing, it never is, but you have a lot of fun. At one stage we got a biscuit called Temptin's because there was the Arnott's Tim Tams—now Arnott's was a wonderful Australian company that had been taken over by the Campbell Soup company in America. So we wanted to get some publicity on this. Our Temptin's created huge publicity because Arnott's took us to court, which was wonderful. Finally they withdrew, but they made our Temptin's just as famous as Tim Tams, which was good fun.

Aviation reform

One of my passions has been aviation reform, and it's been very frustrating for me because I've flown all around the world, hundreds of countries, and I've seen that Australia could be a leader in the world with flight training and recreational aviation, and I've never been able to succeed in that because so many of the bureaucrats tend to not want to take any notice of what's happening overseas. I find that frustrating because all of my success has come from copying the success of others, and I just know that if we copied some of the rules and regulations from overseas, we could employ thousands more pilots, we could have a booming aviation industry. As it is I go out to Bankstown airport and there's hardly anyone flying. We've almost destroyed our wonderful industry that Kingsford Smith started.

I was delighted when Bob Hawke appointed me as chairman of the Civil Aviation Authority. I then later became chairman of the Civil Aviation Safety Authority. Each time I was able to do some reforms but only about 20 per cent of what should be done, what is necessary for Australia, because everyone would come out attacking. The unions and the business people—everyone resists change in aviation. It's very sad because we could employ so many more people, and it would be so much better for country Australians to be flying rather than going by road.

I wasn't everyone's favourite boy and in '99 I resigned as CASA chairman, basically because there were just too many attacks and we weren't getting anywhere. But 2002, I think, I was appointed on an aviation reform panel, and I'm hoping soon to be able to get involved back in aviation reform because it's a passion and I think it's so neglected. The current government has no vision about aviation and that's a real pity.

My approach with aviation reform is so simple and it's where I got my success in my other businesses. Look around the world, copy the best ideas, bring them back to Australia and put those ideas into one system, and you can't fail. Unfortunately, with aviation, there's so much resistance to change, it's almost impossible.

I have this delusion—I'm sixty-three—that when I'm seventy, I believe I'm going to be called by someone saying, 'Look, come and do this reform that you've been telling us about for twenty years; it's obvious that it should be done'. We're the best country in the world for aviation. We've got airlines, they're pretty good, but the general aviation, the flying schools, the recreational aviation, the small commuter people, they're nearly destroyed. They could be booming, we could be leaders; and that's what I want to do. I want to get lots more people flying, lots more people employed.

The problem is that people don't want change. We used to have this incredibly regulated system funded mostly by the taxpayer. The Labor government in 1988 said, 'No, it's going to pay its own way'. In fact the air traffic control system even makes a profit for government now. So I said, 'Well, in that case you've got to get modern regulations, get the cost down'. That hasn't happened, so we just end up with less and less people flying. You go now to country towns and there's no flying school there anymore, and it's just terribly sad, because we have the best weather in the world, the best terrain ... we could have people coming from all around the world learning to fly here.

I've done 8000 hours of flying. I fly jets single pilot. I'm experienced. I've been able to have the time to travel the world and to ask advice, which normal aviators can't do—they're working in a job. So I've had that ability to do that. And also, pilots and air-traffic controllers are generally picked psychologically to follow rules. We don't want lateral thinkers flying our planes. But every decade, or every couple of decades, you need someone to come along and say, 'Are we doing things the best way?' And that's what I'm good at. I'm good at lateral thinking. So there needs to be a combination of both, and I'm very happy to have the pilots resisting change, as long as we can get some change, using commonsense.

David Hicks

Over the years Pip and I have been very fortunate to be involved in a lot of charitable issues and social issues, especially people, Australians getting a fair go. One of the most important issues is David Hicks, who's been rotting in a jail in Cuba for over five years. I've been assisting the funding of his legal team so we can get him a fair trial, and that's a trial with a jury. I'm not a supporter of David Hicks but I am a supporter of Australians being treated fairly wherever they are in the world.

I know I'm going to win this one, and it's going to give me immense satisfaction because, even if he is a really bad boy, he has been treated fairly as an Australian. And to me a fair go is probably the most important ethos—as an Australian. I have a feeling he's not a terrorist at all—he's just a stupid young man who was at the wrong place at the wrong time—but we should find that out properly. We should find that out properly because it could be any of our sons, and we allow the terrorists to win if we start turning on ourselves and don't use due process and fairness.

Life today

I'm very fortunate because most people think, Oh, successful businessman, he probably didn't see his kids at all. Well, I was so lucky, when Pip and I grew Dick Smith Electronics and Dick Smith Car Radio, I made sure that the business was only about 100 metres from where we lived and I'd even come home for lunch. And even when I flew around the world I organised my family to come and meet me in different places. I just loved being with my family.

Now I have grandchildren, which is absolutely fantastic. And everyone is healthy, so it's wonderful. I think the most important thing is family. I had a wonderful close family with my mum and dad, Herb and Joan, and I want to continue that right through to our grandchildren, and maybe even great-grandchildren one day. Right now my grandchildren are learning to swim in the swimming pool at our home. They come up because they don't have a pool themselves.

Pip and I have been married thirty-eight years. Wow! I first met Pip when she was seventeen years of age and at school. We've had a wonderful life together and I think having a loving wife is incredibly important, and very important for success.

My business is still ticking along only it's a lot smaller now. I only have three or four people working for me. Pip and I, when we sold Dick Smith Electronics to Woolworths and then *Australian Geographic* to Fairfax, we put our money into some commercial buildings and that's how we earn our living. I sit at my desk, working on Dick Smith Foods, of course, but also I get lots and lots of letters from people asking for money. I can help some, which is very satisfying.

Too slow

There's no computer on my desk because I don't believe in them. I use a computer a bit, but look, I don't know if you've ever found this with a computer, but if you ask it something, it can sometimes take ten or fifteen seconds before the answer comes up. Now, I don't have that time to waste. So to me, they're just completely useless, and until they make them instant, like opening a book or asking you a question—you'll answer me straight away—too boring and too slow.

In the early days I used to sell a lot of computers. Ours was the leading company for selling computers, but I still believe they were pretty useless. And people used to say, 'Well, how can you sell them with a free conscience?' And I said, 'Ours are cheaper, so if you want to waste your money, you waste less money with us'. So I always had no problem in making millions of dollars out of them.

Google's fantastic, and Google Earth, so you can plan your adventures, I mean, that's good. But generally, computers, I mean, people are obsessed with them, with the emails backwards and forwards and things like that. Nah, too slow, too boring.

I still build electronic bits and pieces; I'm still an enthusiast. I once built a noughts and crosses computer that would play noughts and crosses using old telephone parts. I was very proud of that when I was a kid, but modern computers, too slow. If they make them a bit faster, that'll be okay.

Dreaming up future adventures

I read, I go walking in the bush. I fly, I mean, there's only ... how many hours? I don't know how many hours there are in a week, but there are not enough.

My love of the outdoors has only grown stronger as I've got older. I still love bushwalking. I bushwalk every day. I must admit I still occasionally hug a tree. And it recharges my batteries and I think that the most wonderful thing is that even if you don't have any money you can walk out into the bush. In Sydney we have a national park to the north and one to the south—we're the luckiest people on earth.

I've read Steve Fossett's autobiography. I've been down climbing over the ice cap in South Georgia following Shackleton's routes. I've naturally read the book on Shackleton. I've been reading books on aviation pioneers. I've read recently Richard Branson's book. I think that's quite motivating, quite an incredible person. I love books by Dame Mary Durack. I love books about Australia. I mean, we're a wonderful country.

My life changed in 1973 when I learnt to fly a helicopter. I'm very fortunate: I can head down to the front lawn, take off in my helicopter to just about anywhere in the world. And the beautiful thing is, it's like a magic carpet: you see the magnificent Australian scenery. Even though I love the ground, I'm probably my happiest when I'm in the air; it's where I've had some of my most fantastic adventures. And to see Australia and the world from the sky, I just realise that I'm one of the luckiest people alive.

And this, of course, is where I dream up my future adventures. I'm still only sixty-two—just a kid. I dream about them when I'm walking, and when I'm flying, and all the time, you know. I'm an adventurer at heart and I dream of these things. I'm planning a flight at the moment over K2, the second highest mountain in the world. I flew around Mount Everest; I thought I should fly around K2.

I built a solar dog: it's a solar-powered little car that maybe will take me to the South Pole, but Pip says it's just a dream and I'm too old for adventuring like that. But more walking, and there's a few secret ones I don't want to talk about.

My energy must come genetically. My grandfather Harold Cazneaux was a livewire. I don't think I'm that energetic, but I still have to have four or five things on at once to be happy.

Giving money away

I get lots of requests and can only help 1 per cent. But what a fortunate situation to be in, where people are harassing you for money, and they're normally lovely people who are writing letters, people with disabled kids who want a vehicle or something like that. I'm honoured to be asked, and Pip and I feel disappointed that we can't help everyone.

But we've been fortunate; for the last ten years we've always given at least $1 million a year away. And we're proud we pay over $1 million tax a year, and I can tell you, if you still pay over $1 million tax, and you've given $1 million away, most of which is tax deductible, you're not really suffering, are you? You're doing okay. So we've been very fortunate and I get immense satisfaction out of paying tax, because we have fantastic roads, schools, defence and all the rest of it. And even more satisfaction when Pip and I can help people who are less fortunate. I tell you what, one day they'll help us when we're less fortunate.

Looking ahead

Inheritance ... look, what we've decided, we will give our girls some money so they're comfortable, and we're loaning the money for their businesses which they're working on. But at the normal bank interest, because I think they would be really horrified just to be given large amounts of money. And our plan is to give our money, the bulk of the money, away to a charity. And hopefully I'd love to give it all away before we die, because then you get the satisfaction from it.

I am a bit pessimistic about the future. I don't see how capitalism can reconcile with a closed environment that we have. So I think the system's got to collapse, but hopefully it's quite a few generations away. Every civilisation has destroyed itself. And the fact that human beings are on this earth now is because we've removed anything that's threatened us. I don't know if we can actually change. I'm hoping we can. We're very well educated now and there is a chance, if we can raise the standard of living of countries like China and India and Africa enough so the population growth goes down, we could solve the problem and we might have in front of us 1000 years of wonderful times when we're living in harmony with our environment. Wouldn't that be great? I somewhat doubt it.

I've been so fortunate. I mean, to be born in Australia in the '40s is winning the lottery of life. And to have been successful when I never thought I could be. And I have the most wonderful freedom to say what I want to say, and I think I'm just the luckiest person alive.

I don't really care if I'm remembered. I donate money away, but there's no Dick Smith Foundation; I don't want anything like that. I donate money for selfish reasons: it makes me feel good. So I don't want to be remembered in any way. It'd be great if Dick Smith Electronics lasted. It's lasted for, what, forty years or so. Wouldn't it be wonderful if it lasted a long time, employing thousands of Australians? It now does $1 billion a year turnover. I'm really proud of that. It's owned by Woolworths, a great Australian public company, and that's the proudest thing to me, to start a little business that now employs tens of thousands of Australians that's doing well and is owned by Australian shareholders. I think it's wonderful.

> I think I'm most proud of creating a business that employs lots of people, that's always been honest, that's got a good name, and that's owned in Australia and basically the profits stay here with Aussie shareholders. I really love that. It shows that everything doesn't have to be American, you know America's a great country, but I really think we should own our own things, and we should try and keep profits here, and we should be proud in our own way.

NANCY-BIRD WALTON
Aviator

Screened 10 April 2006

Nancy-Bird Walton is one of Australia's true living legends. She wanted to fly from the age of four, and was taught to take the controls by Charles Kingsford Smith himself. In 1950 she formed the Australian Women Pilots' Association so women who flew would have a friend in every state. Nancy's lifetime as a pilot has seen aircraft progress from canvas, wood and wire to the new generation of super jumbos. Now in her nineties, she remains passionate about the beauty of flying.

> They say something happens to my face and my eyes when I get in an aeroplane, but I'm not aware of it. I think it's just the exhilaration of flying, the freedom of the air, the freedom of flight. You completely remove yourself from the world, and you can voluntarily remove yourself from everything that's near and dear to you. And you voluntarily return.
>
> You're completely and utterly responsible for yourself. The beauty of the air, from the air ... you haven't seen Australia unless you see it from the air—the coastline, the colours of the inland, the claypans, the forests—it's just all so beautiful. You'd never see that from the road. People climb mountains to see these things. You see that every time you take off.

Wanting to fly

When I was young, I did imagine I could fly. When I had nightmares, and tigers and lions were chasing me, I could lift myself above them ... and they'd run underneath! And also on the swing, I'd say, 'Push me higher ... Push me higher. I'm a bird. I want to fly'.

I was born in Kew on the north coast of New South Wales. And at the age of about one or two we moved to Kendall. And then we moved to Collaroy, Dee Why and, finally, Manly. I was born at the same time aviation started coming to Australia. Six hundred servicemen who'd gone away as light horsemen with the Australian forces came back to Australia as pilots, and they wanted to bring aviation to this great, vast land. They could see the possibilities of it, and the need for it.

Even at four years of age, I was climbing the back fence, jumping off and calling myself an epiplane. The only reason a child of four would've known that would've been the conversation of the adults, and, of course, that was the year, 1919, that the Vickers Vimy was the first aircraft that successfully flew from England to Australia. You can just imagine the excitement of people when they got the newspaper each day predicting 'those darn fools' wouldn't get to Karachi, you know, 'they'll never make it to Darwin' and so on, and I was swept up in the enthusiasm, even then. And anyhow, they arrived—they completed the flight, which was fantastic.

I think the first aeroplane I saw was from the school grounds at Manly, doing some skywriting over the harbour. I can remember being late into school because I was watching, and a sewing lesson was on and I was making a pillowslip or something and I got into trouble for being late. But I must have been absolutely fascinated by air, and I wanted to learn to fly. Nobody thought I'd ever do it.

A practical child

I was the second eldest of a family of six. And my elder sister was the star. She was the clever one, and she was the one who became a prefect at school. And she had her own bedroom. I shared a bedroom so I was a bit untidy as a result. And I was very glad to have her hand-me-downs later on, especially when I was out west. But if you're the second eldest of six, you help with anything. You're helping your mother all the time, because she needs help. The potatoes needed peeling, I peeled potatoes. If the nappies needed hanging out, I hung the nappies out. If the place needed sweeping, I picked up the broom. I was the practical one, and that's probably why I was selected by my father to be his offsider in his business in the Manning River.

My father ran the general store in Mt George. He was a very hardworking man. He believed in working sixteen hours a day. And he thought everybody else should. He had to have somebody to help; he needed somebody who could cook and he needed somebody who could housekeep and he needed somebody to help with the books. I didn't like school very much to be quite truthful, and I was only too glad to have something worth doing. I started working when I was not quite fourteen. There was no running water, there was no electric light, there were no facilities whatsoever, but you accepted that in those days. You tipped the tank to see if there was enough water, had a bath once a week, washed in a big basin every morning, cold water. Oil lamps had to be washed every morning, and there was no refrigeration, of course. Boiled things in a copper, hung them out on a line. Mother stayed in the city for the education of my brothers and sisters.

A mother's influence

It's taken me ninety years to realise how very much I got from my mother. People talk about their fathers, but they very seldom refer to their mothers, and it's often from your mother that you get all the good things, like a good reasonable education, even if you don't go to school. You get an appreciation of good music, classical music—my grandfather was an associate of the Royal College of Organists and largely responsible for bringing the London College of Music to Australia—a good religion, a good background in religion, etiquette, good manners, respect for other people; all those things came from my mother.

She loved pretty things, she loved beautiful things. She couldn't afford very much but she never left the house without a posy for somebody in her hand, or a batch of scones. Generosity. All those things were things that I learnt from my mother, but I didn't realise it until years later, until, as I say, at ninety years of age I realised what a tremendous contribution she made to my life.

She paid for our education. We had private college educations and I think they were legacies she'd got from her family in England. I think that probably even paid for my father's business in the Manning River. But, you didn't know those things in those days. You didn't know it was your mother's money that was providing your home and your education. It was just there.

Learning to fly

My chance to fly came when I went to an air pageant at Wingham, and took a ten-shilling flight with Reg Annabel. That was the thing that convinced me that I must fly. I paid him an extra pound to do aerobatics for me, so he took me up and did loops and spins and all sorts of things. My sister said I came down looking a bit green, but I just loved it. Flying was the ruling passion of my life.

I bought a book on learning to fly, Frank Swoffer's *Learning to Fly*, an English book. I studied it very closely. There was a boy who rode a horse across the paddocks in the Mt George area every night to read the paper and he'd learnt to fly and he told me to get this book. His name was George Campbell. He had done a little bit of flying and was the only person who didn't think I was crazy.

My parents just thought it was a childhood dream or something, I suppose. Nobody thought I'd ever do it.

When I came down to visit Mother, I went out to Mascot in

1930 and had a trial instruction flight with Captain Leggett. And that convinced me that that was what I wanted to do. So I bought myself a flying helmet. I was so thrilled that I came home and told my father I wanted to learn to fly. He didn't discourage me. He said he didn't mind if I had a few lessons. Of course, he knew I was 200 miles from the nearest aeroplane and not old enough to learn to fly. But anyhow, at fifteen, when I came again to visit my mother, I went out to Mascot and had the first flight in 1930 at the Aero Club, that was it. I knew that this was what I wanted to do. So I went back to the country to grow up and to save up.

When Charles Kingsford Smith opened his flying school at Mascot I was one of the first, if not the first, to sign up for flying lessons. He was rather preoccupied with going off to England to attempt the England–Australia record, so he only gave me my first few lessons, then he handed me over to Pat Hall, his chief instructor, a very excellent instructor.

There were no runways. There was no control tower. You just opened the throttle and taxied out and faced into wind and took off. There was no planning or anything about it; you kept your eye open for other aircraft coming in or going out, but there weren't very many. We mostly took off to the south, as the wind was often in the south or southwest. By the time you got around, did your left-hand turn and it was time to turn into the airport, you smelt the tannery, and the tannery was such a terrific smell that it was a wonderful landmark. You just turned there, and started your S-turns into Mascot.

I asked Tommy Petherbridge, who died with Smithy, to teach me engineering, and they thought, Ah, a woman learning engineering, what a laugh; give her some spark plugs to clean, give her the dirty work, that'll put her off. So I donned a pair of overalls and started cleaning spark plugs of the *Southern Cross* in black petrol with a wire brush, no machines in those days, and then I learnt to grind in a valve, and hemstitch the fabric after the inspections and so on.

And then when they talked about flying boats coming in, well, I learnt semaphore from a young army officer, and PG Taylor asked me to teach him semaphore.

Smithy was a very likeable person. He was generous to a fault. His colleagues had a very great respect for him. And he was happy-go-lucky and pleasant company but a very, very great adventurer. I don't know that he was particularly keen about instructing, and when I was instructed by him, he was planning the England–Australia record in the Percival Gull, but when I finished my lessons he just said, 'You're okay, you'll learn'.

I started flying on 11 August 1933. And I got my 'A' licence on 27 September 1933. Then I had to get an advanced 'A' so I could carry passengers. And then I had to wait until I was nineteen, and had 200 hours solo, before I could sit for my commercial licence. It was a great feeling of achievement. I really felt I'd done something.

I didn't meet the people, or have the opportunity to meet people, that I was likely to marry. I was dedicated, very dedicated to aviation.

There were no jobs in aviation for the boys—not even Kingsford Smith. The prospects were very, very poor. I had to make a job for myself in aviation because my parents had bought me an aeroplane, which was quite a big thing for them.

I must have told my great aunt, because the great aunt did tell my father she would put up £200 if he could match it, and we could buy a second-hand aeroplane, and that's how I got my Gypsy Moth. It was being rebuilt from a crash; it was a bit of a rattle trap. It took off on its test flight from Mascot aerodrome and landed on the golf course just over Cooks River with a forced landing, fortunately with a chief instructor flying it. And so it was towed back. We christened it with a bottle of champagne. My little aunt stood in a box and broke it over the propeller, which of course you shouldn't do. Then it had to go back into the workshop, and I worked on it.

Barnstorming

I read in *The Country Life* newspaper of all these shows and race meetings all around the country that follow one another—Tamworth, Inverell, Warialda, Boree and so on—and I decided to land in the nearest paddock to them. Everybody said, 'You can't make a go of it, barnstorming around the country; it's been done to death after the First World War; there's nothing in it'. But I had nothing, I had to do something.

I went to the Shell company, and told them what I wanted to do. They were just absolutely marvellous, gave me a credit card. I could use as much petrol as I wanted, even though I didn't have two bob to my name. So I organised this tour to follow the country shows.

I found a co-pilot, a very good co-pilot, another woman. You wouldn't have dreamt of taking a man around the country in those days; there would have been a scandal. And I was very lucky ... most of the women who flew in those days were women of independent means ... all of them who flew were, and they weren't interested in barnstorming round the country. But Peggy had done the same exam as I had done, commercial licence.

Peggy McKillop was a member of a distinguished family in Orange, the Dorkham family, and had even been accused of being 'wicked' learning to fly, because she was an only child. But she was so keen on flying that she agreed to come with me and, of course, she didn't have to be paid. But I told her I'd give her 10 per cent of the takings if there were any, and so we set off together on this tour.

They told me that I couldn't make a go of it. 'You'd be lucky if you got ten shillings.' Well, I was perfectly happy with ten shillings. So long as I could keep flying, and build up time and experience, I was happy.

People would come to see the aeroplane, but had no intention of flying. They were a bit nervous about flying with a couple of women pilots. And my job was to talk them into flying. And you could get people to the stage where they'd even dare one another to fly with 'one of those girls', you know. He'd say, 'I won't go up myself, but I'll pay for my friend. Bring him down green, won't you?'

'Big Bird' and 'Little Bird'

We didn't call ourselves that we were called that from Inverell. The first place we went to was Tamworth, where the mayor was so thrilled to have two young ladies land in the town. The next day we had a civic reception and we had no sooner finished the biscuits and tea than he popped us in his car and took us up the nearest hill to see the view. We'd only been circling it the day before, round and round and round.

And then onto Inverell—and that's where we were christened 'Big Bird' and 'Little Bird', because we were given a dance program and invited to the ball, the race ball. And all night long I had the handsomest men saying, 'Are you Big Bird or Little Bird?' And that's the sort of thing that happened all around the country.

It was very enjoyable. You had the air to yourself; I had the whole of western NSW to myself, just about. There was no other aeroplane there—when the weather was bad you'd have to get right down on the road or the railway line to know where you were going, and hope nobody else was flying in the opposite direction. They were your lifelines: navigation was by compass on the floor and a pencil and the Shell road map.

There weren't many women pilots, certainly none travelling around the country. Women flew only as a sport, and they were almost entirely well-to-do women who had some connection with aviation, or their husbands or boyfriends did, and they gathered at the aero club and socialised and had a little flying. They even had an air race at one stage. But I wasn't in that category at all; I had to make flying pay for itself.

Beyond Bourke

When I was in Dubbo, I met the Reverend Stanley Drummond, who was the superintendent of the Far West Children's Health Scheme. And he asked me if I would go to Bourke and station my aeroplane there and do their regular clinic service, outback and beyond Bourke every six weeks, and also be there for ambulance work if it was required ... fly a doctor out or a patient in. And that's how I started work with the Far West Children's Health Scheme. It was the first time a woman pilot had ever been used commercially in Australia.

All the women who flew in those days ... several of them got commercial licences; in fact, Phil Arnott was the first to get a commercial licence, but of course she never used it: she came from a wealthy biscuit family. But I had necessity, the greatest of all incentives. I had to earn a living, so I had to use mine. And it took sixteen and a half years before they gave another woman pilot a paid job in aviation.

Once I was stationed at Bourke, my job was to do anything I was called upon to do, to help people in emergencies, in illness, or transporting anybody when the roads were impassable and things of that sort. I was just available for anybody who wanted me; or if the Far West Children's Health Scheme wanted me, of course they took preference. It was only when there was an emergency that I operated as an ambulance, because I could only carry a patient and a doctor. I had bought a Leopard Moth, a cabin aircraft, so I could do this.

I was living at the hotel, which was unusual in those days for a woman to live on her own at the hotel. But the owner of it, Mrs Fitzgerald, gave me a very special rate of £2 a week for full board for the children's health scheme. And I'd get up, and first of all if I could do anything on the aeroplane—like cleaning it—I would walk to the hangar. And I remember I wore a topi, and I remember the manager of the local store saying, 'Hat, where are you taking that little girl?' But I would then work on the aeroplane, see that it was fuelled up and everything and get somebody to help me to pull it. I couldn't pull it out on my own. But the Shell man would probably come out and help me pull it out and fuel it up.

That's when I really flew under conditions that nowadays people laugh about: no engineers, no radio, no landing ground. Bourke had a landing ground then, but you picked a lot of landing grounds from the air, you know, claypans or open spaces that you flew over a couple of times to see there were no logs or anything lying across the path.

You'd land in any paddock that you could find. If people were expecting you, I'd often ask them to run a truck over the ground at 40 miles an hour into wind, and that would make enough dust for you to get your wind direction. And you landed behind it: you'd know that the truck would get the stumps first and it was safe to land in that spot. But you just picked them from the air and that's what you did.

I flew on the Shell road map. And there's not much on it west of Bourke, I can assure you. A few lines like the border fence and things like that, they're good landmarks. You just develop a sense of direction and you make a few mistakes that teach you quite a lot.

We'd been taught in those days to land an aeroplane on the top of trees without killing yourself or to land in a very small space and take the wings off the aeroplane if you can't stop it, and things like that. I was very, very well trained to cope with that country. I remember the instructor saying, 'You always have a landing ground in sight'. That's a bit hard to do sometimes, but it's amazing what you could land on if you had to. Stay with the aeroplane and land it. Even if you've got to land it on the top of trees or in the water or whatever ... if you're landing and you've got trees ahead of you, try and get it so you take the wings off with the trees and that'll slow you down. There are all sorts of things you learn to save yourself in an aeroplane crash.

I was a very safe pilot. I was too conservative, probably. I didn't get the best out of an aeroplane, by using it for display and showy things. But I didn't, I was a very conservative pilot.

The only time I've felt fearful was when I had taken off from a place that we'd had to clear a few trees and things away from, little trees to make a spot to take off from. I was frightened the wind would change. Took off, got into the air, and the engine started running roughly. And I had to go back and find that little strip that we'd created, and land in it again.

A cabin aeroplane

I had to buy a better aeroplane for charter work because you've got to take two people, a stock buyer and his agent, and for ambulance you've got to have a cabin aeroplane to take a doctor and a patient. And that's when I chose a Leopard Moth, which was the Cadillac of the light aeroplane ... beautiful aeroplane with a cruising speed of about 110 to 120 miles per hour and low fuel consumption, very reliable engine. And I did the rest of my flying in that. It landed in a very short space, a few hundred yards; it also had very good take-off and it also had brakes, which of course the Gypsy Moth didn't have.

I always wore a dress once I got a cabin aeroplane. With the Gypsy Moth I had to have overalls because it was an open cockpit aeroplane. But once I got the cabin aeroplane I always wore dresses because people expect you to look like a grease monkey, and I went the opposite way. I always looked feminine. I wore feminine clothes. As a matter of fact, most of the clothes I wore were hand-me-downs from my elder sister, and not quite suitable for flying in, but that didn't matter.

I was stationed at Bourke for about twelve months. But then I moved into Cunnamulla for financial reasons, because I was paying off an aircraft and they offered me free accommodation. And it was only about another 100 miles north. And that suited me better to operate from there. Also the Far West Children's Health Scheme subsidy of £150 a year was withdrawn by the government, and they could no longer afford to pay me.

I've never made any money out of flying. I ended up with the capital I started with—£400. But I led a very interesting life.

'My God, it's a woman!'

That was in Cunnamulla, actually. I walked into a stock and station agent's office one morning as he was speaking to his client on the phone. He said, 'You won't get out, it rained heavily last night, the road's impassable'. He [the client] said, 'I've got to get out'. He said, 'I'll send the aeroplane for you'. He didn't even know there was an aeroplane in the district. So he said to me, 'Take the phone, get some landing instructions'. So I took the phone, said 'Hello'. Dead silence, and he gasped, 'My God, it's a woman'.

I must say, as a nineteen-year-old, twenty-year-old girl I didn't realise until I had children of my own what it meant to some of those women who lived … When I went back there and they named the terminal after me, a man came up to me and said, 'You know, you saved my life'. I said, 'What did I do?' He said, 'I was a premature baby and you flew the doctor and the equipment out'. Another one came up and said, 'You were my first Santa Claus'. I said, 'What did I do?' He said, 'You brought out toys to us at Christmas time, and we'd never seen toys. And you gave me a pop gun'. And here's this bald-headed gentleman telling me about the pop gun I'd taken him out. Things like that, that you didn't realise. And as I said, I didn't realise until I had children of my own that that woman who lived 130 miles northwest of Bourke and had a baby, the whooping cough, or she thought it might be whooping cough, and she couldn't face the journey into Bourke, six or seven hours on the road. When I had my first child, I had not one but twenty-one doctors within a telephone call. But women said to me, you know, 'You can't know what it meant to us to know there was an aeroplane there that could bring a doctor out if we needed it'.

In 1936 I entered the Brisbane–Adelaide Air Race. It was such a wonderful thing to be able to do, to take part in an air race, and associate with all the colleagues I'd known at Mascot and throughout eastern Australia, and so I decided I would take part in it. I decided to fly solo in the race. I had a fairly newish aeroplane and I weighed about 7 stone 7, I think. I flew into Brisbane, I joined the crowds there. I made a lifelong friend of Arthur Baird, the chief engineer of Qantas, who looked over my engine for me and said I was the only person who paid him the bill before I left. I did fairly well in the race for times, and the fastest time of all starters between Melbourne and Adelaide, which was a great surprise to me. But I had surveyed the course: I had taken my little sister with me and flown the course beforehand. Reg Ansett won the race and said it gave him the money to start his airline.

I left Australia in 1938 because I couldn't see any future for a woman pilot in Australia. It would have meant an extra expense to the airlines if they had had them in the cabin crews or anything. 'Biologically unsuitable', that was one of the excuses they had. I went to England as the guest of the Dutch airlines to try and fix myself for a ground job in aviation. But because I'd organised an exhibition which I showed in Sydney and Melbourne, I had to come back to Australia when the war started. If I'd stayed in England I'd have probably been in the Air Transport Auxiliary. But today I am so proud to think that women pilots are everywhere. There are sixty-four on the flight deck of Qantas, and eleven of them are captains.

A shipboard romance

I met my husband on a ship, the first time I separated from an aeroplane. It was a complete coincidence that it happened at all. I was on a ship in Lake Mead in America. I met a woman who told me her husband was the purser of the *Maraposer*. I was coming to Australia on the *Maraposer*. Steerage, of course—that was all I could afford to travel. But when I got on, I had an introduction to her husband, and when we got to Honolulu, I said, 'Look, I'm in a cabin right over the propellers with six other people in the cabin. Do you think I could move upstairs if I got some more money from Australia?' And he got me moved upstairs and sat me next to Charles Walton and himself, to restrain my exuberance.

I knew that that was the man that I would marry the moment I met him. I don't know why I did; it just flashed through my mind. He was a very attractive, well-spoken gentleman. And my mother ... I had been brought up to believe that an English gentleman was an English gentleman, you know. That was mother's idea of the perfect man.

And the war came and, of course, I was active during the war years, and then I had two children close together, one after the other, and became a mother and housekeeper and so on.

Women in war

Well, there was no flying for women pilots in Australia, because we only had three women with 500 hours at that stage, and they were not available. But in England and America they were so desperately short of pilots that they allowed them to fly the little light aircraft. Of course, they ended up flying everything that came out of a hangar. So it was fantastic, what they did. If I'd stayed in England I probably would have been a Lear transport auxiliary, but in Australia we weren't really an aircraft-producing country until late in the war. By that time, we had enough servicemen returned from active duties to do any of the ferrying that was necessary.

Commandant of the Women's Air Training Corps 1942–1945

That involved training and recruiting people for the WAF, and before the WAF was formed, it was our work that brought about the WAF. For years before that we had been working in voluntary capacity for the air force. People weren't allowed to use their cars—remember, petrol was rationed. But if a girl could drive or we could teach her to drive, she could borrow Dad's car and drive the air force officers around and provide useful transport for them. We did all sorts of work. We trained, we did drill and everything so that we were there if we were suddenly needed, the women. But the government didn't want women in the services, because they were afraid they would take men's jobs and not want to give them up.

It wasn't until an air marshal came out from England with two daughters, both of whom were WAFs in England in their uniforms, and he said, 'You can't have a full war effort unless you use the women'.

Looking back

Last year [2005] I celebrated my ninetieth birthday with a lavish dinner put on by Qantas, which was really one of the events of the year, and something that I'll always remember and appreciate. It was their eighty-fifth and my ninetieth; I'm older than them. In fact, it was supposed to be secret but they had to ask me for a few names for family and very close friends and addresses, so I had to know a little bit that something was happening, but I really didn't know who was running it.

I was a little bit overwhelmed by it all, because the astronaut Andy Thomas flew in from Adelaide to present me with a copy of my book, which he had taken with him nearly 6 million miles in the *Discovery*. And that was a great thrill. And then, of course, to hear that they'd named the new Airbus after me—*Nancy-Bird Walton*. I just was flabbergasted. I was completely overwhelmed. It was a fantastic evening, and then of course there was a big party put on by the Women Pilots, and the International Club had another party. My birthday went on for a fortnight.

What is it like to be ninety? I think it's a very great privilege to reach that age. And I've had nothing to do with it at all. I think the good Lord just forgot me on his waiting list. Maybe he didn't know what to call me. Whether to call me Bird or Walton. And sometimes I don't know either.

What is my greatest achievement? I think survival, surviving to ninety in a competitive world. I think it's been a very great privilege to reach that age. To be a survivor, literally, of the 1933 period, is quite something.

Recently, I was invited to attend the Qantas eighty-fifth anniversary celebrations in Brisbane. And what a tremendous affair that was. There were 600 guests. And they put on a magnificent display of aviation memorabilia. The very big thing of the whole evening was the A380 being wheeled almost into the hanger, right into the hangar, and John Travolta showed us around it, and to have the first Qantas one named after me is a very great honour and a far cry from the little Gypsy Moth. Never in my wildest dreams could I imagine an aircraft like that could be named after me.

Aviation today

Aviation is the thing I'm still interested in and that I'm really quite savage about, because I'm horrified at what's happening to aviation in Australia. There is no country in the world more suited to aviation than Australia. We have the enormous distances, we have the good weather, the good visibility, low terrain and bad roads, or inadequate roads. And yet, we've got Qantas, who have built up the aviation industry throughout Australia, eighty-five years of it, and now we have foreign airlines wanting to come in and take part of their most lucrative routes. They already have two competitors on the Pacific route, which is their most lucrative route, Air New Zealand and United Airlines, and others are trying to come in. No foreign airline is interested in the development of Australian aviation; they just want the money from a lucrative route or to share a lucrative route, and we've just got to be loyal to our own. I can't understand why the government will allow any other foreign airline to come in and snavel in on Qantas's most lucrative route.

I think that the government has done the wrong thing in selling the aerodromes. They were built and paid for by the people, and they should be retained by the people. If they'd floated them on the stock exchange and let the mums and dads of Australia buy them, it would've been a different cup of tea. No, it's quite wrong. They've popped the prices up 100 per cent in places like Bankstown, and people who've been in the aviation business for thirty-seven, forty years have got to move out—they can't afford the increased rents. There's not enough money in aviation to pay for it. I don't know what is going to happen with the future of aviation if this policy of selling everything to private enterprise goes on.

I still have a pilot's licence. But I can't fly in command anymore. I passed the medical, which is the requirement nowadays, but because I'm out of date with all the rules and regulations, I haven't taken my flying tests and I don't want to. Because today it's so easy to walk onboard an aircraft and arrive where you want to go.

The principle of flight hasn't changed. But, of course, I don't understand all that instrumentation now. With me, I had less than half-a-dozen instruments, including a throttle. I didn't have all this technical knowledge that you have to have today.

I enjoy the social contact with the people in aviation, to know what women pilots are doing, to see how they begin, and how they go on, and what they bring to aviation. And it's just been my life. And I have done everything I can to encourage women to fly, and we even have a scholarship for women over forty-five because you haven't seen Australia unless you've seen it from the air, in a low-flying aircraft. And we think a lot of women could take up flying just as a pleasure. Then of course we encourage young women to go in for engineering and flying as a profession, and it's a very active organisation now. The Women Pilots' Association is in every state.

I don't go anywhere unless I fly. There's nothing easier than getting in a taxi, getting to the airport and walking on board an airliner. All you do is sit back and relax it's just wonderful. I haven't lost the love of flying nor the ease and comfort of it.

I think I was born in a very interesting period of aviation development when people knew one another and knew what one another's ambitions were, and the struggles that some people went through to make a place for themselves in aviation, and the dedication of people—it was a very great period of aviation development. Today it's much more impersonal, much more mechanical, much more computerised and so on. You probably have to be a lot brighter now to cope with developments, but the days of flying for the sheer joy of flying are behind us.

> I love flight and I love people. And through aviation I see a lot of both. I'm always very happy in an airliner. People say do I wish I was up front? I'm completely and utterly relaxed in airliners. And I'm perfectly happy with the period that I've been privileged to have had in the aviation world.

[P.S. The A380 for Qantas, to be named *Nancy-Bird Walton*, is due for delivery in August 2008.}

KEV CARMODY
Musician

Screened 21 May 2007

Singer and songwriter Kev Carmody has spent the past thirty years telling the story of his people. His colleague Paul Kelly said that he was drawn right away by Kev's blending of politics and prayer, poetry, anger and pride. Together they penned 'From Little Things Big Things Grow', inspired by the 1966 Wave Hill-Wattie Creek walk-off by Aboriginal stockmen, an event that continues to resonate through Kev's life.

> I was so proud, September last year, 2006, to be invited back to the fortieth anniversary of the Wattie Creek walk-off. And it was just an absolute buzz to get all those young kids on stage. It becomes a collective then, not an ego thing of Kev Carmody. It made me so proud that that young generation know the history and it's carried in song. It's carried in song, in the old oral way.
>
> > Gather round people let me tell you a story
> > An eight-year-long story of power and pride
> > British Lord Vestey and Vincent Lingiari
> > Were opposite men on opposite sides ...

Early days

I was born in Cairns in 1946. I've got a younger brother whose name is Laurie. He's three and a half years younger than I am. Dad was a second generation Irish descendant and Mum was a Murri woman, and her grandmother's country was Bundjalung country in northern New South Wales. My dad was a fairly quiet sort of a man but very fair. He had an ingrained sense of justice and he would certainly act if things weren't being done in a fair manner. He volunteered for the Second World War and he was in the Red Berets as an instructor. He used to do parachuting and stuff like that. In fact, my Aboriginal grandmother had the best curtains in Queensland because they were made out of parachute silk.

My mother worked as a seamstress in Brisbane when she was sixteen years old. And she was just an amazing bush woman. I had so much admiration for her. She taught us so much. She could track, she could ride horses, she could fence—she could do everything, you know. The women were the cement in any outback community.

Dad was a good bushman himself. Before the war he lived out there by himself, milking cows in that really hard country. And he was living off the land then too.

At that time, so-called mixed marriages were virtually a no-no. But up here in the Cairns area it was multicultural, before the concept was even thought of after the Second World War. I mean, you had Aboriginal people there, you had Torres Strait Island people, you had Maltese people, Yugoslav, Greeks, Italians; all came in to do the hard work on the cane. And it was a matter of everybody pulling together. Where we lived was around a football oval. On Saturday they'd play rugby league and on Sunday they'd play this new game called soccer. And the women would put all this food out, and it was a way of getting the community together with all those nationalities.

We moved to southern Queensland from Cairns in early 1950. My dad and my grandfather on the Irish side drew what they call a goanna block. The government in the Depression was trying to get families out as cheap labour in a way around the big stations. So they opened up all these little blocks, and it was a total social experiment that never worked. And of course they had conditions on it; it was only lease land—they could kick you off at any time. Dad volunteered for the war, went away, and he was up there four years doing quite okay. And they said, 'Unless you come back you're going to lose the land, we're going to take it off you'. And Dad thought. We need to have an anchor somewhere, so it forced him to come back there. You were virtually like tenant farmers or serfs.

A goanna block is a term used in the outback for a block you just can't live on. In other words you can't run one goanna to 1000 hectares. It just won't support that amount of life. It was huge scrub country, ironbark and cyprus. But it could run a few cattle and packhorses, and it was a base. It might've been leased or rented, but at least it was a base. And of course Dad had the big station to work on, as well as all the droving, so there was employment. He did mustering, he did contract branding, fencing, and he was well known throughout the district as a really good worker.

A droving life

Mum and Dad were drovers and they moved the cattle along the stock routes, which were ten chain wide, ten cricket pitches wide. They normally followed the river systems down for water.

Dad worked for Anderson brothers at Chinchilla. For two years we never stopped, Christmas Day and all. They just kept moving. There were lots of people making a lot of money that didn't own an acre of land. They'd buy a mob of cattle out at Charleville, 500 or 600 head, and they'd move them for two or three months, you know, fatten them up, and they'd sell a few, maybe 200 at Roma, and they'd buy a few younger ones that are a bit poorer, then back on the road again. It was a constant move.

My mother knew so much about the bush. For the first three years, from 1950 to about 1953, moved 8 to 10, 15 mile a day with no electricity, no running water, no fridge. Managed to put huge meals on the table three times a day, plus smokos, and it didn't seem to be a big problem for her.

We loved it as kids. I mean, I was on a horse when I was four year old. We just loved it. You were moving, we had all these skills, we could track. Once the cattle get, what we call 'broken in', after about two weeks on the road, they know what's happening. You move this far, you pull up for smoko, you go along, dinner; night-time you settle in one place, you ring them around. The only problem you ever really had was when the cows were calving on the road … you couldn't make the stage; you know, you had to do 8 mile or 10 mile a day so you wouldn't eat the squatters' feed. So they give you a permit, and if you didn't make that stage they wouldn't give you a permit, so you couldn't drove. So if the cow started to calf, they wouldn't make the stage, and Mum would have to put them into the truck.

If you've got cows and calves, around two o'clock in the morning the cows would get up in what we used to call the false dawn: you get this glow in the eastern horizon; they'll get up and feed the calves and settle back down again. You always had to be wary of what we called the 'rush', because if you get 500 to 800 head of cattle hit their feet in an instant, you don't know which way they're going and you just hear it, puts the fear of God into you.

We loved the life too because you were so in tune with the environment. You had to be; otherwise, you wouldn't be able to get feed for your cattle or find water.

We worked the whole thing with dogs. We had about twelve dogs. They were specially trained. Each dog had a certain personality, might be a left-hand dog or a right-hand dog or a lead dog. Then you had your heelers at the back. They knew the whistles, so you could keep a huge amount of cattle together if you had well-trained, well-fed and well–cared for dogs.

Because we were so poor we had to exist from the land. So that's where Dad relied on Mum so much, you know, in the early stages just to get our sustenance on the table every night. Mum would catch freshwater crayfish and freshwater fish and she'd use herbs like this lemon-scented tea-tree to flavour the food. And, you know, you're walking through a giant supermarket—you've just got to have the knowledge to know where it is.

The 'Droving Woman' song, it's nine minutes long and twenty-one verses. I could've done five flaming hours telling about the tremendous respect I have for Mum, and for all the women who did that. You know, she'd go ahead at each stage. She'd set up the billies so that we could have a cup of tea at smoko, then move ahead, dinnertime, and at night-time she'd move on to the camp. Just amazing!

And the majesty of a night-time, looking at the night sky, and that feeling, that total spirituality, the quietness—you can feel infinity touching you, or eternity touching you if you're religious. The experience was just phenomenal. After the evening meal the twilight goes, the stars come out, the fire's going, you've got that smell. All your senses are totally attuned, and this beautiful quietness descends. It's almost like a curtain goes down, and a curtain goes up on the night, the cycle of the moon, the night calls … just that feeling of oneness with the universe, you couldn't ignore it.

The only interruption we had was the ABC Radio, because we'd listen to the radio most nights for a while.

Music on the wireless

The big innovation for us in the early '50s was Dad acquired an old dry-cell battery wireless. We could pick up the ABC, and it was just phenomenal to us, from an oral tradition, to sit down and listen to. In the morning you'd get hillbilly music and you'd get gorgeous classical music. It opened up just this huge, huge flaming world to us.

We were absolutely gobsmacked that we could turn this knob here like this and all of a sudden there were these voices coming through this box. We used to get the hillbilly music, and this more modern music, Frank Sinatra and stuff, after six o'clock. And then of an evening you'd get the classical music, and to hear that when you're looking at the night sky, you know, Beethoven starts to make sense. The *Pastoral Symphony* does start to make sense. You know, Chopin's *nocturnes*. Music makes sense if you're looking at this, well, video clip of reality.

Music, I feel, was always part of me. My old grandfather, quiet man that he was, always used to say to us, 'Always listen to the wind. You're surrounded by sound, boy—it's the wind in the leaf, it's the rain on the earth, it's the cry of the newborn baby, it's the brolga cry, dingo cry, crocodile cry, and you've got to know all those languages or you won't be able to survive. You don't just have to know homo sapiens languages, you've got to know the language of the animals, because they change all through the year'. And then of course around the campfire, there'd always be somebody saying poetry and they'd pass songs from one camp to another.

Taken to school

I didn't go to school till I was ten year old. I thought that with all the skills I had here I was right for life. You know, I'd have this job, stockman, I could break horses, you could track cattle, you could do all that stock work. We've got all these skills and then they put us in school and said, hang on, you need these skills. What for? What for? I could earn a living as a ten-year-old kid. That was quantum change, or you could say the brick wall, that I hit as a young fellow when they put me in the school and said, 'Those skills were irrelevant; we want you to want to socially engineer your intellect this way' ... Cultural clash.

When we were young, in the '40s and '50s, it was government policy to take the kids away from their families. They'd had their eye on us for years, but we were this moving little camp. And it was pretty hard to nail us because we were taught that as soon as you heard a motor car you just ran into the bush and you didn't come out until one of your relatives, or someone you knew, came and got you.

Mum and Dad were given the option, either the kids go to school or that's it. They could put Mum on a Palm Island or somewhere. It was a trade-off. But we were allowed to come home twice a year. And Dad really stretched those holidays from four weeks until about eight. He'd write a letter and say, 'We're not near a rail head so the kids can't get on a train to come in'.

My brother and I wound up at a Catholic boarding school in Toowoomba. It was sort of a subsistence farm. The school was run by nuns, and what we found was a complete lack of human love. Discipline, of course, was very heavy and cruel. We never had had a hand laid hardly on us as kids, and then to get into this context where everything was so regimented. It was unbelievable, the physical punishments they used to hand out to little kids. Little tiny kids. It was unbelievable. The other thing we found was that they seemed to think we weren't clean, and many's the time we were sent back to scrub our skin because of the colour.

There were only a few of us there. It was that clash of cultures. We got floggings for switching an electric light on and off ... it was just kids' curiosity. We knew what an electric light was, but not how the mechanism worked. And they'd flog you for it. And the food ... holy mackerel, after coming from this lovely fresh food, and plenty of it, to this place where you were virtually on a starvation diet.

Up to ten year old you had to develop a fantastic memory. Those old people that I knew couldn't read or write, they could give you genealogies that were in their hundreds, in their thousands, and you had to have a really good memory. So at the school I caught up fairly quickly because it was all rote learning, 'The cat sat on the mat'. And as soon as I'd see the picture, I knew what they were talking about, so I bluffed my way through. But I was a big kid, ten year old, sitting in the Year 1 classes, so I was treated as a dunce right from day one, and I got flogged for it, because I couldn't read.

There was a bitterness in there towards coloured people. After school I just went back to what we knew best: droving and stock work.

Wave Hill-Wattie Creek

In the '60s, the Wave Hill-Wattie Creek walk-off was a very big, significant thing in my intellect. We'd hear stuff on the grapevine all the way through because the drovers would come across the Northern Territory down the Boulia Track, you know, in on southern Queensland, across the border, and the grapevine was working real well too. And we heard that there were things happening there before the strike actually started. Then Mum heard it on the ABC Radio one evening, that the Gurindji Wattie Creek mob had walked off Lord Vestey's station and gone on strike. We thought, Whoa, what's going to go on here? They're going to be looking out through the pigeon hole; they're going to lock them up or they're going to shoot them or something. We were just so taken aback that this step had been taken. It really hit us; this was big stuff.

Don't forget, at that particular time, I was twenty year old. I was not a refugee, I was not an illegal immigrant, I was not an illegal alien. I was not a queue jumper or a boat person. All of us Aboriginal people, you know, we were just non-citizens, we were nothing. We were something: we were flora and fauna, under the Act. So this was a huge move when we heard that this mob had stood up. And we knew, well, we hoped and we knew, that they'd made this decision and they weren't going to go back on it. They were driven to that point, as we were, to actually say, 'Right, we've had enough of this'.

The thing that amazed us so much was the tremendous building of support for the Gurindji struggle, and we just found that so positive after all the racism we'd encountered.

Paul Kelly and myself went on to write a song based on that called 'From Little Things Big Things Grow'. Paul had the idea of a love song, from the little thing a big thing grew. And I told him about

Wattie Creek and what a big impact it had on us. The song grew out of that. I said, 'It's a cultural love song, about the culture and the land'.

Marriage and fatherhood

The referendum was held in '67 and technically I became a citizen. I married at the same time, which was very fortunate ... terrible to get married to a non-person.

I got married to Helen and we had three boys, and the children moved with us with the jobs.

Being a father, to me was the most amazing thing. At that time you weren't allowed to go into the maternity ward or anything. And they bring this little, tiny little human being out to you with all these bruises on him and you think, Holy mackerel, they bashed the poor little fella around. But, yeah, it's just an amazing thing. Again, it's a really spiritual thing.

I wrote a song back in 1968 called 'I've Been Moved', and it was just things that moved my spirit as a young man and a young father, and there's a line in there that goes, 'I've been moved by the crying of a newborn', and that's in reference to my eldest son.

Collective money

There was tons of work around in those days. Labouring work: you sewed the wheat bags, you lumped the wheat bags on your back, you did stick picking, cane cutting, you did wool pressing; and you put all those jobs together through the year, you had more work than you could do. Because we were really good workers and the same people would ring us up again. We were reliable; we didn't drink. It was constant flaming work.

Our money went into a collective account, so Mum used to be in charge of the money. For about three years after we were married, all the money went into a central pool. She fanned it out where it was fair ... Never had a vehicle. We used to travel all around the place, borrow a car here or get Dad's old ute to go over and do the jobs.

We didn't think there was any other way to do it. Everybody had to benefit from it. If uncle had a job over here, Dad had a job over here, my brother had a job over there, or I had a job over here, it went into this central pool and it was fairly distributed.

I think it was a collective consensus that this was the best way to do it. It was no good me having $100 if my brother or my mother or father were out in the cold. There was never a fight over it, goodness me, no. I mean, it was just the way we were socialised. Again, social engineering of our intellect in the economic sense was that way.

To me the really selfish, selfish way of distributing wealth is to have the individual being the sole arbitrator of who gets what. I've put it in songs everywhere—'Pillars of Society', 'Comrade Jesus Christ'.

Music studies

In the mid '70s we moved to Toowoomba and I worked for a number of years in a welding shed. I wasn't interested much in watching TV of a night-time but I was totally interested in music. So I started to study classical music by correspondence. And I did the AMEB, the Australian Music Board exams, because I was really interested in how music was constructed. And I taught myself the basics of classical guitar or finger-style playing from books.

And when I was in the welding sheds I actually got a teacher and she said to me one day, 'Gee, Kev, you're at a standard that's miles higher than, you know, the Institute'—it was the Institute then—'that they require for entry'. And I thought, Gee, anything's better than, you know, working in the welding sheds. I'll go and give it a go.

So I went out in my overalls and auditioned, and they accepted me. It opened up this huge world, not just classical music. We're talking ethnomusicology, experimental music, composition. It was just fantastic. You know, just opened up this world, just like the radio did. And when I had to attend my classical music theory classes I'd hop on the old motorbike with the overalls on and the big black beard and used to wind up sitting in a group of twenty-odd or so young ladies to be able to study the music theory. I don't know what they thought about it, but it certainly didn't bother me.

The university took me on probation for twelve months. You know, it's a sad thing to say that in the mid '70s I'd never been in a library. I'd never been inside a library and I'd never read a book. So for half a day I sat in the library right near the reference section and I pulled out the hugest book I could find to make out I was studying, but while I was there I was watching how they got the book out of the library. And I actually taught myself how to get a book out of the library. I thought if I went and told them, oh boy, I'd be back in the welding shed.

I came to the University of Southern Queensland in 1978 and I couldn't read or write very well at those times, and they allowed me, my first tutorial, to take in the guitar so I could put a bit of my oral history background into the tutorial, which was a quaint little way of conducting a tutorial, but it worked. At least it got me started, because I was practically illiterate. I graduated with a BA in history, geography and music.

I completed a Diploma of Education, at Queensland University, then I did master's work, then I did PhD work, but I had to defer when I signed a record contract.

A recording contract

We sort of decided as a family ... I had all this backlog of songs, and the Bicentennial was coming up and I thought, Even if I become a number-one academic, there's only going to be a tiny percentage of this population is ever going to hear what I put down in dissertations or essays. Maybe music can help bridge that gap. So I recorded on a little eight-track recorder. They were still bolting the studio together in '87 and all of a sudden, whack, Bruce Elder from *The Sydney Morning Herald* picked it up and did a review on it, and that's when I signed a contract.

The first record contract in 1987 was with a small record label in Sydney, just before the Bicentennial, and I've made five albums since then. And, of course, we never get any commercial radio airplay and there's a very good reason why we don't. Indigenous music in this country and a lot of other music in this country is subliminally but very rigidly censored out, because we're playing to them, the powers that be, the programmers and whatnot, politically incorrect music. They want commercial, retail, politically correct music. I knew that my music, even before I recorded it, would be censored out, but my reason for recording it was as an oral record, not as a commercial venture; because I've never made money out of it.

Being indigenous, you were political whether you liked it or not; you were forced into that category whether you liked it or not. To me the music is beyond political. Some of it is, but I tend to think we look at the larger picture, which is human existence on this planet at this time, which goes beyond indigenous.

I mean, if you look back across our Aboriginal history in music, I can name the five, on your hands, that have made mainstream. Harold Blair, Uncle Jimmy Little, Lionel Rose at the end of the '60s, and then you've got a huge gap. A huge gap to Yothu Yindi and then Troy Cassar-Daley, and that's it.

A sense of justice

I suppose I inherited my political justice sort of focus from the fact that I'm indigenous and from my old dad's sense of right and wrong and fairness.

If you look at the '88 protests in Sydney, that was a huge coming together of Aboriginal people from all over Australia, plus a huge support crowd of non-indigenous people. It really was so positive to be part of those huge marches down to Lady Macquarie's Chair.

I've often been called a protest singer, as a lot of other people have. And to me it's derogatory and it's too narrow and it ghettoises the music for a start: 'Oh, it's protest, it's negative stuff', you know? Whereas if you really listen to a lot of the lyrics in my stuff, there's lots of positivity in it. The category 'protest singer' is a convenient little box so they can understand me. They don't have to put in the intellectual work they'd have to put in to listen to the lyrics.

Over the years I've felt it very important to interact with our brothers and sisters in incarceration. At the turn of the millennium I was invited down to the opening of a new concept in prisons in New South Wales just outside Brewarrina, at Yetta Dhinnakkal. There was an open prison on a 26,000-hectare property. And to see the transformation in those young fellas was just so satisfying, just in the few days that I was there. The main thing was, we were allowed to light a huge fire, and for the first time some of those lads actually sat down and talked as men, really talked about what concerned them. And a lot of them wanted to learn how to circular breathe with the didge as well. And I just found it so empowering and satisfying to see that transformation in young people.

The pain of playing

Playing today for me is a, well, to put it literally, a pain. I've got this degenerative sort of thing in my spine ... it hasn't stopped me talking. Because of this thing in the spine, I can move the fingers, but I can't feel them much and sometimes I can't feel them at all. It does make it harder to perform but I can pull it off. And to me, I don't care if I make a mistake. I tell the audience, 'If I make a mistake, that's cool'. You get old and you can't feel your fingers and you make a bit of a blue here and there, but that's a live recording, it's real. It's not virtual reality. If you want virtual reality or the sterile version, go and buy the CD, my friend. And once you explain it to them, that's great.

I've never really loved performing. People have asked me, 'Do you get nervous before you go on stage?', and I can honestly say that I've never been nervous when I walked on the stage because what you see is what you get around the campfire or the lounge table.

When I'm performing on stage, as people that have seen it know, I spend 40 to 45, even 50 per cent of my time speaking to the audience, because to me the song has no relevance at all unless it's in the context of a story. The story and the song to me are one and the same thing. I'm just doing a musical version of this story I'm telling you here, and I can elaborate with word images and stuff in the story just as much as I can in the song.

Make poverty history

Last year I was invited to perform at the Make Poverty History concert. And it was just a privilege to play with Paul Kelly and John Butler on stage, acoustically. And I said to the audience, 'We're helping the environment here. We're not using Marshall amps and all that electricity. We're playing acoustic!'

The brief little time that I talked to Bono down there at Make Poverty History, he was just blown out with the age ... 'There's twelve year olds, there's fourteen year olds out there ... we could network this all round the world with their SMSs and their IT technology. We can change things.' The thing I was picking up from him is that we can change things as people.

The best part for me at the concert was the fact that I had a unique T-shirt that they did for me. Everybody else had on their T-shirt, 'Make Poverty History', and mine had, 'Make Indigenous Poverty History'. So it was a real privilege to wear that.

Cannot buy my soul

My friend Paul Kelly, singer/songwriter extraordinaire, the poet of Australia, really, that man, has organised a tribute album called *Cannot Buy My Soul*, where these fantastic musicians sing songs that I have written. The whole album is a collective; it's not a Kev Carmody thing. It's all of us together in the oral tradition, again passing it on to future generations. And I hope 100 years down the track the same thing happens again, and they change it to suit their particular place in history.

It will go on, and the concepts that are on that album people can build on, add their own too ... Again, it's an alternate voice to what's being force fed over the mainstream media.

As an Aboriginal person, and my Irish heritage, it's got that huge oral tradition with it. And the songs, in a way, are a series of stories or, you know, a series of statements. And I'm just so blown out that that generation can see that what's being said in those songs still relates to today and is still relevant.

Certainly you know the basic melodies; nothing's contrived in them, and the fact there is a story behind them. Bernard [Fanning] rang me up and just wanted to know the background to the song 'Ellie'. Was it a true story about that person? Missy Higgins, the same, emailed me.

> For humanity is more important here
> Than that constant quest for gold
> Well, you may take life and liberty, friend
> But you can never buy our soul ...

When I first sang that song on stage in the '70s I said, 'I use the word soul not in a Christian sense, but it's easier to rhyme ...' I was going to use the word spirit. Anyway it came out 'cannot buy my soul'. What does it mean? Well, I suppose if you look at people—you know, like Nelson Mandela—you can incarcerate the physical but you can't chain the spirit. It's as simple as that. If I look back at my grandparents, what they endured, and in my sixty years the things that I've been through are nothing compared to what they went through. And the thing is that they came out totally with dignity, with strength.

You know, our spirituality, to my way of thinking, has gone out on this huge bungee cord that's almost at breaking point. And in some instances, I'm damn sure, it's snapped. I think that's why those younger people relate to it. I mean, if you look at what the Last Connection did on that album, what the Herd did, they've updated it in the old folk tradition. The Cronulla riots are in there; Palm Island is still relevant. So the younger generation can see the theme is still relevant. We'll just put our new words to it, new melody, change it completely, but the theme is still pretty well the same.

Songwriter

I always start with the music, and I might carry that scene for ten years. I mean, Paul Kelly is the same: you carry those little guitar riffs or you carry that beautiful chord progression or that little finger-style thing for years until all of a sudden a theme will just arise around you, you'll see something and you'll say, 'Wow! That fits that little chord progression that I had, or that little melody that I had'. And in that sense, it's a long-time thing. The lyrics to me just go *zap-zap-zap*, because, again from my oral tradition, I was taught in storytelling that you had to speak in word images, so that they stuck in a person's intellect without the written word.

In one of the songs that's on the album, I remember Granny saying to us when us boys were being a bit rough, 'You got to be gentle, you got to be gentle, boy. You got to be like that moonlight, gentle, soft on your skin, you got to be that'. And you know, Sara Storer sings a song, 'caress of moonlight on my skin'. So you learnt to speak in word images so it would stick in their heads.

I think it was just natural, and not having a grasp of the English language for ten years, we named all the birds from the sounds. Just speaking in those word images, like a shorthand in some ways.

The power of song

I always say now when I'm doing these music and song-writing workshops out there, 'Now just think about the reasons you're doing this. We know you can do it. You can do the best hip-hop song in the whole wide world, but I really want you to think about why you're doing it. Are you doing it for the three E-concept: Economics, Entertainment and Ego? Or are you doing it for the old reasons? Think about it before you start, sing about country, land, things that make you happy or sad. Sing real music, or do you want to become an Idol? You can still do all those things, but sing something that gives you a strength and a dignity and an empowerment'.

And you can see it happening in the workshops, as soon as you take the motherf–ing, rubbish, New York, the city stuff, out of it and say, 'I want to hear language, I want to hear about your community' and put the butcher's paper up, wow! They write the most amazing songs lyrically. And the other thing is it gets them back on the loop. They're straight away on the computer, they've got 2000 drum tracks they can pick from there. Again, just trying to keep that old way of passing things on and speaking reality instead of the stuff you see on video clips.

The family network

Grandma Helen is my former wife and we are still good mates, unless she has a go at me and I have a go at her, but we get on pretty well, most times! We usually argue about food. I have three boys and a girl and, to this point, eleven grandchildren. If I remember rightly, there are twenty-two first cousins on one son and his wife's side, and seventeen on the other son and his wife's side, and three on the way.

Our family networks are our security. That's the most important thing—they're our safety net. And the thing about indigenous culture, the older you get, they listen to you more. You don't become redundant like you do in mainstream society. I think that's the strength of our culture, that the older people have a say, and they have the say first.

One of the grandchildren said to me last Christmas, 'Grandad, what do you want for Christmas?' I said, 'Nothing'. I've never given presents at Christmas, ever, or birthdays, because I said you've got to give every day of your life, even if it's a bag of potatoes for the family. You give all the time.

Spirit of the land

The land is always featured in my writing as a songwriter. It was so inculcated into me for ten years before I went to school, the importance of your custodianship and care for the land. Something I was taught as a young person was that everything has a spirit. The spirit of the trees, the spirit of the wind, the spirit of the cloud, and we as homo sapiens were equal with that. It just concerns me a little that in this modern sort of technological age we are divorcing ourselves in some ways away from the reality of existence and more into the virtual reality of existence. You know, we can't exist without electricity, we can't exist without a car, we can't exist without a supermarket. Well, the thing is, my indigenous family, we could exist out there without any of that, and we did. So if you run into trouble, you fellas, you know, just come and talk to us.

Whether we recognise it or not, we're absolutely connected to everything in existence out there. We've divorced ourselves from that, but it doesn't mean we can't reclaim it.

I feel that we did have a proper way of interacting with this land and this earth. Now if you look at the problems that we're running into here, now in the short term which are going to be here for the long term, like water and our electricity supply, we're going to run out of this stuff unless we really start modifying, and the only way we can modify is not go for more but go for less. That's exactly how we existed, five of us, with a 1000-gallon tank, with a baby.

I'm fortunate at the moment in my life to live on 60 acres of just beautiful, gorgeous, spiritual country. Three national parks join in this area in southern Queensland. It's huge granite country. It's just unbelievable when a storm comes through. Blue lightning comes cracking through the mountains, shakes the house; in fact, it blew the telephone connection to the other side of the wall one night.

I find it a bit of a drain coming to the city. The sounds of the city, the smells—it breaks that continuity of being attuned to everything around you. Like up in the bush where I am ... your morning, you have this whole symphony orchestra of sounds, of the birds, the calls that are around you. You're totally attuned to it: you don't have to think about it, you just know exactly which way the wind is coming from. To come to a city and find signs on your door, 'Lock your door of a night-time', it's a bit disconcerting to me that we have intellectually engineered our society to the point whereby you don't need a prison anymore; you just lock yourself in of a night-time voluntarily.

Retirement I don't really comprehend, because I just feel that you still have so much that you have to do. And especially passing on the bit of knowledge I have acquired to other people. I mean, I'm on borrowed time now if you look at the statistics. I should've been gone ages ago, ages ago.

> I'm proud of the fact that, you know, right now, this very day, my son and my little grandson, they're up there in that country, you know, looking around with this old man who's about eighty-six year old and he's giving them all the concept of what the history is of that huge area up there in that mountain country. So, that's what I'm proud of most: that ancient history, if you like to call it that, or traditional history, is being passed on.

[P.S. In May 2008 Kev Carmody received an honourary doctorate from the University of Southern Queensland.]

DENISE DRYSDALE
Entertainer

Screened 1 May 2006

Denise Drysdale's pub-owning parents sent her to ballet classes to avoid the sight of the six o'clock swill. She danced her way onto the screen, became a go-go girl and, in time, a TV fixture, most notably as Ding Dong on *The Ernie Sigley Show*. As she reveals here, she has spent a lifetime sending herself up.

> I guess I got the reputation for being a bit silly and mad—zany, if you want to say that—but I've been doing things like that all my life, and still do them. My father had a gorilla suit in the back of the car when I was a kid, and we used to go out into the country for picnics and he'd stop for petrol, go and put on the gorilla suit, and come out to pay the guy and frighten the hell out of him ... He'd sneak up in the bushes if people were playing tennis and things like that ... Just mad. The maddest family, the Drysdales—they were just all crazy and this has rubbed off—and so that was my upbringing as a kid, and then as a teenager ... a bit of a daredevil. So I've been doing it for years.

Pub days

I have very fond memories of Port Melbourne, the Fountain Inn Hotel, where I was brought up. I was three and a half when Mum and Dad got the pub, and we lived there for about eleven years. It was a fantastic time for me. We had all male boarders. It was a residential place, and I was spoilt rotten—had all these aunties and uncles. And 'Uncle Billy' used to take me and get me ten comics with a bottle of Coke and a big block of chocolate on a Saturday night, and Mum and Dad usually went out to the Chevron. And I used to sit in Mum's fur coat with my chocolate and comics and my teddies, and watch the telly and do Dad's tills. I would have been about eight or nine, I think.

I think this is where the humour comes from, and also maybe the bit of gumption that I've got. They used to say when I was a little kid, 'There's a packet of razor blades, go and play in the traffic'. These would be the drinkers when I came home from school in the afternoon. There was always this banter ... and the other thing, I lived in a hotel with male boarders; they were gentlemen, I remember them all. I used to have to call them 'uncle'. I had that many uncles and aunties in the pub, but those men were gentlemen. But I wanted to say that because there was a lot of things said about that era now, and about schools and things, about how people were abused. Those people were gentlemen.

The pub had six o'clock closing and it was a six o'clock swill. And on the weekends, because there was no trading on the Sunday at that stage ... and Mum thought it was a bit rough and it did seem a rough crowd, and they'd be swilling it down and taking their bottles home at six o'clock. And so Mum thought it was better if I was out of the way, and so that's how I started dancing at May Downs's.

Dancing with May

May Downs was an amazing woman. She's taught a whole lot of kids that are still around, doing different things. And she taught us

150 per cent is what you gave in any performance, or don't bother. And of course, that's got me into strife over the years. But that's what she did to us, she made us work so hard, like the discipline of not sitting in an outfit. To this day if I'm dressed for a show, I don't sit down. And if I have to do a commercial and it takes all day, I don't sit down in the outfit. I've seen kids sit in beautiful ball gowns with a cup of coffee and think, Oh my God, if May was here she would kill you.

The discipline that she taught with that has stayed with me, and got me into a lot of trouble, because every time I go to work, that's the thing that's in the back of my head. You do what is totally necessary to, well, I suppose, to get a laugh now or anything to do with it. You just go for it. The extra 50 per cent is probably 'off centre' … go where someone doesn't expect you to go.

She used to say I was 'tits and teeth'. She meant exactly that! If you had that, then no one was watching your feet. You could get away with anything. You still can, you know. You can have ten people in a ballet line-up, but if you do a step like that and nine others do something different, they go, 'She was right'.

At May Downs's we used to do every competition and concert, pantomimes every summer, and I think I was about ten and a half and there was an audition at Channel Nine—they were starting up *The Tarax Show*—and they wanted some junior ballet. And May sent a whole lot of us in to audition, and I was one of the ones that got in. And it was a fantastic time, except I used to leave school early, and I had a note to get out, but the nun that was teaching me at the time wouldn't let me. She used to keep me in and then Dad would have to come down from the pub to South Melbourne and then to Richmond; it was a bit of a ritual. I don't think she liked dancing very much … I don't think she ever tap-danced herself.

I went to Kilbride Ladies Convent, South Melbourne. I was a left-hander, the Devil's work, and I had already been dancing for three years, so by the time I got there, the nuns didn't like me much.

There was one day when I had had enough at school—and I forget what had happened—and I came home and I came in the door of the chicken bar that Dad owned at that time and said, 'That's it, I'm not going back there'. And Mum and Dad weren't high on education; they would prefer me to have been in show business. I suppose I was lucky in that respect. And they went, 'Well, what are you going to do?' And I said, 'There's auditions coming up at Channel Nine for the senior ballet. I'm going to see if I can do that'. And I was lucky enough to get in there. I think, because they were never educated as kids, education was never offered as an alternative to what I was doing.

Sacked from the ballet

Sacked from the ballet! Oh God, I can remember it. We'd been on holidays, I'd been there about a year and a bit, and on the holidays I had put on weight, but not much, but the girls were very slim, and as you know, if you put someone in a nice tutu, they don't have bosoms—they have very flat chests. Pete Smith always said, 'You grew boobs; they had to get rid of you'. They couldn't do it today. They said I was the weakest link in the ballet. Is it too late to get them, do you think? Take Channel Nine to court? And I've suffered to this day. I still stand on the scales six times a day to check whether I've put on half a pound or a pound. And I still watch what I put in my mouth because of you bastards!

Imagine, I was sixteen. I can remember I was devastated. And Russell Stubbings said to me, before this cliché was made into a joke, 'One door closes and another opens'. And I auditioned for *A Funny Thing Happened on the Way to the Forum* and got in to that. That was with Betty Pounder; she was another fabulous teacher. And I did a bit of theatre for a while, and *Kommotion* happened. I could've still been in the ballet and missed doing all those other things. For some reason, every time something bad happened, it just served to make me stronger.

Luck again! Barry Bell at Channel Nine had taken some photos of me in a bikini for *Everybody's Magazine*—and that magazine had gone over to Vietnam, and American soldiers saw me, got in touch with *Everybody's Magazine*, said, 'Oh, I think she's really fabulous', and so they gave me Girl of the Year.

And in the meantime, there was a new show coming up, *Kommotion*. I knew the choreographer, so I was on tour singing with Ray Brown and the Whispers, and they were auditioning for *Kommotion* so I didn't go to the auditions: I just came back and had a job as a go-go girl. And *Kommotion* lasted for a couple of years. I actually got the sack from that because I wanted to sing. But I got reinstated when the other guy got the sack.

I get the sack all the time. It's fabulous. But then I went to the ABC to do *Dig We Must*. They tried to get rid of me once. I sang live:

'Robin's singing,
In my backyard,
In the treetops …'

Oh … Cried my eyes out and then he [Barry Langford] said, 'No, no, I think she's got something', and he gave me comedy songs to do.

Vietnam

And at the end of that year I was invited to Vietnam with Patti Newton, the Strangers and Doug Owen. And off we went—it was September 1967. Unbelievable! Well, it was our first trip overseas. Patti and I were beside ourselves. We actually went on a plane with about 120 young boys. My sandals went missing, and when I got them back at the end of the trip they'd all put their initials on them, over the sandals. I do wish I had kept them. We went off—it was what you call a captive audience. For us at the time, we did almost what we'd been trained to do, which was to give 150 per cent and to be pleasant, because neither of us were political. And I think you've got to remember that. In this day and age it would be totally different. But when we went there we touched these soldiers, and still I get people coming up saying what a difference we made. We didn't know the difference then—it was just part of it—but the Vietnam vets now to me are a very important part of my life because I realise what we did for them, and it makes me feel pretty special.

Again, no education, so our idea of war was John Wayne and John Mills—the English versions and the American versions. We didn't actually think that anybody really, really got hurt. In this day and age it would be totally different. And so to Patti and me it was an adventure.

They were so pleased to see us and to see someone from home, and we didn't realise at the time how important it was. I still say we were lucky to have gone, but they go, 'Oh, but you came', you know. 'You were so important.' And as I've gotten older, it's become more important to me that I did go, because we gave so much, not knowing at the time.

Years later I had this lovely guy came up to me, and he was really emotional and he said, 'You did something for me that made my life different'. And I've gone, 'Oh God, what have I done?' And he said we had met him in the afternoon at a barbecue, and then the next day he'd gone out in Nui Dat, and the next time I saw him was in hospital and his face had been really badly smashed from, whatever, and I kissed him. And he said, 'I mustn't have looked very pretty'. I said, 'It wouldn't have made any difference to me'. And he's remembered that and come back to say ... And he had to go because he was crying, and then he came back and he went, 'I just want you to know how much I remember it and to say thank you'.

[Denise went back to Vietnam in 1969 as part of a six-month tour of Asia with the Digger Revell Revue.]

Because we weren't government sponsored, we were working for the American bases; we'd be staying in all these terrible places. One day the guys that had organised to take us to the market came and said, 'We're not going, eight people have just been killed with a bomb there'.

It was only after *The Deer Hunter*, when that movie came out, and you realised what was going on. That was when I realised, My God, all the stories that they told us were true. Men are made to think that if they don't want to go to war, they're a coward, but sometimes I think you're a coward for not standing up that you don't want to be killed, you know? Life's precious.

At one stage they wanted us to go back to Vietnam and I felt it was very unsafe, so I didn't go back. I went to London.

London

I didn't have a lot of money over there, and I worked really hard. And I learnt lessons, like how people can really use you—this is just doing waitressing jobs—and how people use other people to get free employment for the day. They'd test you out, and take your tips and then give you four bob or something.

And I came home probably thinking that I never wanted to starve again, like in *Gone with the Wind*: 'I'll never starve again!' I worked for Samaritans in London. And when I came back I thought, That's the work that I'd love to do. And so I got in touch with Lifeline here, but you have to have theses, and all these things after your name, and I had nothing so I just decided I'd look after my friends.

Meeting Ernie

Patti Newton was over visiting in London, and we were on one side of the street and Ern [Ernie Sigley] was on the other. And he took us in and bought us a drink ... think he took Patti out that night, and then he went back to Adelaide to do his show.

I went over to Adelaide a couple of times when I came back to work with him, then he was asked to do the night-time show. I started off doing the sketches, and then I was asked to do the barrel, you know, the wheel. Steady job, barrel girl, if you can get it. It's a great segment, and it's audience participation. You've got to use your head, it's everything, because there's no autocue. This is what's ruining our business, autocue, because none of these people have to think on their feet. The autocue fails, they can't talk.

So in the '70s we did *The Ernie Sigley Show*—'74 and '75—and that was when I was lucky again. I talk about luck all the time. That was fantastic! Ernie and I just hit it off. We worked together for over twenty-seven years. I gave him the best twenty-seven years of my life, but we had a lot of fun, and it was at a time in television where there weren't the restrictions on what you could do.

We used to go on in the '70s, and I'd say to Max Morrison, the stage manager at Channel Nine, 'Oh, Max, could you blow this up? I'll be doing this', and da, da, da. And he'd go, 'Yeah, no problems, darl'. He'd be the only one that would know what I was going to do. But now there's meetings a week before and unless you've got a safety officer and the WorkCare guy, and then there's an executive and then they bring in three firemen, and then Auntie Nellie's sitting at the back to make sure … You can't do it.

But I'm still the same. If someone rang and said, 'Look, we need someone to hang off the top of something. Could you hang off there?', I would. But the thing is, I was always in control of not hurting myself. I think that's the important thing to remember. Even though the things that I've done may be a bit dangerous, I was always certain I wasn't going to hurt myself.

The time with Ernie in '74 and '75, I started off doing the sketches in the afternoon, then they asked me to do the barrel, and it just went from there. We won Logies. It was phenomenal, and you've got to remember for the first six months … I was going to the show on the tram, two trams to get there, so I didn't have a penny. And when that show started I was actually wondering where I was going to get the money for the rent, so I just flew from there. Again, lucky, so lucky.

Ernie had a secretary when he did radio called Denise Bell, so because of the bell they called her Ding Dong. And when he heard my name was Denise he automatically went 'Ding Dong'. But imagine what he could have called me. You think of pet names that he could have given me in those days that would have stayed with me. So, I'm really glad it's Ding Dong. I love it! Some people go, 'Ding Dong? I don't know your name'. I don't mind it at all.

At the end of '79 I actually got married, and then very quickly followed two children: there's only nineteen months' difference. And I was still working on shows. I still worked when I was pregnant with Peter—I did a show out of Ballarat—and when I was pregnant with Rob I did *Beauty and the Beast* with Derryn Hinch. So I've worked all the way through. I was always working—never stopped.

But then the opportunity came up to work with Ernie on *The Morning Show* in Melbourne only. And in the meantime they asked me to do *Hey Hey* when Jackie McDonald left. I was remembering when I was a sprinkler on *Hey Hey* ... I was attached to a hose. You had to come dressed as something in the garden, so I had a sprinkler on my head, and every time that Daryl [Somers] went to speak, I'd let go of the hose, just enough so Daryl copped it. It was great. I loved it, I really loved it. So I did that for a year. That was fantastic because people hadn't seen me on national television. That was fabulous for outside work on ads, and everything like that.

I left that, and Ernie and I worked together then for about seven or eight years, I think. And I thought I'd had my day in the sunshine, and then I got the opportunity to do *In Melbourne Tonight* with Frank Holden.

I know that there were years there where they'd think, Oh, get Denise, 'cause she'll do it. And I've never been a lot of trouble, really—maybe a little bit—but game for anything, and still the same, except conditions have changed. I was always top of the desperate list, I used to say. They'd get people they wanted, they'd be working ... 'So, get her. She's at the top of the desperate list'.

I was just thrilled to be asked to be anything. And that's the basis of it ... happy to do anything because I'm thrilled to be working. Anything! I go, 'Oh, that's lovely. Oh, yes'. I'll get a job for ... I don't know, for a talk somewhere, and I go, 'Oh, yes, another one! Good, beaut'.

Aspirations

I suppose people are in more control now, but you've got to be at the top of the tree to do that. I was always just sloshing around in the middly-bottom bit, so I wasn't in control. I've been so lucky. People say to me, 'You've worked hard'. I have worked hard, and things that people wouldn't do, jobs that they wouldn't ... 'Oh, too hard, I'm not doing that'. I've done those jobs, but then I've known people who have done equally the same, but just not had the luck.

I wanted to be an all-round entertainer like Toni Lamond. I'd watch Toni: she'd sing—that fabulous voice—she'd dance, she'd do comedy, she'd hosted her own show, she did all of that stuff. I just wanted to be a really good entertainer. In dancing, we did everything, from ballet, tap, national modern ballet, we did everything. Singing, I was shocking. I would've given anything to be able to sing like, you know, Reba McEntire, with this catch in her voice when she sings. I haven't got it. I'm trying.

Years ago, I mean, I couldn't sing, I wanted to sing, and I have developed a voice. I've been singing for ages, so now I'm quite good. But one of the best things that I've ever done, I worked with the Australian Pops Orchestra, New Year's Eve—I can't remember what year it was—and I sang 'Impossible Dream' with them, and I nailed it right at the end.

A professional

I reckon once you've got your make-up on and your frock on, just keep going, no matter what. That's true and that's happened. You'd get to a job and the band can't play, or there's no stage, there's no lights, the microphone breaks down. Do whatever you can possible to entertain and get your cheque and go home. Or sometimes we got cash.

I couldn't do it if I was going to be nervous of doing it. No I couldn't. That's what I mean—stupidity ... never any nervousness about hanging from anywhere, or going abseiling down the side of a building. I've abseiled off a Turkish mountain outside of Bodrum. And it took three-quarters of an hour to come down, and we did those spirals where you go round and round and round. And that was fabulous. But to do with show business, I used to come down from the ceiling, just holding on to, you know, a bar, and go straight into the act. And when I finished, come back and go up on the bar. I am just like that. I just love that sense of adventure, and you feel like you're alive too.

I cry. Of course I do. Oh God, I've been in situations, about to go on television and I'm upset, but then that trooper thing, I don't know if you're born with it, or whether you achieve it, but the show must go on, always did.

A show of her own

In 1998 I got a phone call to do my own show on Channel Seven, and I was absolutely thrilled. I couldn't believe that it had happened, because I thought I'd had my day in the sunshine, and as you're getting on, just because you've worked in show business doesn't necessarily mean that you have a job. So I was thrilled and it was great fun. And I also realised what I didn't know about being the host, starting segments and finishing segments. I still can't finish segments. The producers would be tearing their hair out.

I had a four-year run with *Denise* and met so many fabulous people and guests, and I had a ball. Heaven! Here was I, after seven years with Ern on *The Morning Show*, thought that was it. Get *IMT* for a couple of years ... thought that was it. How lucky, how lucky. And then all of a sudden I was offered the show at Channel Seven, which I did for four years ... lucky. It opened up a whole new lot of things that I hadn't done. And I learnt a lot—like how to finish an interview.

And then I did some work for Channel 31 with *Dig & Dine*, which was probably the most fun I've had doing a show because we were out and about—nothing in the studio. And there were only four of us, and we were left to our own devices.

Depression

I think it's either in you or it's not. And it's definitely in my make-up. I've had an up-and-down life. All issues that people have got ... Same things. I'm no different to anybody else. I've covered it well. I'm just sorry I didn't seek help earlier.

I had a lovely psychiatrist who I went to for a while and chatted to him about various problems and felt really good again, and when I went back to see him he'd retired. He probably thought, If this is the calibre of patient ... He was only young, too! He was in his thirties. I don't know ... He probably thought, If this is what I'm going to cop, I'm out of here. I'm going to get out of the job.

I just thought that I should be strong enough to do it on my own. That's what I really thought. A lot of people make that mistake. I was probably lucky I had the work to go to: that lifted me, and gave me so much. But there are people who haven't got that to go to, and they sink deeper. And now is probably the best time of my whole, entire life, and I'm sorry I waited so long to get it in order.

Country living

We've been up in Gippsland since 1979. I just absolutely love it. And in that time, we've been up here, gone down to Melbourne and rented, but now I'm back here and I just love it. I think I love it more than I ever have. I love the view, the people, the peace, and it's just a lovely way to live, and the city's so close. I'm very, very lucky.

But there are a few things to do with the country that I'm not that keen on, like going down to the pump and having to turn it on, and each time when the weather's hot I think there's going to be some crawly thing. And only last week I came down to turn the pump on and a big black snake slithered just over my gumboots, and I nearly died. I got up that hill—I could have been in the Commonwealth Games and won a gold medal. There's that and there's the mowing. But it's a beautiful place to live. You just have to adapt to it; it doesn't adapt to you. That's one thing I have learnt.

Even though Chris and I divorced in '91 or something, we're still good friends, and his partner, Carmel. Chris built this place and the boys think of it as their family home. I hope it stays in the family for many years.

The two boys—Rob, who's twenty-three, and Pete, who's twenty-five—they live in Melbourne. They're very lovely boys and they've got lovely manners, which I always thought was important. And I think they'll probably end up working and having a business together in hospitality, a little bar somewhere. Very suited to that, the whole family ...

Deb Cooper and I have known each other thirty years. She's done wardrobe, she's done absolutely everything from producing, editing, but she can do anything, she's that clever. So, she finally opened a florist's shop in Elwood. I enjoy it. I love going down there. And people, when you serve them, get quite a shock. But then what's happened is Fay next door has opened a shabby chic shop, so I help her too when I'm not busy. I just love it down there.

I've always loved clothes, and that's why I'm really happy to be doing these fashion parades, and we're doing it with a bit of a difference, where I get into clothes that are too small, I look terrible, then change it around and just show you how wonderful clothes can look just if you've got a bit of know-how and expertise. And the good thing is a percentage—20 per cent of the money raised—goes towards a charity, and I've got so many charities I'm involved with, so that's fantastic.

Charities

I'm ambassador for the oncology ward at the Traralgon Hospital. It's selfish work: I feel good. And just last week I was with Susie O'Neill, who works with children that have been burnt and have got third-degree burns, and these kids have so much courage and they are gutsy kids. They're unbelievable.

I'm very proud of this—I was arrested for twenty-four hours by the local police and had to get bail money. We got all the money for the skate park in Neerim South. But do you know what? When I rang people for bail money, they said, 'We'll give it if they keep you in'. And I thought, I've never done anything to you!

Vietnam vets

Over the years I've done a lot of things for the Vietnam vets, maybe paid shows, or maybe charity shows. I think I've met nearly all of them, put it that way. But there's a group—the sub-branch, East Gippsland—up at home, and they have a picnic every year. And it's grown in size—there used to be about twenty people; now there's about 200—and it's just people getting together because there's still things that aren't resolved with these men. And to get together with other people, it's very, very important. They're still letting out secrets, and that's why I think they've gone through so much, because they've kept so much in. We're still getting some of the men come up and go, 'I haven't talked about this ever, but I find in this environment I can'.

It was an awful war. I mean, it was a war that they didn't know who they were fighting, and it was a different war, it was a dirty war. These were young kids, they'd never had a gun, and all of a sudden they're firing at villagers, and ... it was against the grain of an Australian.

I rang one of them, John Ricardo, and I said, 'John, do you know anybody who can do a couple of odd jobs around the house? I'm just snowed under ...' And he said, 'Don't worry'. So seven guys have come round and done the most beautiful dry stone walls out of all the rubble that I had round the house. And they'll never know what they've done for me, because it's exactly how I imagined this house would be, and I've been there for over twenty years.

I love living up here, and one of the really great things about that is that I have two friends that live about five minutes away, Jack and John. John, I used to dance with years and years ago in the ballet with Graham Kennedy, and we play cards—we play Canasta and Bolivia. And a friend of theirs and mine, Laurie, comes up, and they're all ex-dancers and they're all in their seventies. But I laugh my head off, have the best time ever. I suppose it's the simple life, isn't it, really?

I haven't got a moment lately in my life that doesn't make me feel terrific. Because I feel I'm in control, just of my own self, and I've got really great friends, same friends that I've had for years, that I really love. My two boys are gorgeous and they're happy. You know, they're finding their own way. And I've got all my animals, and I've got a beautiful place in the country, and I've got work. And I'm pretty healthy, basically.

I just feel really good, and I'm lucky. We are lucky, we are lucky to still be in a business that we love, doing things, and entertaining and making people laugh. You can't ask for more than that.

> I left school at just on fifteen ... there's been times in my life that I wish I would have something to fall back on. But show business is all I've ever known, so any time I went to do something, they'd say, 'Oh, have you got this degree?' or whatever. I wanted to actually do social work at one stage but I didn't have the background, and so I'd say to anybody, 'Get an education', because if it doesn't work out in show business you have got something else that you can do.

ACKNOWLEDGEMENTS

While our 'talking heads' are the stars of the show, they were able to share their talents and knowledge and experience through the efforts of a hard-working team behind the scenes. We would like to extend our thanks to the Brisbane-based *Talking Heads* production team of executive producer Jack King; series producers Gary Johnson and Nick Lee; production co-ordinators Nadya Reich and Kerrie Wells; regular field producers Deborah Boerne; Peter Cooke, Jennifer Harrison, Catherine Ledingham, Neil Proud, and Tracey Spring; researchers Caroline Page, Ramya Sundrapandi and Megan Hazlett; senior editor Brad McCrystal, and publicist Adrienne O'Connor.

A special thanks to the talented crews who shot the show over the years, the editors who cut the programme and our ever-helpful archive and library teams throughout the country.

Pauline Turnbull
Peter Thompson